Obedient To The Heavenly Vision

Printed by the
White Wing Publishing House and Press
Printing division
of the
Church of God of Prophecy
P. O. Box 3000
Cleveland, TN 37320-3000
1997/1M
27747
ISBN # 1-889505-07-2

DEDICATION

This book is dedicated to all those who minister the Word of God. May the grace, mercy, and strength reflected in these pages inspire all in fulfilling their call to preach the gospel.

The Publishers

FOREWORD

Change is inevitable and often painful. It has been said that *"the only thing permanent is change."* This is true of all living *organisms* as well as *organizations*. Sometimes the change is observable and somewhat predictable as in the metamorphosis of the caterpillar to the butterfly. Sometimes the change is so gradual as to be almost imperceptible. This process of changing from simple into a more complex form can, after time, redefine the organization sometimes for the better, or on the other hand, change can render the organization something considerably less than the original. If properly understood and managed, change can be positive. However, if unchecked, the process can subtly change the goals and objectives on which the organization is based and thus redefine both its original purpose as well as its structure, fulfilling the maxim — "form follows function."

As the life cycle of an organization continues, it may appear that its fundamental foundation begins to erode. It is then that a desperate cry to stop the erosion can be heard. This cry brings to light the need for corrective measures. For the organization known as Israel, a cry was heard from prophets like Isaiah, Jeremiah, and John the Baptist. For the organization known as the Church of God of Prophecy, the entreaty came from the Holy Spirit to the General Assembly in 1984 by an Assembly committee.

> *"This Committee knows of no greater need to bring to this Assembly's attention than the need for repentance — the need to fall on our faces before God, confessing that we have drifted in many ways from a vital relationship with the Holy Ghost, confessing a self-centeredness lacking in deep compassion for a world of people who are living now under the judgement of God to eternal damnation, rededicating ourselves to being the Church of God of the Bible"* (79th Assembly Minutes, 1984, p. 127).

As a ship that quietly drifts from the dock until, suddenly, it can no longer be reached, the Church of God of Prophecy had, by the ripples of time, drifted in many ways from a vital relationship with the Holy Ghost. The solid spiritual heritage of Holy Spirit infusion and confirmation so evident at the turn of the century had evolved into a self-centeredness that lacked deep compassion for a lost and condemned world.

As God began to inspire His ministers with messages calling for repentance, rededication, and restoration of a vital relationship with the Lord, there was a prophetic voice that began to rise. Billy D. Murray, then the Assistant Editor of the *White Wing Messenger*, official publication of the Church of God of Prophecy, began to speak with unction the divine message that was already burning in the hearts of others, as God mercifully worked with His people. For six years, Brother Murray's Assembly sermons articulated the urgent need for restoring a vital relationship with Jesus Christ — flowing in grace instead of bondage to law. Often he would amusingly admit to preaching the same theme, only changing the title. But the theme was inspired of the Lord and a reflection of the vision for return to God's original purpose.

In 1990, Billy Murray was unanimously selected General Overseer of the Church of God of Prophecy. Since his selection as General Overseer, Bishop Murray has continued a prophetic proclamation of a vital and living relationship with Jesus Christ, the Head of the Church.

True leaders are, by the very definition, visionary. It is visionary leadership that "casts the vision" for the organization and helps to articulate its objectives as it moves forward. Brother Murray's leadership has been the outgrowth of the vision given from Heaven and inspired by the Holy Ghost. It is this vision that gave birth to the current focus of "Turning to the Harvest" that was launched in the Assembly of 1994.

This book, a chronological account of Bishop Murray's messages and a reflection of his unfolding leadership, is presented as a witness of how God inspired a man whom He is using to lead the Church in its quest to recapture its original purpose and to revitalize its lost relationship with Jesus Christ.

John Pace
Cleveland, Tennessee
June 1996

CONTENTS

Chapter	1	Lord, Open Our Eyes, That We May See	9
Chapter	2	Then Shalt Thou See And Flow Together	21
Chapter	3	Have Faith In God	33
Chapter	4	Thy Kingdom Come	47
Chapter	5	He Shall Be Satisfied	61
Chapter	6	Upon This Rock	75
Chapter	7	A Vision	89
Chapter	8	Our Commitment	97
Chapter	9	Form And Substance	105
Chapter	10	Text: John 4:31-38	119
Chapter	11	Where Is The Passion?	131
Chapter	12	"And Sinners Shall Be Converted Unto Thee"	139
Chapter	13	Vibrant Local Churches	149

ASSEMBLY PRESENTATIONS AS GENERAL OVERSEER

Chapter	14	A Spirit Of Reconciliation	157
Chapter	15	Jesus, Take Charge!	181
Chapter	16	Reaching Forth	209
Chapter	17	88th General Assembly Sermons	241
Chapter	18	Engaged In The Harvest	261

Lord, Open Our Eyes, That We May See

1

79th General Assembly
White Wing Messenger, Nov. 17, 1984

"That the God of our Lord Jesus Christ, the Father of glory, may give unto you the spirit of wisdom and revelation in the knowledge of him: The eyes of your understanding being enlightened; that ye may know what is the hope of his calling, and what the riches of the glory of his inheritance in the saints" (Ephesians 1:17, 18).

The Syrian army had surrounded the city of Dothan by night, for the purpose of taking captive Elisha, the prophet of God. In the morning Elisha's servant arose early and beheld the Syrians with their horses and chariots as they encompassed the city. Being seized by a feeling of helplessness, Elisha's statement, ". . . they that be with us are more than they that be with them" (2 Kings 6:16), meant little to the servant, until the prophet prayed, "Lord . . open his eyes, that he may see. And the Lord opened the eyes of the young man; and he saw: and, behold, the mountain was full of horses and chariots of fire round about Elisha" (v. 17). What a difference it made when the Lord opened his eyes.

Blindness to the existence of a thing, or of a condition, in no way alters its reality, but only prevents its perception by the person who is blind. While none of us relishes the idea of being physically blind, inasmuch as it would deprive us of so much which we are able now to behold, there is a blindness that is much worse than physical blindness, and that is to be blind spiritually.

A person who is physically blind recognizes and acknowledges the fact that he is blind. However, a person who is blind spiritually does not know that he is blind. To the church at Laodicea Jesus said, "Because thou sayest, I am rich, and increased with goods, and have need of nothing; and knowest not that thou art wretched, and miserable, and poor, and blind, and naked" (Revelation 3:17). They were blind and did not know it. They thought they had good perception.

This fact adds to the awfulness of spiritual blindness, or deception. A person who is deceived does not know he is deceived. A deceived person believes he is right. We may wonder how many right now, even among us, are sharing the condition of the Laodiceans. If, indeed, that be our case, how could we know it? They did not know they were blind, and if they had been asked, they would have denied it, possibly replying, "We are a part of the Church of God, and if anybody has light we surely must have." Their assessment of themselves was that they were prospering, having need of nothing. But Jesus' assessment was that they were blind, and wretched, and poor, and naked.

If, indeed, a person, or a church, who is spiritually blind does not perceive that he is blind, but supposes that he is seeing clearly, how can he receive help? A person will not seek help who is not aware that he needs help. For a person, or a church, to be in such a state is frightening, indeed.

The only hope for receiving help in such a case is a merciful, divine visitation which opens one's eyes. This is what occurred in each of our lives when we were brought to repentance—the repentance which preceded our being born again, becoming new creatures in Jesus Christ. When this visitation came, which we commonly call Holy Ghost conviction, and our eyes were opened to the terribleness of sin, we saw ourselves as we really were—lost, miserable, poor, wretched, blind and naked. We felt like crying out as did Isaiah when he saw the Lord in the year that King Uzziah died: "Woe is me! for I am undone" (Isaiah 6:5). Such hopelessness caused us to want to fall down before the Lord and beg for mercy.

This is exactly what we did, and a gracious God responded by forgiving all our transgressions. In an instant we felt clean, forgiven—transformed by His marvelous grace. As Paul wrote, we were "delivered . . . from the power of darkness, and . . . translated . . . into the kingdom of his dear Son" (Colossians 1:13).

Reflecting upon that moment of deliverance one feels like lifting his heart to sing "Amazing grace! how sweet the sound, That saved a wretch like me! I once was lost, but now am found, Was blind, but now I see." Our eyes were opened, and within this new kingdom of light into which we were translated we beheld things which, as Paul wrote, "Eye hath not seen, nor ear heard . . . But God hath revealed them unto us by his Spirit" (1 Corinthians 2:9, 10).

No comparison can measure up to what really took place at the time of this transformation. Words cannot describe it—it is joy unspeakable and full of glory. By one act of faith we stepped into a new kingdom, leaving a kingdom of darkness, wherein we walked blindly, and entered into a kingdom of eternal light. It is a kingdom of righteousness, peace and joy in the Holy Ghost.

It seems that no one, once he has entered into such a marvelous relationship with Almighty God, could possibly be drawn back into the kingdom of darkness from which he was so wondrously delivered. The fact is, if it was so clear-cut, so pronounced that a person recognized what was happening to him and what he was doing, he surely would not return to his former wretched state.

The Christian's adversary, however, is a master at deception, using such insidious means as to be unrecognizable to the child of God who fails to maintain spiritual vigilance. If he can somehow cause us to leave off those things which are essential to retaining a close communion with God he will be successful in starting a drift backward toward our former state.

To the Corinthians Paul wrote: "Who also hath made us able ministers of the new testament; not of the letter, but of the spirit: for the letter killeth, but the spirit giveth life" (2 Corinthians 3:6).

The letter, or the law, brought condemnation unto death. But we have been made ministers of the Spirit which giveth life. Rules are for people who cannot follow principles. This is why the law was given. But the Church of God is not under the law, and if it is to be a spiritual house then it must find its life in the Spirit. Those principles outlined and demonstrated by Jesus Christ, seen first in Abraham, must abide in us. They must be seen in us if we are to fulfill our purpose of showing forth His excellencies to a debased world.

We must admit that right now there is far too much carnality among us. Inasmuch as carnal people are not sensitive to the Spirit, there is a tendency to want to revert to legalism in an effort to force members to "line up." But remember, the law could not correct sinfulness in the Israelites and it will not solve the problem of carnality among us. We must get to the root of the problem.

The Church of God cannot be a house in which Isaac and Ishmael both dwell. As Paul addressed this problem with the Galatians, who were being tempted to revert to legalism, he wrote, "Nevertheless what saith the scripture? Cast out the bondwoman and her son: for the son of the bondwoman shall not be heir with the son of the freewoman" (Galatians 4:30). A legalistic approach will never perfect the Church. "For the law made nothing perfect, but the bringing in of a better hope did; by the which we draw nigh unto God" (Hebrews 7:19).

This better hope came to us in Jesus Christ. In this new and living way, God's Word is written within soft and responsive hearts. This writing cannot be done by any mechanical efforts; it is a writing which only the Holy Ghost can do. And when His Word is written in the heart by the Holy Ghost, man's legislation will not be needed.

Lord, Open Our Eyes, That We May See

We must have a relationship with God which lifts us above a routine that can be carried out methodically. This relationship involves much more than mere adherence to rules which produce a religious form. Rules do not produce growth. Life in the Spirit does.

Now this is not to imply any disrespect for the written Word of God—the Holy Bible. Indeed, the Word of God is the foundation for our faith. But the Bible must be more for us than just written rules and regulations. It is fitting that each of us join the Psalmist in praying: "Open thou mine eyes, that I may behold wondrous things out of thy law" (Psalms 119:18).

It is through the illumination of the written Word that we behold the beauty of divine principles, that we receive our proper concepts of God. For example, the commandment, "Thou shalt not kill," when illuminated, reveals to us not just the sanctity of human life, but that we are to respect God's purposes for that individual whom He has created for His glory. The recognition of God's sovereignty in all things and respect for His purpose is most important. Therefore, hatred for a brother is equated by God as murder, because such hatred is directed against God's creation and will manifest itself in attempts to demean, belittle and prevent that brother's becoming all that he can become for God's glory. We have no right to hate God's creation. We should hate sin, but never people.

The legalist looks at the commandment, "Thou shalt not kill," and counts himself righteous in that he keeps that commandment, even though he may be nurturing grudges against one of God's children, grudges which would cause him to belittle or degrade a brother's efforts. The spiritual person, on the other hand, perceives a divine principle in this commandment which goes far beyond the mere taking of another person's life.

"Thou shalt not commit adultery" is a command of God, but Jesus gave further illumination by saying, ". . . whosoever looketh on a woman to lust after her hath committed adultery with her already in his heart" (Matthew 5:28).

Here again would be the failure to respect the woman as a creation of God, a person whom He made to be a temple of the Holy Ghost, viewing her instead as an object to be used for selfish gratification. This is wrong and is judged by God as sinful.

To the legalist, the keeping of rules establishes and demonstrates his righteousness, but to the spiritual person the exaltation of God is paramount. This is something which is difficult to understand for people who are blinded by their own self-importance. We need our eyes opened that once more we can see the Lord. A vision of God will bring us at once into the dust of humility.

A divine principle prominent in the New Testament is that of self-denial. Jesus said, "If any man will come after me, let him deny himself, and take up his cross, and follow me" (Matthew 16:24). To the Romans Paul wrote, "For even Christ pleased not himself; but, as it is written, The reproaches of them that reproached thee fell on me" (Romans 15:3). There is no place within Christian principles for selfishness. "We then that are strong ought to bear the infirmities of the weak, and not to please ourselves. Let every one of us please his neighbour for his good to edification" (vv. 1, 2).

From time to time we hear murmurings about the Church's teaching against wearing gold for ornament, based upon its interpretation of First Peter 3:3, First John 12:16 and First Timothy 2:9, "In like manner also that women adorn themselves in modest apparel, with shamefacedness and sobriety; not with broided hair, or gold, or pearls, or costly array." Some have decided that the Church's interpretation is wrong, and no matter what the Church says, or how their brothers and sisters feel, that they are going to do as they please. Such an attitude certainly is not in keeping with the cardinal Christian principle of self-denial and submission to one another, which was addressed by Paul as he wrote that we are not to please ourselves, but "Let every one of us please his neighbour for his good to edification." Spiritual people will not be insensitive to the feelings of others. O how we need our eyes opened! Self-sacrificing love for one another will bring peace and edification to the Body of Christ.

To walk with God is to walk in the light, something that each member in this Assembly covenanted to do to the best of his ability. This is a progressive march which will require a conscious and determined effort, an effort which our coming together in this Assembly should reflect. (The stated purpose of having an Assembly is to search the Scriptures for additional light and knowledge.) Paul's prayer for the Ephesians seems appropriate for the Church in this 79th Assembly: "That . . . God . . . may give unto you the spirit of wisdom and revelation in the knowledge of [Christ]: The eyes of your understanding being enlightened; that ye may know what is the hope of his calling, and what the riches of the glory of his inheritance in the saints."

We must continue walking in the light. Jesus said, "Walk while ye have the light, lest darkness come upon you: for he that walketh in darkness knoweth not whither he goeth" (John 12:35). John wrote: "But if we walk in the light, as he is in the light, we have fellowship one with another" (1 John 1:7). Walking is much different from drifting. Walking is an action word; in drifting one is passive. A person who is drifting is being acted upon instead of acting—acted upon by forces surrounding him. It is easy to drift. Just don't attack and oppose the forces which encompass you, and they will carry you along in their wake. Many Christians have drifted far from the spiritual reality they once experienced. In so doing they now possess a dullness of spiritual perception. Their spiritual eyesight is very dim; indeed, some have become totally blind. Adding to the sadness of their plight is the fact that they are unaware of what has happened, supposing that they are capable of seeing quite well. In fact, some of these are very vocal in diagnosing the needs of the Church, being blind all the while. I feel like praying, "O Lord, open our eyes, that we might see."

The Church of God was described by Peter as a spiritual house, and it must be a spiritual house if it is to glorify its

Builder. In a waning relationship with God we lose the sensitivity to His Spirit that is vital for retaining our spiritual stature. Oftentimes, as the freshness of our spiritual experience passes and the fervency of our love diminishes, we find ourselves settling into a routineness to which we feel only an obligation for faithfulness.

For a non-spiritual person these routines of being faithful can become quite comfortable. You see, they do not make the demands upon an individual which life in the Spirit makes. (He has been told by the Assembly what to do and what not to do.) Agonizing prayer, for example, is virtually unknown to the religious conformist who would tell you he is a faithful member of the Church of God. After all, he doesn't curse, smoke, swear, gamble or drink intoxicating beverages, and besides that, he pays his tithes and attends services fairly regularly. He may even be present in this Assembly, feeling, as did the church at Laodicea, that he has need of nothing, that he is doing fine.

What is most important, however, he overlooks, and that is the quality of communion he enjoys with God through the Holy Ghost. A true spiritual house must be built up of lively stones—alive unto God through the Spirit.

It is not enough to learn a certain discipline and follow a set of rules. The Pharisees that Jesus encountered could do that and boast of their faithfulness, but communion with God was foreign to them. Jesus called them "blind leaders of the blind," going on to say, "And if the blind lead the blind, both shall fall into the ditch" (Matthew 15:14). O Lord, open our eyes that we may see!

Right now the Church has some problems, and it is important that we recognize the root of our problems. It will be much more beneficial to treat the disease which is afflicting us than to continually treat our symptoms. (Cancer cannot be cured with bandages. Smallpox cannot be cured by putting Band-Aids on the sores which break out. This would only make the sores more conspicuous, calling attention to one's sickness.)

Amidst the carelessness and indifference which in many places is so prevalent, some of us, out of frustration, are calling for more rigid rules to discipline our members. While the Church bears a definite responsibility for exercising certain disciplines, the solution to the problems we are facing is not more rules. We must address the root of our sickness.

If we are to learn from those sayings which were written for our learning, we will see that rules were given to people who could not observe divine principles, people who had a faulty relationship with God. The root of our problem lies in our relationship with the Lord.

Abraham believed God and became the father of those who would serve God through faith. God talked with him and he talked with God. Paul tells us in Galatians 3:8 that Abraham had the gospel preached to him. Through the strength of the relationship he had with God, he observed certain divine principles, and since divine principles are immutable—they never change—these principles later were taught by Jesus Christ to His Church.

In the course of time Abraham's descendants drifted far from God. In order to show them how far they had drifted God gave them the Law at Mount Sinai, which we call the Ten Commandments. The Law was not given to correct their condition, but rather to manifest their sins. Paul wrote in Romans 5:20, "Moreover the law entered, that the offence might abound." These commandments were given, as Paul wrote in Romans 7:13, "that sin by the commandment might become exceeding sinful." The Law simply revealed sin and placed the people under condemnation before God. But thanks be to God for Jesus Christ who came to deal with the root of the sin problem! He brought a new and living way! In the eighth chapter of Romans Paul wrote: "There is therefore now no condemnation to them which are in Christ Jesus, who walk not after the flesh, but after the Spirit. For the law of the Spirit of life in Christ Jesus hath made me free from the law of sin and death. For what the law could not do, in that it was weak through the flesh, God sending his own Son in the likeness of sinful flesh, and for sin, condemned sin in the flesh: That the righteousness of the law might be fulfilled in us, who walk not after the flesh, but after the Spirit" (Romans 8:1-4).

Feet Washing is a prominent teaching of the New Testament, but it is possible to practice this observance faithfully and never be illuminated to behold its real significance. Jesus used this to teach servanthood—a reversal of the worldly system wherein those who were great exercised lordship over others. And Peter was reminded that unless he could submit to this reversal of order he would have no part with Christ.

Jesus said to His disciples, "Ye know that they which are accounted to rule over the Gentiles exercise lordship over them; and their great ones exercise authority upon them. But so shall it not be among you: but whosoever will be great among you, shall be your minister: and whosoever of you will be the chiefest, shall be servant of all" (Mark 10:42-44).

Now, we are to appreciate and respect government. Peter described the Church as a Holy Nation, and a nation has government. There are those who would discount the need for governmental structure, but that which they advocate, wherein no one has anyone over him, has no support in the Scriptures. Anarchy is not acceptable to God. The Bible is clear in its call for government in the home, in the nation, and in the Church. Paul wrote to the Thessalonians: ". . . to know them which labour among you, and are over you in the Lord, and admonish you; And to esteem them very highly in love for their work's sake" (1 Thessalonians 5:12, 13).

This esteem was to be given them for their work's sake. Their work was to lead, to nurture, to feed the flock of God. A leader's work in the Church of God is a work of love. Never is he to be a "lord over God's heritage." Rather, he becomes a servant who serves by love. This is very different from the worldly order, but the Church of God must take its stand against worldliness, a worldliness which we must admit has made its intrusion among us. It would be better for leaders to dwell more upon the word *responsibility* rather than on authority, the *responsibility* of servanthood.

When I observe some of the attitudes and dispositions with which we are beset, it causes me to wonder how far we have drifted from those divine principles which must guide the Church of God. Many religious denominations came into existence with good intentions. Often it was to escape the dullness and routineness into which their parent bodies had drifted, in an effort to follow the New Testament pattern more closely. In the course of time, however, they lost their spiritual vitality and became like that from which they had tried to escape. Historically, when those groups had drifted as far off course as it appears to me that we have drifted from the paths charted by the pioneers in the early part of this century, they never found their way back. Nor do I believe we will be able to make a gradual return.

Individual Christians who become possessed with carnality do not make gradual comebacks. My observation has been that they return to the Lord in times of a crisis experience. They, mercifully, receive a divine visitation—at times this visitation seems severe—and if they repent they are forgiven and find a freshness of relationship with God. I believe this is the way it will have to be for the Church today.

The Lord's message to the church at Laodicea was, "As many as I love, I rebuke and chasten: be zealous therefore, and repent" (Revelation 3:19). There can be no repentance without confession There will be no confession until our eyes are opened. It was when Isaiah's eyes were opened and he saw the Lord that he was ready to confess, "Woe is me! for I am undone . . . I am a man of unclean lips."

Being blind, the Laodiceans were saying, "All is well—we have need of nothing." I can say to you tonight, I believe, certainly, by inspiration of the Holy Ghost, that all is not well. It is time for confession—a confession to be followed by repentance. Divine intervention, an intervention which opens our eyes and leads us to repentance, a crisis experience—only this can bring God's Church into a right relationship with Him. Until then we will continue treating only the symptoms of our real problem. I pray, "God, please send conviction upon us! O God, please open our eyes!"

Then Thou Shalt See And Flow Together

2

Preached at the 80th General Assembly
White Wing Messenger, Nov. 17, 1985

"Arise, shine; for thy light is come, and the glory of the Lord is risen upon thee.

"For, behold, the darkness shall cover the earth, and gross darkness the people: but the Lord shall arise upon thee, and his glory shall be seen upon thee.

"And the Gentiles shall come to thy light, and kings to the brightness of thy rising.

"Lift up thine eyes round about, and see: all they gather themselves together, they come to thee: thy sons shall come from far, and thy daughters shall be nursed at thy side.

"Then thou shalt see, and flow together, and thine heart shall fear, and be enlarged" (Isaiah 60:1-5).

Unity is a principle that God insists upon for His people. When we view the fractured structure of Christianity, with its thousands of denominations, we may wonder whether the Lord's plan for Christian unity is indeed possible. We must remember, however, that such divisiveness is a work of Satan among God's children, and Satan's works must be exposed and destroyed from among us.

His kingdoms will continue to exist within this world all right, until that time when he will be bound for a thousand years, but the power of this deceiver must not be given any place among the blood-bought followers of Jesus Christ, who are not of this world.

The Son of God was able to say, " . . . the prince of this world . . . hath nothing in me" (John 14:30). The Church which He purchased with His own blood, that blood which sanctifies wholly, has the privilege of having the same testimony: "the prince of this world . . . hath nothing in me." At the present time, however, the Church cannot rightfully make such a claim.

There are some who view strife and divisions as something to be tolerated, but this is not the view of God. According to Paul's letter to the church at Corinth, the Corinthians seemed willing not only to tolerate divisions, but to boast against one another in their party loyalties. The apostle's message to them was piercing: "Now I beseech you, brethren, by the name of our Lord Jesus Christ, that ye all speak the same thing, and that there be no divisions among you; but that ye be perfectly joined together in the same mind and in the same judgment. For it hath been declared unto me of you, my brethren . . . that there are contentions among you. Now this I say, that every one of you saith, I am of Paul; and I of Apollos; and I of Cephas; and I of Christ. Is Christ divided? was Paul crucified for you? or were ye baptized in the name of Paul?" (1 Corinthians 1:10-13).

He thus reminded them of the One who deserved their total loyalty, the One who was crucified for them and in whose name they were baptized. Jesus Christ alone is the focal point for Christian unity. Any unity achieved apart from Him does not bring glory to God. (There was a unity which the builders of the tower at Babel possessed, but its purpose was to bring fame and glory to man.) The unity that has been purposed by God for His children will be arrived at in such a manner that no man will receive any glory in our having attained it. For Christians to be united with one another is not enough; their unity must be in Christ.

For several years now there has been a call in Christian circles for ecumenical unity, and we have seen some denominational mergers. The unions that have occurred, however, are a far cry from the spiritual unity ordered by God for His children.

Since the early part of this century the Church has proclaimed a message of corporeal unity, a gathering together into one body all the saints of God. We have proclaimed with great zeal the message of one Fold and one Shepherd. This is a message we must continue to preach, without apology, "Till we all come in the unity of the faith, and of the knowledge of the Son of God, unto a perfect man, unto the measure of the stature of the fulness of Christ" (Ephesians 4:13).

Unity of the faith, as I understand it, implies unity of doctrine or, as Paul expressed it to the Corinthians, "that ye all speak the same thing." In such unity there is no room for doctrinal differences. Why should there be? After all, we have no right to any doctrine of our own. We are sent to declare the words of the One who sent us, the One who is the Head of the Church. It is His doctrine, not ours, and His doctrine bears the mark of His immutability. It does not change. Jesus Christ is the same yesterday, today and forever, and so is His doctrine. Notwithstanding, the understanding of His Word comes to us in varying degrees of illumination, becoming richer and fuller as spiritual light shines more brightly.

While unity of the faith is an important goal for all the children of God, something more immediately pressing, I believe, is unity of the Spirit. Paul wrote, "With all lowliness and meekness, with longsuffering, forbearing one another in love; Endeavouring to keep the unity of the Spirit in the bond of peace" (Ephesians 4:2, 3).

The unity designed by God for His people is much more than physical, corporeal unity; it is spiritual. Without a unity of the Spirit, people conceivably could be members of the same church and agree perfectly on doctrinal issues, while at the same time be of such attitudes as to be hardly on speaking terms with one another. And this condition does exist. It cannot exist, however, where there is unity of the Spirit. If we can keep the unity of the Spirit, although our degree of spiritual illumination for the moment may not be the same, as we yield ourselves to the Spirit's guidance we will ultimately arrive at the unity of the faith.

Let us notice our Lord's prayer for His believers' unity as recorded by John: "That they all may be one; as thou, Father, art in me, and I in thee, that they also may be one is us: that the world may believe that thou hast sent me. And the glory which thou gavest me I have given them; that they may be one, even as we are one: I in them, and thou in me, that they may be made perfect in one" (John 17:21-23).

Is this not the key to divine unity for God's Church—"I in them, and thou in me"? Where Christ is enthroned in human hearts, where His lordship is truly experienced, it will not be difficult to have the unity of the Spirit. And I cannot see how such people can disagree for long on what is His will as outlined in His Word.

Jesus said, "If a man love me, he will keep my words: and my Father will love him, and we will come unto him, and make our abode with him" (John 14:23). Each of us made a verbal commitment to keep His words upon becoming members of the Church of God. Our names were then added to the membership roll. Now that was an important step for us to take, and I am glad to know that my name is still listed on the membership roll of the Church of God.

I am afraid, however, that some are putting too much trust in the fact that they took a covenant and that their names are on the book. It is more important that they make certain their names are inscribed in the Book of Life. Paul wrote, "Nevertheless the foundation of God standeth sure, having this seal, The Lord knoweth them that are his. And, Let every one that nameth the name of Christ depart from iniquity" (2 Timothy 2:19). Church membership will not save you. It is important, all right, but of overriding importance is your relationship with Jesus Christ. Neither will membership in the Church of God automatically create the unity for which Christ prayed: "That they all may be one." This unity must come about, but it will happen only as we find the relationship of which Jesus spoke: "I in them, and thou in me."

It is not enough to be united in one body, we must be united in one body in Him. The life of the body relates to our relationship with Jesus Christ. Our likeness must be to the branches of a vine rather than to a bundle of sticks that are somehow bound together. Such sticks have no life, nor will they bear fruit. When we know the relationship of "I in them, and thou in me," we will be as the branches of a vine, all bearing the same kind of fruit, the fruit of the Spirit.

It is very possible at the present time to be a member of the Church, yes, even a minister in the Church, and be as lifeless as a dry stick. It is possible to be a member, or a minister and even be steeped in iniquity. However, this will not continue to be so.

Last year, in the Assembly, God issued a call for repentance. I wonder how seriously we have taken that call. At the time this call was given through the Questions and Subjects Committee, practically everybody present went to their knees in prayer. Such a spirit prevailed that many tears were shed. The same thing took place in the ministers conventions. As the Business Acts of the Assembly were ratified in the local conferences this call of repentance again brought people to their knees all around the world.

Our response to this call from God, however, requires more than praying; it requires more than tears. It necessitates a change. Praying, even with tears, is not repentance. Repentance involves turning away from what is wrong and turning toward what is right. It means giving up our own ambitions and surrendering to the lordship of Jesus Christ. It literally means giving His Church back to Him. Until this has been done it cannot be said that we have repented.

Right now, there are mixed feelings among us. Some seem to be wondering what we have to repent of; to them the repentance they made when they got saved is the only repentance they feel to be necessary. To them the Church is doing fine and all we have to do is to "stay the course." Others feel that a spiritual drift has taken place, leading us to a place of near-rejection by God. There certainly is the need for a clear perception, a divine perception of our spiritual status. And I believe we can have it if we will only be willing to give heed to the voice of God. Sometimes we need to stop talking and listen.

At this late date we do not need the confusion of a thousand voices; we need to hear one Voice loud and clear. The spirit of Babylon can exist within as well as outside the Church. Such confusion should find no place in the Church of the living God, the pillar and ground of the truth. It is time for Zion's watchmen to "lift up the voice," the singular Voice of the Son of God.

God's judgment is against Babylon, and He is saying to His children today, "Come out of her, my people, that ye be not partakers of her sins, and that ye receive not of her plagues" (Revelation 18:4). The Spirit of the Church and the spirit of Babylon are diametrically opposed to each other.

When leaders within the Church give uncertain sounds, it is confusing to the people. We need to speak the truth unequivocally. There should be no cause for a man who is sent by God with a divine message to hedge or to appear uncertain. God's Word must be preached with boldness. If it is His Word you have all the authority of heaven and earth behind you. If it is not God's Word, don't preach it.

It is important also that our message be matched by our lifestyles. Double-standards breed confusion. If the message calls for self-denial, then don't be grasping and greedy. Live a life of self-denial, otherwise, don't preach it. The love of money has destroyed many a person. Covetousness is a work of the flesh. Being overtaken by this fleshly lust, many have "erred from the faith, and pierced themselves through with many sorrows" (1 Timothy 6:10). Ministers, of all people, should be examples of those who deny themselves to take up the Cross and follow the Saviour.

When John the Baptist was preaching his introductory message of the kingdom of God, a message of repentance, even the soldiers who came to him were told to be content with their wages. This was only preparation for the gospel of Jesus Christ.

A worldly spirit should be given no place in God's Church. For men who have been called of God to be aspiring to higher positions, to bigger churches or states, to more prestigious positions, is worldly. Where people look up to their spiritual leaders, expecting to see the Master's life and teachings mirrored in them, and instead detect a worldly spirit of grasping for personal gain or advancement, such self-centeredness is confusing to sincere Christians.

Among the voices of Babylon in our age has arisen a cult which preaches prosperity and the absence of suffering for God's people. This perverted doctrine appeals to the flesh, and many fleshly-minded people are being caught up in its corruptness. The fellowship of Christ's sufferings and His lifestyle of self-denial are foreign to these "ticklers of carnal ears."

When this life has ended and we are gathered together with the saints of all ages, how comfortable would these peddlers of the no suffering, prosperity doctrine feel with those faithful martyrs who sacrificed themselves totally for the Lord? The writer of Hebrews described them as having, "trial of cruel mockings and scourgings, yea, moreover of bonds and imprisonment: They were stoned, they were sawn asunder, were tempted, were slain with the sword: they wandered about in sheepskins and goatskins; being destitute, afflicted, tormented" (Hebrews 11:36, 37). I would like to feel that my fellowship with these precious people will be genuine, along with all those who at the present time are suffering privation and hardship, some being in prison right now. If our fellowship is to be real, I must join Paul in desiring to know the fellowship of my Saviour's suffering. Such fellowship will preclude any greediness on my part. I will rather follow the intent of Paul's instructions when he wrote: "Look not every man on his own things, but every man also on the things of others" (Philippians 2:4).

Yes, it is time for Zion's watchmen to lift up the Voice. His sheep will hear His voice, because they know Him. But what about those among us who are simply trusting in the covenant relationship of His Church, who really do not know Him. Remember, " . . . they are not all Israel, which are of Israel" (Romans 9:6).

In our zeal for the message of "one Church for all," we have at times almost disassociated the Church of God from the kingdom of God. Sometimes it comes across in our messages that "we" are the Church and "they" are the kingdom. But we must not remove the spiritual, invisible kingdom from the Church. The Church's life flows through the kingdom. "The kingdom of God is . . . righteousness, and peace, and joy in the Holy Ghost" (Romans 14:17).

We can have so much pride in being the Church and spend our time boasting of it, that the root of the matter is a wordly attitude, totally unbecoming to a child of God. It would be more profitable to search for and cultivate those spiritual qualities of the kingdom, thus concentrating on being the Church. Otherwise, we could find ourselves polishing the brass on a sinking ship.

Without the kingdom's vitality the Church becomes a dead, dry organization, which would be able to operate mechanically, but its members would not know God in the vital relationship which He demands. God's call to repentance in the last Assembly was for our having drifted from a vital relationship with the Holy Ghost.

"For the kingdom of God is not in word, but in power" (1 Corinthians 4:20). We might know all the right words, being able to articulate Church doctrine very expertly, yet be woefully lacking in spiritual power. Theology is important. The Church's theology must be correct, and we are taught to earnestly contend for the faith; that is, we must not allow the doctrine which was once delivered to the saints to be watered down or weakened in its application.

At the same time we must have the power. It was the power of God which brought about the addition of three thousand souls on the Day of Pentecost. It is the power of God today which draws men and women to God. They cannot be educated into salvation. Clever arguments of defense for doctrinal positions do not convert sinners. This is not to minimize the importance of solid biblical teaching which is necessary to establish Christians in the faith. We just must make sure that our presentation of the gospel is in demonstration of the Spirit and of power (cf. 1 Corinthians 2:4).

The Holy Ghost is our Guide. Now, in an area with which one is very familiar, he will feel no need for a guide. He feels assured that he knows his way around, and that he can maneuver quite well without help. This is true in the natural. Some seem content to continue in a spiritual area with which they are familiar, where they can maintain control, where they need no guide, but the Holy Ghost is here to guide us into all truth. All truth contains areas into which we have not moved as yet. Still, God has decreed that His Church will move into all truth, that she will come to the measure of the stature of Christ's fulness. For this, we need our Guide. We must have Him.

In the power of the Spirit the Church must proceed with its ministry. We will never succeed otherwise. Apart from this power we will never be, as was said of the Early Church, "of one heart and of one soul." I believe the time is at hand when we will see and flow together. This verse from Isaiah may be applied ultimately to all God's children everywhere, but our first concern is its application within the Church of God of the 1980's.

I do not believe we can train ourselves into this unity. There must be a melting together by the Holy Ghost. The snow which blankets much of this continent during the winter months does not begin flowing together until it melts. As the melting process takes place, it leaves its fixed position and starts moving toward a meeting with other melted snow, finally joining it in one great river. Of course, only that which is of the same substance will melt. As the snow melts and moves toward unity with other melted snow, things which do not melt will be left behind.

The snow is composed of water from the heavens. While the power of the sun melts it, the sun has a different effect upon the mud next to the snow. The same sun that melts snow causes the mud to become crusty and hard. Paul wrote, " . . . The first man Adam was made a living soul; the last Adam was made a quickening spirit. . . . The first man is of the earth, earthy: the second man is the Lord from heaven. As is the earthy, such are they also that are earthy:

and as is the heavenly, such are they also that are heavenly" (1 Corinthians 15:45-48).

"Then thou shalt see, and flow together." What shall we see? We shall see Jesus, not a mere character of history who walked in Galilee long ago, but the living Lord who even now is walking in the "midst of the seven candlesticks" (cf. Revelation 1:13). As our eyes are opened to behold His glorious presence, we will feel as did John the Revelator who said, "And when I saw him, I fell at his feet as dead" (v. 17).

If we are of a melting substance, those things separating us from the full glory of His fellowship will appear in the paltriness with which they really should be regarded. Petty bickerings will end; jockeying for positions will come to a halt; there will be no seeking for promotions, nor will there be attempts to destroy someone else's influence who, you fear, may be outshining you. Instead, we will be, in the words of Paul, "kindly affectioned one to another with brotherly love; in honour preferring one another" (Romans 12:10).

Our eyes must be opened to those things which are hindering our forward march. We must identify the things which God has condemned us of in calling us to repent. He has literally asked us to change our ways! To the church at Ephesus He said, "Remember therefore from whence thou art fallen, and repent, and do the first works; or else I will come unto thee quickly, and will remove thy candlestick out of his place, except thou repent" (Revelation 2:5).

I believe God right now is giving us space to repent. That which He has purposed from the foundation of the world, in which He has invested the blood of His only begotten Son, He will not allow to fail. He will thoroughly purge His floor, "and gather his wheat into the garner; but he will burn up the chaff with unquenchable fire" (Matthew 3:12).

A revival is on the way! A renewing is at hand! It is going to result in a flowing together. And Jesus Christ will appear, and He will present unto Himself a glorious Church without spot or wrinkle, or any such thing. It shall be holy and without blemish!

The question that each of us must ask himself is, "Am I of the substance which melts before His presence?" Do we possess the "earthy" nature or the "heavenly"? Carnal people will not melt, but spiritual people will melt before His presence and flow together!

Have Faith In God

3

81st Annual Assembly
Wednesday, September 3, 1986
White Wing Messenger, Nov. 15, 1986

"And Jesus answering saith unto them, Have faith in God" (Mark 11:22).

The writer of Hebrews wrote: " . . . for he that cometh to God must believe that he is . . . "—that He is God, so great and high above man as to be incomprehensible in the totality of His being. If man was only a physical and intellectual creature, he could not know God at all. But he is also a spiritual being, and it is in this aspect of his makeup that he may perceive that which is divine. "That which is born of the Spirit is spirit." We have formulated some words in an attempt to understand some things the Scriptures teach us about Him. For example, we say He is omnipotent, omniscient, and omnipresent. All of these He is declared to be in His Word.

To confess that He is omnipotent, or all-powerful, acknowledges that He is God; moreover, that He is one God, inasmuch as there cannot be two all-powerful beings. The all power of the one would negate the possibility of another's being all-powerful. This fact provides some insight into the nature of the Trinity. Some would have us embrace the idea of tritheism; that is three Gods. This is erroneous. Now, Sabellianism, commonly referred to as the "Jesus Only" or "Oneness" doctrine is wrong, but tritheism is also wrong. It is just as erroneous as the "Jesus Only" doctrine.

There are not three Gods; there is one God in three persons: God the Father; God the Son, and God the Holy Ghost. "For there are three that bear record in heaven, the Father, the Word, and the Holy Ghost: and these three are one" (1 John 5:7). This is one aspect of God's being that is incomprehensible except by faith. " . . . he that cometh to God must believe that he is . . . ." Have faith in God!

To say that God is omniscient is to say that He is all-knowing. The Psalmist wrote: "Thou knowest my downsitting and mine uprising, thou understandest my thought afar off. . . . For there is not a word in my tongue, but, lo, O Lord, thou knowest it altogether" (Psalms 139:2, 4).

To have faith in God is to have faith in His omniscience—that He is all-knowing. Our lives, all our actions and activities, even our thoughts are an "open book" to Him. The fact is, He knows our thoughts before we think them. He understands our nature completely, the nature of our hearts which produces the quality of thoughts that we think. He knows the sincerity of our devotion to Him, or the lack of it. This faith in His omniscience provides assurance to a true worshiper of God. He knows God understands him completely, knowing his motives which often may be misunderstood by others.

There is an obvious lack of faith in this aspect of God's being among those who are deficient in sincerity and integrity. True faith in God will not allow unchristian thought or action. It is evident that some people, even in the Church, are putting their faith in themselves—in their ability to scheme, to maneuver, in their ability to manipulate people to achieve their own selfish desires. Such people are to be pitied for their willful ignorance.

Then there are those who have placed their faith in the operation of the Church's organization, in the system, drifting along with a feeling of security that as long as they can stay in the Church they will be secure, or as long as they support the system, that it will support them. Let it be stated emphatically that faith in anything or in anyone, other than faith in God is misplaced faith and will result in eternal ruin.

It is not enough to have faith in a form of regular church attendance, going to the conventions and to the Assembly. This is commendable, but a person can be ever so faithful to attend all these gatherings, trusting in this aspect of his faithfulness to save him, rather than in a vital relationship with the Living God. This is a mistake!

As the Church of God our faith must not be in ourselves, that is, in the Church. That would be a grave error, a fatal error. It must be in the Head of the Church. Israel had faith in themselves, in their heritage. Their faith told them that they could not fail. They knew they were a covenanted people and felt sure that God would not forsake them, that He would not fail them. They failed to consider, however, the consequences of their failing Him, of putting their faith in their role as the chosen of God instead of putting their faith solely in God. Let us not repeat their error! Only God is infallible; we certainly are not. What He has purposed to perform is infallible. His purposes cannot fail, but these purposes do not have to be fulfilled in us!

In the eleventh chapter of Hebrews, which we commonly call the "faith chapter," our attention is drawn to Abel, to Enoch, to Noah, to Abraham. These were men who believed God to the point of being willing to walk with Him, to work for Him, to obey Him. This is not so much an account of God's miraculous gifts to them, as though their faith turned Him into some kind of giant Santa Claus. Rather, it speaks of their sacrifices for Him. It speaks of a faith which commanded Noah's faithfulness to a task which drew few converts: of a faith which made Abraham confess that he was a stranger and a pilgrim on this earth.

It speaks of people who were tortured, who had trials of cruel mockings and scourgings, who suffered bonds and imprisonment, who were stoned and sawn asunder, who were slain with the sword. These people's faith in God enabled them to wander about in sheepskins and goatskins, being destitute, afflicted and tormented (cf. vv. 35-17).

Contrary to a popular "faith in faith" philosophy which guarantees material prosperity and freedom from all suffering, faith in God acknowledges His sovereignty and says with Job, "Though he slay me, yet will I trust in him" (Job 13:15). It acknowledges His infinite goodness in the face of our very limited understanding. When we are unable to understand why things are happening to us as they are, faith in God says, "And we know that all things work together for good to them that love God, to them who are the called according to his purpose" (Romans 8:28).

We are in a constant warfare with Satan who is trying to weaken and destroy our faith, or cause us to somehow place it in something other than in God alone. Our leaders in the early part of this century had little to put their faith in apart from God. Their finances were very meager, they had not heard about a "Big Business Program," there was little organization or system, but one thing they had—freedom in the Spirit and faith in His power. They knew God would sustain them in every circumstance; furthermore, that He would guide them and give them souls for their labor. And He was sufficient! The record of their work attests to the wisdom of this approach.

When David faced Goliath, his faith was not in the weapons that were available to him. Without being an officer, having no rank (which seems to me to be a worldly term), his faith was not in a position or a title, but he faced this giant with faith in God, and that was sufficient.

Now in this Assembly, in our decision-making, we must not place our faith in the majority—that would be putting faith in the judgment of people. The majority can be wrong, and often is. The account of the twelve spies who were dispatched by Moses to the land of Canaan illustrates the fallacy of majority rule. It is our business to put our faith in God and to know His mind. We must turn from fleshly judgment to spiritual discernment. This can be done only by a spiritual people.

Then, there are those who profess to have faith in God who seem to care little for His demands of righteousness. This is not sound faith. A person whose faith in God meets divine approval will live out his faith in compliance with the divine will. All unrighteousness is sin and God cannot fellowship sin. Those people claiming to possess great faith while yet living unrighteous lives surely do not have faith in God. It would be profitable for them to evaluate, to examine, to question in what, indeed, their faith is placed.

Let it be emphasized also that God is a God of judgment. His judgments are not always executed speedily, but they are, none the less, sure. To have faith in God is to have faith in the certainty of His judgment against sin. His judgments are not haphazard. Nothing escapes His eye. Some might prefer to regard Him as an ancient old man who lives in a remote place called heaven, far removed from the busy details of modern life. The fact is, His omnipresence provides that in Him we live and move and have our being. It is in His power that we exist, that we live. There is no place where God is not. He is here right now in this Assembly, not somewhere far-removed, as though He had left everything in our hands.

Would His visible presence on this platform tonight make Him more real to you? Would it make any difference in your manner of worship? Would His visible presence in your home make any difference in your conversation and conduct there? Though He is the invisible God, His presence is no less real than were He visibly recognizable. He is not the "man upstairs." In fact, this is a term that is degrading and should not be used. He is Almighty God, God of majesty, power and glory.

The quality of our faith will be determined largely by our concept of God. Too many, even among us, have a low image of God. This accounts for the replacement of true spiritual living with a form of godliness which is carried on in the strength of the flesh, often bearing the marks of carnality.

This accounts also for the legalistic approach toward government within the Church—depending upon rules and regulations for ethical conduct which should not be necessary for a spiritual people who have a high view of God. Whenever we begin compiling a set of rules there arises the immediate danger of minds being turned toward the observance of these rules instead of seeking the face of the Lord and enjoying His presence. The joyful life cannot be known apart from a joyous relationship with Him. It certainly will not come through the mere adherence to a list of rules.

The legalist labors under the impression that, as long as he is faithful to the rules, he is spiritual. Now there might be things not included in the list of rules that are just as important, and maybe more so, than some of the things that have been spelled out. But the legalistic mentality tends to ignore what is not specifically stated in the rule book. To the scribes and Pharisees, who were guilty of this very thing, Jesus said, "Woe unto you, scribes and Pharisees, hypocrites! for ye pay tithe of mint and anise and cummin, and have omitted the weightier matters of the law, judgment, mercy, and faith. . . . Ye blind guides, which strain at a gnat, and swallow a camel" (Matthew 23:23, 24).

How much better it is to place one's faith in the Omnipresent God and to establish a relationship with Him that exalts and glorifies Him in a life of true holiness and righteousness.

The prominent teachings of the Church, of which we may boast, do not bring God's delight except as the principles behind them abide in us. Holiness, for example, does not consist in those external observances that are often associated with it, but in the principle which creates an absence of sin in one's life.

Faith in God means faith in His holiness and in His demands for holiness in the lives of those who serve Him. Such faith will go beyond mere profession, that of giving verbal assent to this teaching; it will cause a person to embrace the provision of the sanctifying blood of Jesus, thus becoming wholly sanctified, then holiness will be an inner quality, reflecting that person's oneness with a holy God. Without a sound faith we may stop short of the spiritual experience, all the while dwelling upon the "externals."

What we say we believe is not nearly so important as what we believe. What you really believe is what makes you the kind of person you are.

The "rule-book" mentality of legalism poses real dangers for the Church of God, which is described by Peter as a spiritual house. Israel's numerous ceremonial laws and ordinances did not make the Israelites a spiritual people. They did create in some a self-righteous and judgmental spirit, as was evidenced among the Pharisees of Jesus' time. Our Lord condemned these legalists, saying, " . . . they bind heavy burdens and grievous to be borne, and lay them on men's shoulders; but they themselves will not move them with one of their fingers" (Matthew 23:4).

Jesus, the great Emancipator, cried to these people, "Come unto me, all ye that labour and are heavy laden, and I will give you rest. Take my yoke upon you, and learn of me; for I am meek and lowly in heart: and ye shall find rest unto your souls. For my yoke is easy, and my burden is light" (Matthew 11:28-30).

Spiritual freedom was upon the minds of those Early Church fathers who were present for the Jerusalem council, when they wrote, "For it seemed good to the Holy Ghost, and to us, to lay upon you no greater burden than these necessary things; That ye abstain from meats offered to idols, and from blood, and from things strangled, and from fornication: from which if ye keep yourselves, ye shall do well" (Acts 15:28, 29). Earlier in this council Peter had asked, "Now therefore why tempt ye God, to put a yoke upon the neck of the disciples, which neither our fathers nor we were able to bear?" (v. 10).

From time to time we hear the clamor for more rules, or for the desire to make some of our present advice and teachings more binding upon our members. I cannot feel this is the proper course to follow. Some place must be given to Christian conscience. Paul wrote, "For the grace of God . . . hath appeared . . . teaching us that, denying ungodliness and worldly lusts, we should live soberly, righteously, and godly, in this present world" (Titus 2:11, 12). The grace of God is a great teacher.

Since the early part of this century it has been emphasized that we would not be a creedal organization, but that the New Testament, and the New Testament alone, would be our rule of faith. In the New Testament certain principles are given which spiritual people will observe. The Scriptures, for example, give us the principles of moderation, of modesty and of separation from the world. These principles are distinctly set forth in the Word, and to violate them is to violate Christian conscience.

For some reason most every denomination has felt it necessary to make its list of rules to insure the observance of these principles among its members. To enforce these principles of moderation, modesty and separation from the world they have made rules to regulate outward adornment. Some have insisted upon extreme plainness, with the men wearing no neckties and coats with no buttons, while the women's dresses had to cover the ankles, with no frills, no curling of the hair (or straightening, as the case may be), no makeup, no jewelry, etc.

One group forbade motorized vehicles, stating that the members should ride only in vehicles pulled by animals, so as not to be worldly. Later a group separated themselves from the parent group and altered their stand to allow the use of automobiles, but insisted that they be without any ornamentation. Any chrome had to be removed or else painted black, the only color that was acceptable to them. To have chrome on the automobile, to them represented excessive ornamentation which characterized the pride of life, or worldliness, and they were very sincere in their belief. To them these rules were necessary to maintain a standard of separation from the world. Were they correct? They were sincere in wanting to please God, and suffered persecution and the ridicule of society as a result.

Now we have not altogether escaped this kind of rule-making, which most all denominations have employed to set forth their distinctives. We might not have been as extreme as some other groups, but to be the Church of God, the One Fold for the gathering together of the children of

God, we must be willing to examine, in the light of the Scriptures, every position we have set forth, in total honesty and openness. If in our zealousness we have acted without knowledge or wisdom in the formulation of some of our statements, we must have the courage to correct whatever might be an impediment to true Christian unity.

To place our faith in whatever the Church has said and cling to it tenaciously, with no willingness to reexamine or walk in a greater light, is not wisdom. Any position we may have taken which cannot bear reexamination is not one upon which I would want to stake my eternal destiny. Our faith must be in God, being sensitive to His enlightenment of our hearts and minds. God alone is infallible. The Church is composed of flesh and blood people who are fallible. We are capable of erring; only God is not!

It is better to stand upon divine principles than upon rules. God's principles for His people never change. The rules we make in an effort to enforce His principles are what create problems.

When I was in high school about forty years ago, it came time for purchasing high school class rings. I was told that the Church was opposed to its members wearing class rings, but that it was all right to buy that same set that was in the ring and wear it in a pin on my lapel. I had some difficulty understanding the principle behind this kind of distinction. Today, when I hear of members, and even ministers, wearing diamond-studded watches which may cost a thousand dollars or more attacking another Christian who is wearing a relatively inexpensive wedding band, teaching against that other person's excessive ornamentation, I still have problems understanding the correctness of their position.

Now I do not propose that we start examining everyone's watch, neither do I suggest standing in the parking lot to check the automobiles they arrive in to see whether they are too expensive or have too much chrome on them, so that we can judge them as being worldly. Some things are better left to the conscience of the individual. Each of us must make certain, however, that his conscience remains sensitive to the Holy Ghost.

It seems sometimes that we are more interested in rule-making and rule-enforcing than we are in observing divine principles—loving God and loving people. Rules tend to breed a spirit of legalism, with accompanying judgmental attitudes, while embracing from the heart the principles of moderation, modesty and separation from the world brings glory to God, who called us and chose us to be a people who would shine as lights in the midst of a darkened world.

The power for illumination must work from the inside, outward. This was the essence of Paul's message to the Colossians when he wrote, "Wherefore if ye be dead with Christ from the rudiments of the world, why, as though living in the world, are ye subject to ordinances, (Touch not; taste not; handle not; Which all are to perish with the using;) after the commandments and doctrines of men?" (Colossians 2:20-22).

There are those today who feel that by keeping such ordinances as Paul mentioned—touch not, taste not, handle not, they can keep themselves undefiled and thus shine as lights in the world. Defilement, however, does not come from what is touched, tasted or handled. Jesus said, "Hear, and understand: Not that which goeth into the mouth defileth a man; but that which cometh out of the mouth, this defileth a man. . . . those things which proceed out of the mouth come forth from the heart; and they defile the man. For out of the heart proceed evil thoughts, murders, adulteries, fornications, thefts, false witness, blasphemies: These are the things which defile a man . . . " (Matthew 15:10, 11, 18-20).

Separation from the world involves more than leaving off outward adornment or staying away from places of worldly amusement. The surest marks of our separation from the world will be denoted in our interpersonal relationships—in how we treat one another, in how we respond to one another (cf. Romans 14:4, 10-22). Of the Early Church it was said, "Behold how they love one another." Jesus Himself said, "By this shall all men know that ye are my disciples, if ye have love one to another" (John 13:35).

When Jesus prayed, "That they all may be one . . . that the world may believe . . . " (John 17:21), it was not just for the organizational unity of His disciples. People can be fellow-members of the Church of God of Prophecy, without possessing the oneness for which Jesus prayed. It was, " . . . as thou, Father, art in me, and I in thee, that they also may be one in us . . . ." Our oneness must be in Him. It is only when we are in Him, abiding in Him, with the power of His life flowing through us, that our "other-worldness" stands out. There is no worldliness in Him, neither will it exist in the Church which He presents to Himself "a glorious church, not having spot, or wrinkle, or any such thing."

We might be ever so careful to keep all the "ordinances," as Paul mentioned to the Colossians, while at the same time possessing malice, guile, hypocrisy or envy, speaking evil of a brother or sister (cf. 1 Peter 2:1). Whatever is in our hearts will be manifested in our interpersonal relationships, and it is here that our separation from the world will be most vividly manifested.

Some people pride themselves in being keepers of the "Advice to Members" while at the same time they have no reservations about being critics of brothers or sisters who have a genuine relationship with God. Contained in that advice is, "Don't be a critic. Guard your conversation. Be careful what you say about a brother, sister, or anyone else." It is excellent advice also to "spend as much time as you can in secret prayer. Give yourself all you can to intercessory prayer. Daily prayers and study of God's Word are necessary and very important for the spiritual welfare of each child of God."

It might be noted that this part of our "Advice to Members" is listed ahead of the part which deals with moderation in dress, adornment, and worldly amusements. Why would a person want to skip right over this advice that is primary, which would help him to become a more deeply spiritual person, which is, indeed, our most urgent need with the Church right now, and dwell upon the "externals"? Without a renewed emphasis upon that which is basic, we will continue "swatting at mosquitos, all the while ignoring their breeding places."

A ritualistic religion is usually negative rather than positive in its character, strong in the elements of its prohibitions. Ritualistic religion can be carried out through the flesh for the purpose of building one's ego, of asserting his self-righteousness. Instead of leading a person closer to God, it all the while causes him to drift from a personal relationship with Jesus to the inflating of his own personal pride, whereof he can boast, as did the Pharisee, "God, I thank thee, that I am not as other men are" (Luke 18:11). This fosters a judgmental attitude toward others who are not keeping the rules as well as he considers himself to be doing.

Perhaps it was Peter's background of ceremonial law that caused him to ask, "Lord, how oft shall my brother sin against me, and I forgive him? Till seven times?" (Matthew 18:21). He wanted some rules. This new way Jesus was introducing where forgiveness works from within, from the heart, was foreign to him. If Jesus would just give him a number, then he would know when he had been faithful "to the teachings."

It seems so easy to drift into the condition of the Pharisees who busied themselves with all the "externals." Jesus called them hypocrites, saying, " . . . ye make clean the outside of the cup and of the platter, but within they are full of extortion and excess. . . . ye are like unto whited sepulchres, which indeed appear beautiful outward, but are within full of dead men's bones, and of all uncleanness" (Matthew 23:25, 27).

There is no point in trying to preserve dead men's bones in God's Church. The Church is not a repository for preserving corpses; it must be a vibrant, living organism, showing forth the power of the Living God. Our faith is in the God of the living. God is alive and He is wanting His Church to grow up in Him, into His life.

Life in Him is never stagnant, but growing, changing. When our faith is in ourselves, in our rules, in our control, the tendency is to fear change, lest we lose control. When our faith is in God, knowing He is in control, we welcome the changes which He orders. They are always for our good and for His glory.

I want to reiterate that it is wrong to place our faith in anything other than in the Living God. Luke provides us an interesting account of an occurrence as Paul was aboard a ship, sailing for Rome. "Then fearing lest we should have fallen upon rocks, they cast four anchors out of the stern, and wished for the day. And as the shipmen [those in charge of sailing the ship] were about to flee out of the ship, when they had let down the boat into the sea, under colour as though they would have cast anchors out of the foreship, Paul said to the centurion and to the soldiers, Except these [shipmen] abide in the ship, ye cannot be saved. Then the soldiers cut off the ropes of the boat, and let her fall off" (Acts 27:29-32).

Different analogies have been drawn from this account. Some have read it as though Paul had said, "Except ye abide in the ship, ye cannot be saved," thus emphasizing the necessity for staying in the Church in order to be saved. Actually, Paul said, "Except these [those responsible for piloting the ship] abide in the ship, ye cannot be saved." A better analogy might be that if the Father, Son and Holy Ghost abandon the "Old Ship of Zion," we cannot be saved. They alone are capable of piloting this "ship."

Now in Paul's situation, the ship could not save them, but staying in the ship, at the word of the Lord, would save them. Their faith in the ship to save them would have been a misplaced faith. In fact, we read a little farther in this account that the ship was broken in pieces. Paul's faith was not in the ship but in the words of the Lord. He said, "For I believe God, that it shall be even as it was told me" (v. 25).

Faith in anything or anyone, other than faith in God, is misplaced faith. Faith in the General Overseer is misplaced faith. In the church at Corinth one's faith in Paul, another's in Apollos, another's in Cephas was misplaced faith. Our faith must be placed squarely and wholly in God and God alone. "Thou shalt have no other gods before me" is still the word of the Lord.

Faith in the Ark of the Covenant was a misplaced faith for the Israelites in a time when they were engaged in battle with the Philistines. When things were going poorly with them in their battle against these enemies of God, their decision was, "Let us fetch the ark of the covenant of the Lord out of Shiloh unto us, that, when it cometh among us, it may save us out of the hand of our enemies" (1 Samuel 4:3).

But the Ark did not save them. The death of thirty thousand of their men attested to the Ark's powerlessness as an object of their faith. It was a sacred object, all right; God had ordered its construction, but it had no saving power. This account in the Scriptures is to remind us that God's people must put their faith in Him and Him alone. It was Jesus, the Head of the Church, who said, "Have faith in God."

Our greatest mistake would be not to recognize God, and not to recognize Him in our midst—the immediacy of His presence. He is not a distant Being in a far-off place in the sky. He is present among us right now, seeking to draw us into an intimate relationship with Him such as we have never experienced. Will you acknowledge His presence? Will you put your complete faith in Him—not in a creed, a dogma, a set of rules, an institution, but in Him? Will you submit yourself to His power to make of you an instrument of divine power?

He is God. He is all-powerful; yet, He is infinitely caring, infinitely compassionate. His love toward you is perfect. He could not possibly love you one bit more than He does. His grace is abundant, no matter what your need is right now. Are you ready to relinquish your faith in all else in which you might have been trusting, and put your faith totally in Him? Have faith in God!

Thy Kingdom Come

82nd Assembly
Wednesday, September 9, 1987
White Wing Messenger, Oct. 17, 1987

Recently, more and more I have found myself praying, "Our Father which art in heaven, Hallowed be thy name. Thy kingdom come. Thy will be done in earth, as it is in heaven." Our Father which art in heaven—He is far above all that is earthly, all that is carnal, all that is petty and childish, "dwelling in the light which no man can approach unto" (1 Timothy 6:16); yet, we can approach unto Him and call Him our Father. What a condescension He made, coming unto us in our "low estate." It was John who exclaimed, "Behold, what manner of love the Father hath bestowed upon us, that we should be called the sons of God" (1 John 3:1). Paul wrote, "And because ye are sons, God hath sent forth the Spirit of his Son into your hearts, crying, Abba, Father" (Galatians 4:6).

The more we comprehend of our Heavenly Father, of our mighty God, the more we feel like crying, "Hallowed be thy name." In awesome reverence we feel like joining the seraphim seen by Isaiah, crying, "Holy, holy, holy." It is not hard for me to pray, "Hallowed be thy name." We exalt His name, we revere His name; we bless His name.

O the earnestness with which I find myself praying more and more, "Thy kingdom come." The topic I have chosen for this message is the cry of my heart: "Thy kingdom come in my life, Thy kingdom come in my home, in my family; Thy kingdom come in my local church, Thy kingdom come within the leadership of the Church, here in Cleveland and in every state and nation. O God, thy kingdom come!"

It is a kingdom of righteousness, peace and joy in the Holy Ghost. It is a kingdom of power, of authority over all that is in opposition to His rule, over all that exalts itself against God. Now, it is God's purpose that His kingdom be given expression within His Church; the Church was divinely instituted for this purpose. However, the institution itself does not assure kingdom power. The home also is a divinely ordered institution, but every home is not under His dominion; therefore it should be our prayer: "Thy kingdom come within my home." So it is with the institution we call God's Church.

Historically, institutional form has been substituted for kingdom authority, for kingdom power, for kingdom righteousness, for kingdom peace, for kingdom joy. The religious institution into which Jesus was born was not lacking in form. The machinery of institutional government was in place. They had their prescribed forms of worship which they carried out meticulously; they had the written Word to which they gave much lip service with a great show of piety. They even knew how to stone people who did not "measure up." Love for institutional laws apart from love and concern for people is deplorable. Then, there were factions within this institution which enjoyed arguing and contending with one another over points of doctrine, often teaching for doctrine the commandments of men. They frequently were in error, not really knowing the Scriptures, nor the power of God. Of course, they thought they knew the Scriptures; they could have quoted them at length, but they were ignorant of the substance, the life, the power, the inspiration of God's Holy Word.

When the Word was made flesh and dwelt among them, they could not identify Him with the Scriptures they professed to know. And He is still walking among us (as among the candlesticks of Revelation 1:13), but many remain blind and insensitive to His presence, while with legalistic pride they consider themselves to be authorities of the Scriptures. These Jews could not identify the Living Word with the Scriptures they professed to know. In the absence of such knowledge they took refuge in the institution, boasting of their heritage. Eventually this Living Word, Jesus of Nazareth, became a threat to them, to their power in the chosen nation. They could not control Him, and that which they could not control they set about to destroy. First, however, they tried to discredit Him: " . . . out of Galilee ariseth no prophet"(John 7:52), the rulers argued. But there was power about Him, an authority that they could not cope with. In less than three years into His public ministry they determined that He must die. And He did die. But death could not hold Him; He tore its bars asunder. He was God. These people, this institution had been visited by God; moreover, they had been judged by God. They had desired to control God, to make Him fit into their scheme of things, but God will not fit into any mold of man.

What they had received from God, they had corrupted. At Mt. Sinai He had offered to make of them a peculiar treasure, a holy nation, a kingdom of priests. In a manifestation of great power, wherein the mountain was enveloped in smoke, with thunderings, lightning and an earthquake, God descended to give them His Word, covenanting with them to be their God while they would be His people.

When Jesus later walked among them, however, He found a nation that had perverted their covenant. The fruit of righteousness could not be found among them. They had turned His house of prayer into a house of merchandise where greedy men who were in control exploited the common people, enriching themselves at the expense of devout pilgrims who came regularly to worship. (We still see this kind of thing going on.) On two occasions, as the indignation of our Lord was stirred against these hypocrites, He cleansed His temple of their pollutions. Their hearts were not toward God, but their selfish minds were focused upon the material things which appealed to the lust of the flesh.

The sacred trust they had received from God they had not kept. Rather, they had abused their privileges. Therefore, Christ's pronouncement to them was, "The kingdom of God shall be taken from you, and given to a nation bringing forth the fruits thereof" (Matthew 21:43). This new nation was instituted by Jesus Himself, which He called "my church" (Matthew 16:18). It is identified elsewhere in the New Testament as the Church of God.

Its descriptive titles, as given in 1 Peter 2:9, are similar to the earlier designations for Israel—"a chosen generation, a royal priesthood, an holy nation, a peculiar people." The power for this new nation's function is in the kingdom it has received—the kingdom of God. As mentioned earlier, this is a kingdom of righteousness, of peace, of joy in the Holy Ghost, and this kingdom cannot be separated from the vitality of the Spirit. The Church may be separated from the Spirit's vitality, drifting into a dry form, but the kingdom is with power.

So, today we still pray, "Thy kingdom come, Thy kingdom be fully realized in every area of Your Church, that individually and corporately we shall see a reign of righteousness, of joy, of peace."

This kingdom righteousness is the righteousness which God will accept. Paul wrote, "And be found in him [Christ], not having mine own righteousness, which is of the law, but that which is through the faith of Christ, the righteousness which is of God by faith" (Philippians 3:9). Paul had given much of his life to the righteousness of the law, that is, good works by legislation. He felt sincerely that he was on the right track, but when he had his encounter with Christ on the road to Damascus, he at once knew his righteousness was unacceptable.

Kingdom righteousness cannot be legislated; it works from within—and it does work! Some seem willing to excuse themselves for unrighteous behavior, feeling that the grace of God compensates for their failure in righteous living. This is a fallacy. The true purpose behind God's amazing grace is not that we may continue to sin, but that sin's power over our lives can be broken, that we can, as Zacharias prophesied, serve God without fear, "In holiness and righteousness . . . all the days of our life" (Luke 1:75).

Righteousness is not an option for Christian conduct. John wrote very plainly, " . . . whosoever doeth not righteousness is not of God" (1 John 3:10). There are no exceptions. Again, he declared, "All unrighteousness is sin" (5:17). Paul gave a strong warning to members of the church at Corinth: " . . . the unrighteous shall not inherit the kingdom of God" (1 Corinthians 6:9). His is a kingdom of righteousness.

The righteous nature is God's gift to His children, but continuing righteous living is the result of a person's will, something which God will not override. Righteous living is the exercise of one's will to keep himself in the love and grace of God. Jude wrote, "Keep yourselves in the love of God" (Jude 21). According to Jude we do this by retaining a spiritual vitality, "building up yourselves on your most holy faith, praying in the Holy Ghost" (Jude 20). Apart from a blessed relationship with the Lord, an individual will not live a life of righteousness. Such conduct is not guaranteed by a one-time experience in an altar.

Tenure of membership in the Church, no matter how long, or no matter what office one may hold, does not assure righteousness. In fact, many today are hungering for a return to true holiness and righteousness within our ranks to meet the demands of God. They realize the great need we have for a bestowal of God's favor. We must not feel smug and secure through our positions in the Church, but continue to pray, "Thy kingdom come within thy Church—thy kingdom of righteousness." To the Corinthian members who were allowing too much "loose living" Paul wrote, "Awake to righteousness, and sin not; for some have not the knowledge of God: I speak this to your shame" (1 Corinthians 15:34). Sin is still a reproach to any people, and it is righteousness that will exalt this nation that has been chosen by God for His own exaltation.

We gain assurance from the words of our Lord when He said, "Blessed are they which do hunger and thirst after righteousness: for they shall be filled" (Matthew 5:6). Thank God for this hunger, for this thirst, for this desire which is causing us to pray, "Thy kingdom come." We must not be satisfied or rest until God's judgment against all sin brings a conviction to hearts that will result in a Church-wide purging; then righteousness will run down among us a mighty stream (cf. Amos 5:24).

Frustration and distress will no longer be the "order of the day." Instead, peace will reign among us, the peace that our Lord gives. When the righteousness of His kingdom is not prevailing, when sin remains unjudged, there will be a resultant disharmony within the Church. The Church was designed to be a holy nation, not a secular nation where rivalries, contentions and antagonisms are found. These things breed trouble, and they belong to the world, not the Church. Isaiah wrote, "But the wicked are like the troubled sea, when it cannot rest, whose waters cast up mire and dirt. There is no peace, saith my God, to the wicked" (Isaiah 57:20, 21).

When His kingdom comes within our lives, it brings peace. When His kingdom comes within our homes, it will bring peace. When His kingdom prevails within the Church, peace will be assured. "The kingdom of God is righteousness, and peace . . . ."

Another distinctive of the kingdom is joy. This is the joy of which Peter wrote when he spoke of rejoicing with "joy unspeakable and full of glory" (1 Peter 1:8). The writer of Acts told how "the disciples were filled with joy, and with the Holy Ghost" (Acts 13:52). They were partaking of the promise of their Master who had said to them: "Verily I say unto you, That there be some of them that stand here, which shall not taste of death, till they have seen the kingdom of God come with power" (Mark 9:1).

When spiritual power wanes, it is always marked by a decline in joy. Members begin to perform their various functions in the church from a sense of duty, which becomes quite mechanical. Apathy eventually gives way to drudgery. Nehemiah wrote, " . . . the joy of the Lord is your strength" (Nehemiah 8:10). The enthusiasm brought by joy is marked, among other things, by people gathering eagerly for times of worship and fellowship together. It is normal to see such people seated near the front of the sanctuary. As joy diminishes, you observe the front part of our churches becoming less crowded, congregations moving farther back from active participation in worship, not really anxious to become too involved.

A decline in joy goes with a decline in righteousness, which is marked by a decline in the peace that passeth all understanding.

The Church must experience a restoration of the joy of the Lord! A frustrated, distressed world will not be affected and changed by a Church experiencing the same frustrations. Joyful testimonies are exciting. Sound theology is important, but sinners are not stirred by theological reasonings and debatings. What they are touched by is the testimony of a joyful, victorious Christian.

We must move from mere form to kingdom righteousness, peace and joy. The kingdom is not in word but in power, an exhilarating power. It was this power which was experienced by the Early Church that accelerated their outreach. It will do the same for us. It must not be suppressed. It must rather be sought after, it must be prayed for. Prayer is said to be the sincere desire of the heart. That is why I continue to cry many times on my knees, "Thy kingdom come!" My heart yearns for righteousness, peace and joy to fill God's Church.

The righteousness of this kingdom, the peace of this kingdom, the joy of this kingdom is the outworking of the Holy Ghost within us. Indeed, it is the fruit of the Spirit. Adherence to rules does not bring it. It is as we abide in Him and He abides in us that we will experience a divine relationship which outside forces cannot affect. Dwelling in the midst of all kinds of wickedness, our conduct will be righteous. When storms rage around us we can have peace.

Even in severe persecutions we can know the kind of joy that was demonstrated by Paul and Silas in a Philippian jail. With their backs bloody from the beating they received, and their feet made fast in the stocks, at the midnight hour they could still pray and sing praises to God. This is the joy that is not affected by circumstances. It comes through a relationship with the blessed Holy Ghost.

O for leaders who will lead us on into this kind of kingdom power and glory. It will open new dimensions of service and outreach for us. It will of necessity bring change. Why resist spiritual change?

We date the Reformation as being a Sixteenth Century movement, and it is true that some bold moves were made during that century by Luther, Zwingli and others. But can we say that what they began has ended? What they intended to be a reformation led eventually into an attempt at restoration. The purpose of most every Protestant denomination in its beginnings was an attempt to restore New Testament Christianity. They would break away from what they viewed as apostate parent bodies for this purpose.

This, likewise, has been the stated purpose we have embraced—to see the Church functioning again in all the power and beauty of the Early Church, and even going beyond, to a place of readiness for presentation to Christ. Can we say we have succeeded, that the restoration is complete—that we are operating with the same power and glory which propelled the Early Church into all the known world? No, we do not make that claim. But we must not stop until we have succeeded!

The Church's greatest days are not in its past; its greatest days await a people who are praying earnestly and fervently, "Thy kingdom come—in all its power, in all its glory—Thy kingdom come within Thy Church, O Lord!"

What righteousness! What peace! What joy—unrestrained joy! Let no one be guilty of putting on the brakes in an attempt to stop the Spirit's work in this final period of restoration. Let no one feel that he must control the Spirit. We must, instead, yield to His control. O for spiritual leaders who do not feel it their duty to exercise control over the Church, who do not feel themselves to be lords, who do not feel that they must act as watchdogs, but who rather view themselves as true leaders, moving ahead, setting the pace for venturing into new spiritual realms. There surely are dimensions we do not know yet, into which we will have to move, as we approach the consummation, the full restoration and perfection of this Church age.

Leaders are needed who share Paul's feelings toward the church at Corinth, who wrote, "Not . . . that we have dominion over your faith, but are helpers of your joy" (2 Corinthians 1:24). He did not pretend to have any dominion over their faith. Christ alone is its Author and Finisher. He is God's revelation of Himself—of what we are to believe and understand, and this ongoing revelation of Christ is not under the control of any man, but under the direction of the Holy Ghost. Paul saw himself as a helper of their joy, an instrument in God's hand, not controlling, but being for them an example, an example of a yielded heart, a receptive spirit, an eager pacesetter into the fuller joys of the kingdom. Who among us will be this kind of leader?

Position or appointment does not make one a leader. But God will have leaders—leaders who are advancing to heights they have never known previously. But this requires spiritual boldness and courage. A person will never climb higher on a ladder than he is at the present moment until he is willing to turn loose the rung to which he is holding, reaching up to take hold of a higher one. Those who fear heights, and this is applicable to new spiritual heights, often panic and "freeze" onto what they have in their grasp. Such men cannot be leaders for the last days Church of God. "For God hath not given us the spirit of fear; but of power, and of love, and of a sound mind" (2 Timothy 1:7). Fear is paralyzing, and leaders who are paralyzed by the fear of following the Holy Ghost into untrodden paths will create paralysis within the Church.

Our Lord's charge to the Church is "Onward! Upward!" This is no time for cowards to be in leadership positions. We must not draw back from or fear freedom of the Holy Ghost.

Some leaders feel it their duty to hold the line, to merely preserve the standard, but there is more beyond that line they are holding. The kingdom of God is not static, and the Church that is operating with kingdom power will not be static. It will be "reaching forth unto those things that are before" (Philippians 3:13).

When Christ descended into the midst of that nation which professedly were keepers of the kingdom, but from whom the kingdom would be taken, He declared, "And from the days of John the Baptist until now the kingdom of heaven suffereth violence, and the violent take it by force" (Matthew 11:12). It was a time of upheaval. God was moving among His people, but a staid, recalcitrant leadership was resisting any change. To these defenders of the status quo Jesus said, "Woe unto you, lawyers! for ye have taken away the key of knowledge: ye entered not in yourselves, and them that were entering in ye hindered" (Luke 11:52). These lawyers were experts, priding themselves in their ability to interpret the law. (They were the kind of men who could have told you with preciseness every ruling of the Assembly.) They were legalists, indeed, but they had "taken away the key of knowledge," not seeming to know or appreciate the fact that the knowledge of God is expansive, that it cannot be contained within prescribed boundaries or rules. There was more to the knowledge of God than they themselves understood.

As Paul thought on this subject he cried out, "O the depth of the riches both of the wisdom and knowledge of God! how unsearchable are his judgments, and his ways past finding out!" (Romans 11:33). These lawyers were more interested in holding the people to their strict interpretations than they were in pursuing the richness of a deeper spiritual knowledge and fellowship with God. "Ye have taken away the key of knowledge," Jesus said. "Ye entered not in yourselves, and them that were entering in ye hindered."

I have pondered whether we have been more concerned with training than with teaching. The key of knowledge into the mysteries of the kingdom is turned, not by training, but by teaching, leading people into the exploration of the unsearchable riches of God's Word. The word train is used in the Scriptures with reference to children. "Train up a child in the way he should go . . . " (Proverbs 22:6). Children require training. When they are not old enough to understand why, it is important that they be disciplined not to go into a busy street, or to play with matches, etc. But they will never become mature, functioning adults apart from the process of teaching, which gives freedom to explore and make judgmental discernments on their own. Teaching brings illumination. Training does not involve additional light, but is just a how to do—it is the programming of responses.

Animals are trained, being rewarded for performing according to their trainer's desires. They learn what pleases their master and what brings rewards to them. But we are not animals—we are sons of God! And the Holy Ghost has come to us, not as a trainer but as our Teacher, whose purpose it is to lead us into all truth, into the depth of the riches, both of the wisdom and knowledge of God.

Obviously there is need for training in some of the mechanics of our work, but a training mentality is not conducive to spiritual growth. How sad it is to see non-spiritual leaders attempting to train people into spirituality. Is this an attempt to contain and control them within a sphere where such a leader feels comfortable himself! We must have leaders who feel a burden to explore with, and lead others into a deeper and fuller relationship with God.

Even as the kingdom then was suffering violence, or upheaval, so now there is a battle raging. It is a battle between the Spirit and the flesh, and at times the lines of demarcation seem blurred. But these lines will become clearer, and those who are determined that the Church is going to be a spiritual house, operating with kingdom power, will be forceful in pressing into a new dimension of kingdom living.

When Jesus said, "and the violent take it by force," we must not suppose He was advocating any kind of carnal force. We possess our spiritual blessings only by the power of the Spirit—a power which convicts, which justifies, which regenerates, which empowers, which aligns us with the Captain of the Lord's host. Through Him our victory is assured. It is a sure thing that His kingdom will come, that He will triumph gloriously over all His enemies. Paul records it as follows:

"Then cometh the end, when he shall have delivered up the kingdom to God, even the Father; when he shall have put down all rule and all authority and power. For he must reign, till he hath put all enemies under his feet. . . . And when all things shall be subdued unto him, then shall the Son also himself be subject unto him that put all things under him, that God may be all in all" (1 Corinthians 15:24, 25, 28).

Then cometh the end—the consummation of God's purpose for mankind on this earth will occur—the end will come. According to Paul this will be marked by Christ's surrender of His delegated power and authority to the Father, a power that was given Him in His subordinate role in God's great redemptive plan. As God He had all power, but in accepting His mediatorial role between God and man, He received power from the Father. "All power is given unto me," were His words. This is the power which at last will be given up to the Father, being no longer needed. With it He shall have put down all rule and all authority and all power, everything that has exalted itself against the knowledge of God.

This event, this delivering up of power about which Paul wrote, will occur after the Rapture, after the millennial reign, after the final judgment.

This whole earth has been corrupted. It pleased God to reconcile all things unto Himself by Jesus Christ. While this subjugation of all opposing power will extend throughout the entire earth during the Millennium, with Satan being bound, it will occur first within His Church, of which He must be the absolute Head—the absolute Sovereign. Yes, His kingdom will come ultimately to this whole world, where He will rule the earth from Jerusalem. But first, His kingdom must come within His Church. This is so in order for the Church to be cleansed from everything that defiles. It must become a glorious Church—a fit Bride for the Heavenly Bridegroom.

Right now Satan is still enthroned within some hearts among us. He still holds seats of power within God's Church. This will not continue! Jesus is now said to be seated on the right hand of God, "From henceforth expecting till his enemies be made his footstool" (Hebrews 10:13). The Psalmist wrote, "The Lord said unto my Lord, Sit thou at my right hand, until I make thine enemies thy footstool" (Psalms 110:1).

As we pray, "Thy kingdom come," we are praying for an end to all power that is in opposition to His righteousness, His peace, His joy, His authority. There is much yet to be understood about the kingdom's fulness, but I believe as our understanding of this kingdom power and authority increases, so will the fervency of our petitions increase.

The Church, with all its government and organization, with all its methodology, with all the possible innovative ideas which may be set forth, must not divorce itself from kingdom power. And we must not be satisfied until this power is working mightily in us. We must pray with intensified fervor, "O God, Thy kingdom come." Satan will be put down to his complete humiliation and destruction only by the power of Almighty God. "Behold, I give unto you power to tread on serpents and scorpions, and over all the power of the enemy: and nothing shall by any means hurt you" (Luke 10:19). I feel like saying, "Old Satan, your kingdom must come down." He must be given no place within us or among us. Christ's authority and rule over him shall be complete.

He Shall Be Satisfied

5

83rd General Assembly
Wednesday, September 7, 1988
White Wing Messenger, November 12, 1988

"Surely he hath borne our griefs, and carried our sorrows: yet we did esteem him stricken, smitten of God, and afflicted.

"But he was wounded for our transgressions, he was bruised for our iniquities: the chastisement of our peace was upon him; and with his stripes we are healed.

"All we like sheep have gone astray; we have turned every one to his own way; and the LORD hath laid on him the iniquity of us all.

"He was oppressed, and he was afflicted, yet he opened not his mouth: he is brought as a lamb to the slaughter, and as a sheep before her shearers is dumb, so he openeth not his mouth.

"He was taken from prison and from judgment: and who shall declare his generation? for he was cut off out of the land of the living: for the transgression of my people was he stricken.

"And he made his grave with the wicked, and with the rich in his death; because he had done no violence, neither was any deceit in his mouth.

"Yet it pleased the LORD to bruise him; he hath put him to grief: when thou shalt make his soul an offering for sin, he shall see his seed, he shall prolong his days, and the pleasure of the LORD shall prosper in his hand.

"He shall see of the travail of his soul, and shall be satisfied: by his knowledge shall my righteous servant justify many; for he shall bear their iniquities" (Isa. 53:4-11).

At times a person who has gone through a very difficult time or traumatic experience will say, "If I had known in advance what I would have to go through, I don't believe I could have taken it." Indeed, most of us acknowledge that God is merciful in not allowing us to see everything that lies ahead.

Such was not the case, however, with Jesus. He knew what faced Him as He approached the Garden of Gethsemane for a time of agonizing prayer. He knew what lay ahead. He was very familiar with Isaiah's prophecy, of His being wounded for our transgressions, bruised for our iniquities and by whose stripes we are healed. Our Saviour knew this was written of Him, that He was the One who would be led as "a lamb to the slaughter."

We cannot know all that He felt as He approached His darkest night; we do have His testimony, as He declared, "My soul is exceeding sorrowful, even unto death" (Matthew 26:38). Matthew wrote, "[He] began to be sorrowful and very heavy" (vs. 37).

His suffering in the Atonement has been written and preached about extensively, but we are still left to wonder at what He really suffered. The account of His agony in the Garden is enough to melt our hearts as He prayed "with strong crying and tears unto him that was able to save him from death" (Hebrews 5:7). But God's love for us prevented our Saviour's deliverance from what lay ahead. Luke's description is very vivid: "And being in an agony he prayed more earnestly: and his sweat was as it were great drops of blood falling down to the ground" (Luke 22:44).

We can only try to comprehend what was taking place in the One who was truly God and truly man. Surely it was not just His dread of death, although crucifixion was a horrible means of execution. Many others had faced such death, however, without this kind of preceding agony. It was not Christ's fear of being crucified, for He knew that in three days He would arise from the grave.

But here was the sinless, blameless, Son of God, God incarnate, being pressed into the state of tasting death for every man. The Father was laying on Him the iniquity of us all. Paul wrote, "For he hath made him to be sin for us, who knew no sin . . . " (2 Corinthians 5:21). All that this mysterious imputation of our sins involved we cannot know, but to the pure and holy Son of God it was unspeakable anguish.

Could not God in His infinite wisdom have devised another way? Perhaps this is what Jesus was asking when He fell on His face and prayed. "O my Father, if it be possible, let this cup pass from me" (Matthew 26:39). No, God's wisdom is perfect, and this is what He ordained from the foundation of the world. Not only was it designed to satisfy God's righteous law, that the penalty for sin is death, and this judgment had to be met, it also was to show His great love for us. Christ's humiliation and sufferings were altogether for us, undeserving though we be. John wrote, "Hereby perceive we the love of God, because he laid down his life for us" (1 John 3:16).

Except to show God's love for us and His abhorrence of sin, why else would Jesus have been subjected to such shame and suffering? In Isaiah's prophecy it was said of Him, "I gave my back to the smiters, and my cheeks to them that plucked off the hair: I hid not my face from shame and spitting" (Isaiah 50:6). A scourging in itself, as the Romans administered it, was enough to kill a man, which it sometimes did; yet He bore it for us. And can we imagine the sight of His face, whose beard had been ripped out, reminding us of another prophecy, " . . . his visage was . . . marred more than any man"? (Isaiah 52:14.)

After all this cruel suffering at the hands of His tormentors, He retained His consciousness enough that He would attempt to carry His cross to Golgotha. But His agony in Gethsemane plus His inhumane torture had weakened Him too much. Another had to accept this burden.

His sufferings on the cross cannot be adequately described. Suffice it to say that He endured the cross, despising the shame, until He could say, "It is finished," and "Father, into thy hands I commend my spirit," He died. This is the heart-rending account of our Saviour's suffering, but it is encouraging to read in Isaiah's prophecy, these words, "He shall see of the travail of his soul, **and shall be satisfied.**" The scriptural assurance is that His suffering shall not be in vain. He shall be satisfied!

We cannot understand God's desire for fellowship with mankind except that He is the epitome of love and love is a powerful, constraining force which reaches out, extending itself toward someone in need. Thank God for such love that reached out to us in the giving of His only begotten Son to suffer so shamefully for us. Satan had won a victory over man in the Garden of Eden, alienating him from his Creator, but the love of God for His creatures brought forth the means for their reconciliation. O the wonder of it all!

When God called Abraham to become the father of a chosen nation, it was that He might have a people on earth to be a witness for Him to all the world. Through these people He desired to demonstrate the superiority of godliness over ungodliness.

Even as this chosen people dwelt in Egypt's bondage, God's blessing upon them was evident. "And the children of Israel were fruitful, and increased abundantly, and multiplied, and waxed exceeding mighty; and the land was filled with them" (Exodus 1:7). The more they were oppressed and afflicted by the Egyptians, "the more they multiplied and grew" (v. 12).

God brought them out of this nation within which they dwelt to make of them a nation apart from all others—a peculiar nation, a kingdom of priests, a nation that would show forth the excellence of God's rule as opposed to the rulership of Satan that was being exercised among all the other nations.

He Shall Be Satisfied

Following their miraculous deliverance from Egypt, God had descended upon Mt. Sinai to establish a covenant with them. "And mount Sinai was altogether on a smoke, because the LORD descended upon it in fire: and the smoke thereof ascended as the smoke of a furnace, and the whole mount quaked greatly" (Exodus 19:18). "And so terrible was the sight, that Moses said, I exceedingly fear and quake" (Hebrews 12:21).

In such mighty demonstration of power the law was given by God to establish His covenant with these descendants of Abraham. Now there was nothing wrong with the law—it was from God and it was holy. Paul, to the Romans, wrote, "Wherefore the law is holy, and the commandment holy, and just, and good" (Romans 7:12). It set forth God's righteous requirements for those who would be His people. Because, however, these people lacked inward righteousness to match God's requirements, the law served for their condemnation.

It demonstrated the inadequacies of what could be done to create a holy nation apart from the shedding of Jesus' blood. The weakness of a covenant apart from His atoning sacrifice was clearly manifested by Israel's history. The law, even with the sacrifices ordered in its administration, did not have the power to remove man's fallen, carnal nature; it could reveal sin but it could not remove it.

Jesus died, then, to deal with man's sin problem and to provide a new and living way, in a new covenant. "For if that first covenant had been faultless, then should no place have been sought for the second. For finding fault with them, he saith, Behold, the days come, saith the Lord, when I will make a new covenant with the house of Israel and with the house of Judah" (Hebrews 8:7, 8). "This is the covenant that I will make with them after those days, saith the Lord, I will put my laws into their hearts, and in their minds will I write them" (Hebrews 10:16), as Paul said, "not in tables of stone, but in fleshy tables of the heart" (2 Corinthians 3:3).

This new covenant, instituted by God in Christ, has its power in the precious blood of our Saviour. Jesus referred to the cup of Communion as, "the new testament in my blood" (Luke 22:20). This is God's provision for His people today, whereby Jesus one day shall see the travail of His soul and shall be satisfied.

The problem that His Church has faced historically, both in the days of the Apostles and in modern times, is the failure to appreciate and accept the efficacy of Jesus' blood in the new testament as being sufficient. There was then, and there is now, the feeling of the need for something more tangible. This was the case when certain Judaisers came down to Antioch, demanding that the Gentile converts be subjected to circumcision and the law of Moses. They just could not believe that the blood of Christ alone and the inscribing of God's law upon the tables of their hearts was adequate to replace the law of Moses and the religious traditions that had been carried out for centuries. Of course, the resultant strife led to the calling of the Jerusalem council in Acts, chapter fifteen.

The Holy Ghost had done His work, and it was a perfect work, the sanctification of their hearts by the blood of Jesus. He had taken up His abode within these Gentile believers, but these men from Judea who were steeped in their traditions believed the Holy Ghost needed help. They did not trust Him to manage lives apart from the imposition of outward precepts.

This was a problem which Paul dealt with over and over again. His emphasis upon grace rather than law is woven into all his epistles. His letter to the Galatians dealt extensively with this issue, where he said, "I marvel that ye are so soon removed from him that called you into the grace of Christ unto another gospel: Which is not another; but there be some that trouble you, and would pervert the gospel of Christ" (Galatians 1:6, 7). Jesus was all they needed, and the grace He brought could not be strengthened by supplements. The attempt to do so resulted only in the perversion of His gospel. Salvation by grace alone has always been difficult to accept among self-righteous people who see themselves as being partners with God in their salvation. We must remember, however, that it was "Not by works of righteousness which we have done, but according to his mercy he saved us, by the washing of regeneration, and renewing of the Holy Ghost" (Titus 3:5).

In this "new and living way" our life is in Jesus, and Jesus alone. Now we esteem very highly the written Word, but it is possible for us to take the Book which we call the New Testament and approach it with the same mindset that those under the law approached their sacred writings which we know as the Old Testament. With this mindset we attempt to make ourselves subject to what is written. But the New Testament was never intended by God to work from the outside inward, into our inner being. This covenant of grace works from the inside to express itself outwardly, and then its reality can be attested to by what we find written in the Book. It is possible to become lovers of the **Book** of the Lord, while failing to be lovers of the **Lord** of the Book. Some seem to think more highly of the **Church** of God than they do of the God of the Church. They find it easier to talk about the Church than of God.

When this grace of the indwelling Word is absent, it is then that we often find men bringing themselves into the frame of mind where they become mere rule followers, and following rules becomes a substitute for true relationship. This rule following becomes such a way of life for them that they insist on everything being spelled out. This has led in the past to the adoption of creeds and statements of faith to govern their belief and practices. Such creeds, however, have a way of becoming static, rigid, inflexible, with no provision for greater illumination which could make some creedal statements no longer relevant.

The Church which Jesus purchased with His own blood must not subject itself to such creeds. Our body of faith is the New Testament and this expressed outwardly in Christian living, in New Testament lifestyles, from an amazing union of God's Spirit with the individual's human spirit. This Book called the New Testament serves, then, as a gauge or measure for ascertaining the certainty of our spiritual relationship. To impose the Old Testament approach of law-keeping upon the New Testament is to pervert the gospel of Christ.

We do not want to be guilty of treading under foot the Son of God and treating this covenant in His blood as though it were not needed, thus doing despite upon the spirit of grace. There is no way for His Church to succeed in its mission, according to His purpose, apart from life in the Spirit in the new and living way.

Paul's counsel to the church at Colosse is especially timely for us now: "Let the word of Christ dwell in you richly in all wisdom; teaching and admonishing one another in psalms and hymns and spiritual songs, singing with grace in your hearts to the Lord" (Colossians 3:16). This is not burdensome living. When dwelling in us, it works from within. James calls it " . . . the engrafted word . . . " (James 1:21). By the Spirit, in a new way that is incomprehensible to us, our spirits have received a graft of the divine Word. Now a successful graft always produces fruit of its own kind, not of that into which it is grafted. A Golden Delicious apple branch, grafted into crabapple stock, will produce only Golden Delicious apples, never crabapples.

Non-spiritual people who attempt to live the Christian life by the observance of external rules can be expected to display the works of the flesh: oftentimes they will even be crabby, ill-tempered, harsh in their judgmental attitudes. But the engrafted Word will produce only the fruit of the Spirit. This means, as Paul wrote, "It is no longer I that liveth, but Christ that liveth in me." The life of the engrafted Word of life is in the new testament, life through the power of Jesus' blood. It is life in the Spirit.

Life in the Spirit means love; life in the Spirit means joy; life in the Spirit means longsuffering; life in the Spirit means gentleness; life in the Spirit means goodness; life in the Spirit means faith; life in the Spirit means meekness; life in the Spirit means temperance. God's Church is a spiritual house whose life is in the Spirit. "If we live in the Spirit, let us also walk in the Spirit" (Galatians 5:25).

Life in the Spirit means growing, changing. Only God is immutable, unchanging. He alone is perfect, needing no change ever. But the Church is not perfect; so, it must be ever open and receptive to divine illumination, changing from *glory to glory*, till we come into His image, "the measure of the stature of the fulness of Christ" (Ephesians 4:13). Change is unsettling to many people; it makes them uncomfortable. They seem to feel they are losing control, but perhaps that is what we need—for us to lose our control. Change for the Church of God is inevitable. We must not resist it, being afraid to surrender control to the Spirit. He is all-wise, and it is His business to lead us into all truth, and He will be changing us or else refusing us. He will change us or abandon us.

Crossing into Canaan involved a change of direction for the people of God. The manna that had sustained them for forty years would no longer be their food. Until that time their diet had been very "predictable." As we move ahead now in preparation for the Rapture our forms will lose their predictability.

People who live and walk in the Spirit will not require burdensome creeds to which someone must be constantly pointing them in order for them to live right. This spirit of supplementing the covenant of grace with outward precepts, as mentioned earlier, was at work early into the history of the Apostolic Church, and it was not long in making its presence felt in the last-days Church. This was distressing to R. G. Spurling and some others who saw the governing of the Church to be the law of love. But this spirit of legislating increased in strength.

Was not this the spirit that led to the adoption of the Constitution in 1921? The former General Overseer saw this as an error, and in the next Assembly in 1922, called for its abrogation. He asked that we raise high the Book (the Bible) and declare, "This is our only rule of faith and practice. No discipline but this—this blessed old Book." He felt that the Holy Ghost, for His immediate leadership of the Church had been thrust aside and grieved, and he prayed for His return.

Now, sixty-five years later, it is fitting that we take an objective look to see how much we are depending upon those things written in our Assembly Minutes and elsewhere which, as our former General Oversee pointedly reminded us, "have never been regarded as laws to follow." He stated, "We must cling to the blessed old Book for our laws if we keep the favor of God." So, again we must determine whether we are, indeed, practicing real sensitivity to the immediate direction of the Spirit. The addition of supplements to the New Testament is dangerous, which itself is the gauge of the spiritual relationship we are maintaining with God through the indwelling, engrafted Word.

An excellent checkpoint is the Sermon on the Mount, Christ's inaugural message to His Church on the day when He set it in order with the twelve apostles. A greater sermon has never been recorded. It deals with issues of the heart, outlining things that can be carried out only when the Living Word is in control of the inner man.

Relationships within the Church are said to be both vertical and horizontal. Whenever there is an under-dependance upon the vertical and an over-dependance upon the horizontal, there will be spiritual failure. To maintain good fellowship within the church group is commendable, but it is possible to have such group fellowship while at the same time no member of the group is enjoying a vital relationship with God. We may even pride ourselves on what wonderful fellowship we enjoy with one another, while being woefully deficient in spiritual power. This poses a real danger. It is surely time for us to make certain about our individual relationships with Jesus Christ. Is the Word dwelling in us richly?

Paul wrote, "For he will finish the work, and cut it short in righteousness: because a short work will the Lord make upon the earth" (Romans 9:28). If He is going to "cut it short in righteousness," we may well ask wherein is the righteousness. It assuredly is not of our own doing. To assume such a thing was the error of the religious Jews in Christ's day. Theirs was a self-righteousness wherein the Pharisee could boast, "God, I thank thee, that I am not as other men are, extortioners, unjust, adulterers. . . . I fast twice in the week, I give tithes of all that I possess" (Luke 18:11, 12).

In His Sermon on the Mount, Jesus said to His Church, ". . . except your righteousness shall exceed the righteousness of the scribes and Pharisees, ye shall in no case enter into the kingdom of heaven" (Matthew 5:20). This does not mean that we must fast three times per week instead of two, or pay a double tithe. We rather must know a righteousness which they did not know. In that same sermon Jesus tells about it: "But seek ye first the kingdom of God and his righteousness . . . " (6:33). To seek His righteousness is to seek Him, because there is no true righteousness apart from God. It is time for us now more than ever to seek Him.

" . . . For it is time to seek the Lord, till he come and rain righteousness upon you" (Hosea 10:12).

"But of him are ye in Christ Jesus, who of God is made unto us wisdom, and righteousness, and sanctification, and redemption" (1 Corinthians 1:30). There is no righteousness apart from Him: there is no holiness apart from Him. Keeping certain standards does not make one holy. Holiness can never be legislated. One's relationship with Jesus Christ determines his holiness.

Now we believe strongly in Church unity, but the unity of which He approves is that unity which is found only in Him. It is that which He expressed as "I in them, and thou in me, that they may be made perfect in one" (John 17:23). Therein is the unity which exalts and praises His power. Any other unity we might seek could turn into self-praise and even become idolatrous. Such was the unity of the tower of Babel. It was to give the people a name, to make them famous.

Thank God for the atonement of Calvary. Thank God for the victory Jesus won for all time on that awful day. It is through Calvary that He will finish the work and cut it short in righteousness. After fifteen hundred years of the administration of the law, those people were no nearer to fulfilling God's will than when the law was given at Mt.

Sinai, and no more righteous. Another fifteen hundred years would have made no difference. They still would have been far from God, while perhaps, boasting of their own self-righteousness, attempting to live by what was written without the power to do so.

The Bible says, "For the law made nothing perfect, but the bringing in of a better hope did; by which we draw nigh unto God" (Hebrews 7:19). This better hope is our Blessed Saviour, and He will finish the work and cut it short in righteousness. "For the law was given by Moses, but grace and truth came by Jesus Christ" (John 1:17). Some not experiencing this righteousness of His grace are trying to "climb up some other way," by a perverted gospel of good works, but legalism (the doctrine of salvation by good works) is not an acceptable substitute for the marvelous grace of our Saviour. Jesus remains the way, the truth, the life, who of God is made unto us *wisdom, righteousness, sanctification, and redemption.*

What began as some kind advice and instructions for new members in the Church, to offer them some guidance in their Christian walk, has the potential for becoming a legal document as if it was some kind of creed. Some loving advice to members becomes **The** Advice to Members. Then eventually a member may feel that if he adheres to what is written in this document he is a faithful member in good standing with the Church and with God, which may not always be the case. A person may be called "a member in good standing" simply because he has maintained a record of faithfulness in church attendance, in tithing, in participating in the programs of the church and in refraining from going to movies and other places of worldly amusement. He may do all this and have a pleasing horizontal relationship with the other members of the local church, yet because of the deficiency in his vertical relationship he may one day come to hear Him say, "I never knew you."

Nothing is so important as **knowing** the Lord. In fact, the certainty of this knowledge is the undergirding rock upon which Christ declared He would build His Church. A person might know how to defend biblical doctrines expertly and never know the Lord. The knowledge of the Lord involves much more that academics. It speaks of an intimate relationship, a divine union between a man and God. One of the greatest dangers today is in accepting a substitute for this intimate, vital relationship. This not only cripples our effectiveness as the Church of God, it will prevent one's entry into heaven.

The word "know" in the Scriptures is a word of intimacy, especially as it relates to the union which devout believers are experiencing. This mysterious relationship has been entered into through the power of the Atonement; yet, there is a more perfect knowing of Him for which we are yearning. This yearning seems to be becoming more intense among those who are going to be in the Rapture. We hear Paul saying, "I count all things but loss . . . that I may know him," and we identify with his feeling. Certain kinds of knowledge seem to foster pride, but not the knowledge which Paul desired. It is an intimate, loving relationship. He wrote to the Corinthians: "Knowledge puffeth up, but charity edifieth. And if any man think that he knoweth any thing, he knoweth nothing yet as he ought to know. But if any man love God, the same is known of him" (1 Corinthians 8:1-3). It is a loving relationship.

Jesus said, "I . . . know my sheep, and am known of mine" (John 10:14). It is the "people that do know their God" who "shall be strong, and do exploits" (Daniel 11:32). But we must not be so much motivated by the desire to do exploits as we are by the desire to *know our God*. While we long for a more intimate relationship with the Heavenly Bridegroom, especially during those times when we commune with Him in secret prayer. We seem to come to the limit beyond which we are unable to pass. I believe this restriction is associated with our mortality, but that will not always be. John foresaw a time called the marriage supper of the Lamb. This will be the time for the consummation of our limited and restricted knowledge. That will be the time when we will move from mortality to immortality. We shall be like Him; we shall see Him as He is!

Paul wrote, "For we know in part, and we prophesy in part. . . . For now we see through a glass, darkly; but then face to face: now I know in part; but then shall I know even as also I am known" (1 Corinthians 13:9, 12).

The time is at hand when John's revelation will be fulfilled where the angel said, "He that is unjust, let him be unjust still: and he which is filthy, let him be filthy still: and he that is righteous, let him be righteous still: and he that is holy, let him be holy still" (Revelation 22:11). To each of you who can say, "By His amazing grace I am standing in His righteousness alone," I feel like saying, " . . . look up, and lift up your heads; for your redemption draweth nigh" (Luke 21:28).

This redemption is something Jesus won for us, that is, our ultimate redemption from these vile, corruptible bodies. He defeated mortality and death, triumphing gloriously over the grave, clothed with immortality. Those who have an intimate relationship with Him, being filled with His Spirit, even now groan, waiting for their redemption from these mortal bodies, " . . . not for that we would be unclothed, but clothed upon, that mortality might be swallowed up of life" (2 Corinthians 5:4).

Jesus is the way, the truth, the life, and as John wrote, "He that hath the Son hath life" (1 John 5:12). The spiritual death we were experiencing has already been defeated, our spirits regenerated, and we are walking now in newness of life. But now we stand on the verge of immortality, mortality itself being swallowed up of this life which is in Christ, when this corruptible body takes on incorruption.

"For the Lord himself shall descend from heaven with a shout, with the voice of the archangel, and with the trump of God: and the dead in Christ shall rise first: Then we which are alive and remain shall be caught up together with them in the clouds, to meet the Lord in the air: and so shall we ever be with the Lord" (1 Thessalonians 4:16, 17).

He shall see of the travail of His soul and shall be satisfied. He did not suffer in vain.

He will have a Bride who is living in the life of the New Testament, who is walking in the Spirit, alive in the Spirit. Will you be in that number?

Upon This Rock

6

84th General Assembly
White Wing Messenger, October 14, 1989

"And I say also unto thee, That thou art Peter, and upon this rock I will build my church; and the gates of hell shall not prevail against it" (Matthew 16:18).

This declaration by Jesus signaled the formation of a new entity, a new creation to replace the apostate Jewish institution which was rejecting its only hope. It was an institution which had failed in its calling to be a witness to the nations, a witness of spiritual excellence, of the superiority of godliness over ungodliness. Becoming egocentric, they had forgotten their true mission.

While the institution itself was being rejected, the Jewish people would still have access to God; however, this access would be through Christ on an individual basis, the same access the Gentiles would have. Both Jews and Gentiles would thus be joined together in this new creation which Jesus was announcing. He would, as Paul expressed it, "make in himself of twain one new man . . . one body" (Ephesians 2:15, 16). Jesus called this new creation, "my church," and with divine authority, He declared its ultimate triumph over "the gates of hell."

When Jesus made this pronouncement in Caesarea Philippi, He revealed the undergirding principle upon which His Church would be solidly built. There has been much discussion through the years as to what this rock is upon which Christ declared He would build His Church. Some have interpreted the rock to be Peter, but we reject this idea. Others feel that it is Christ Himself. This is correct in the sense that He "uphold[s] all things by the word of his power" (Hebrews 1:3), and that "by him all things consist" (Colossians 1:17).

More specifically, however, it has been generally concluded that He spoke of an understanding between Himself and those believers who comprise His Church, a mutual understanding based, for their part, upon divine revelation. It was by divine revelation that Peter could declare, "Thou art the Christ, the Son of the living God." This was not a display of knowledge he had gleaned from others. His brother Andrew earlier had told Peter, "We have found the Messias, which is, being interpreted, the Christ" (John 1:41), and Andrew had introduced him to Jesus. But Peter's declaration went beyond His being simply the Jewish Messiah. Something burned within his spirit to where he could call Him "the Son of the living God." He acknowledged His deity. Jesus then declared, " . . . flesh and blood hath not revealed it unto thee, but my Father which is in heaven."

Failure to appreciate and respect His deity is cause for a lot of faulty building. Instead of the awesome sense of being in the presence of Almighty and All-knowing God, standing on holy ground, feeling our utter unworthiness of His grace, we can become victims of carnal, political desires, as were seen in James and John who wanted prestigious positions. Whenever divine revelation is received, there is a witness in one's spirit, which Paul called "the inner man" (Ephesians 3:16). This witness goes beyond intellectual perception. To really know spiritual truth, one must know it in his spirit. It was this kind of knowledge which gave Peter the certainty to declare, "Thou art the Christ, the Son of the living God." He would need much more understanding of his revelation, but he had received in his spirit a flash of divine revelation which gave him the assurance that here was the Christ.

When Jesus replied, "And I say also unto thee, That thou art Peter," He was indicating His keen perception of this impetuous disciple whom He would make into a solid believer. He knew Simon's present weaknesses and was able to foretell how he would deny his Master in a time of trial. Jesus also predicted his conversion, however, and knew he would become a rock of strength to his brethren. Jesus knew Peter, even as He knows each of us.

Is not this, then, the rock upon which His Church is being built—His perfect knowledge of each member and the particular nurture each one will require; also, the growing knowledge each member has of Him, which is received by His gracious revelation to sincere, searching hearts? It must be pointed out that His knowledge of us is perfect, while our knowledge of Him must be continually expanding through fresh comprehensions. Yet, the basic premise of "I ... know my sheep, and am known [really known] of mine" (John 10:14), is the undergirding rock which supports Christ's Church.

Even though Peter had received a divine revelation of Jesus' being the Christ, what he knew and what he thought he knew were quite different. It is interesting to note in this sixteenth chapter of Matthew, where Peter made his very positive declaration in verse sixteen, that just five verses later we have an account of his being rebuked by Jesus for his lack of understanding.

Beginning with verse twenty-one of Matthew, chapter sixteen, we read, "From that time forth began Jesus to shew unto his disciples, how that he must go unto Jerusalem, and suffer many things of the elders and chief priests and scribes, and be killed, and be raised again the third day. Then Peter took him, and began to rebuke him, saying, Be it far from thee, Lord: this shall not be unto thee. But he turned, and said unto Peter, Get thee behind me, Satan: thou art an offence unto me: for thou savourest not the things that be of God, but those that be of men" (vv. 21-23). These were Christ's words to a man who had a divine revelation.

Peter could not reconcile what Jesus was predicting with the revelation he had received. Peter's understanding of the role the Messiah was to fill did not fit what he was hearing. He had in mind a king who would restore Israel's sovereignty as a nation, and he believed Jesus was this king. Therefore, when Jesus spoke of going up to Jerusalem to be killed, Peter rebuked Him.

Now, there was nothing wrong with Peter's revelation—it was divine, and whatever comes from God is perfect. The problem came when he made this perfect revelation subjective to his imperfect previous understanding. Whenever revelation from God is made to fit into one's existing understanding, which itself may be flawed, then such revelation becomes distorted. Rather than to continually make divine revelation subjective to what we already think we know, we need a willingness to allow it to replace whatever is shown to contain error.

What Peter believed about the Messiah's role was what the institution of which he was a part had taught him. And, they had taught it from their understanding of the Scriptures. The prophets had portrayed Him as a successor to the throne of David, that He was to be a king. Isaiah wrote, "Of the increase of his government and peace there shall be no end, upon the throne of David, and upon his kingdom, to order it, and to establish it with judgment and with justice from henceforth even for ever" (Isaiah 9:7). Micah had prophesied, "But thou, Bethlehem Ephratah, though thou be little among the thousands of Judah, yet out of thee shall he come forth unto me that is to be ruler in Israel" (Micah 5:2). These surely were prophecies of their coming king, and these Scripture passages had greater appeal to the Jewish leadership than those which depicted Him as a sacrificial lamb, upon whom God had laid the iniquity of them all. That they had any iniquity would have been difficult for them to confess.

Of course, there is a kingdom Christ was introducing wherein He rules in the hearts of men, but there is also a time clearly foretold when He shall be enthroned and rule upon this earth for a thousand years. In his mind, Peter just had Him assuming this earthly kingship role about two thousand years too soon. It is possible to get prophecies out of sequence, and this creates problems. This is what caused Peter and the other apostles such great disillusionment when Jesus was arrested and crucified. Subsequent illumination, however, caused their revelation of Christ to come into better focus.

There is never anything faulty about divine revelation. The problem is that it leaves heaven pure, but by the time it is assimilated into our minds, often being filtered through and colored by misconceptions we are holding, it is less than correct. Yet, we may argue loudly all the while about our divine revelation and condemn others who do not share our views. We should thank God for what He reveals to us, but we should make sure the revelation we proclaim is as pure as when it left heaven.

The truth remains that divine revelation is basic in the undergirding of the Church of God, but we must realize the need for proper understanding of the revelation we are given. Divine revelation the Church has received must not be considered as static, with there being no need for further illumination of what we have received. There is necessity for a commitment to seek for understanding and to walk in the light from now until the Rapture. As long as the Holy Ghost is in charge, we have no need for fear. He will never mislead God's people.

The rock of revelation and understanding supports a relationship apart from which the Church cannot survive, much less succeed in its mission. While this relationship produces a faith that can be articulated and defended, we must remember that it is principally spiritual rather than intellectual. Historically, we have seen what began as spiritual faith evolve into mere intellectual dogma. People who at one time knew the Lord in a deep personal relationship have gone from knowing the Lord to simply knowing what they believe. It becomes no longer "Who" they know but "what" they know.

A pertinent question for all of us is whether the quality of spiritual life we now are experiencing is being determined by "what" we know, or by "Who" we know. Is it "what," or is it "Who"? Is your faith solely in the Church and its teachings, or is it in the living God? Which is it that dictates your actions and your lifestyle? Dogma is learned, it is in the mind, while vital faith is in the heart. Dogma can be committed to memory and even used for arguments; faith, on the other hand, transcends reason and oftentimes cannot be easily explained. Dogma is belief that is outlined in written propositions, while faith rests in a Person, in Jesus Christ. Faith is alive and expansive.

There is a degree to which true faith can be articulated and written in words all right, and it has been, and this is in order. What is written by divine inspiration is to be appreciated and respected, but faith does not begin as doctrine. It begins in a Person, and it must be kept in a Person, in a very personal relationship with Jesus. Doctrine grows from this, but doctrine must never be allowed to replace the relationship. True faith goes beyond merely knowing biblical teachings.

Knowing Jesus never puts one at odds with biblical doctrine. The person who knows the Lord will be living in harmony with biblical doctrine. I surely do not want to de-emphasize the importance of sound doctrine. I hold it to be very important, especially in this day of so many uncertain sounds. The point I wish to emphasize is that one can know correct doctrine and at the same time fail to know the living Lord.

Even God did not regard His written words as being all-sufficient for mankind's needs. He gave His law through Moses and the prophets; yet, something more was needed than words on stone or on paper. Thus came the Incarnation, God being manifest to us as a Person, and then inviting us to join in a mysterious union with Him, to where we could experience His life and power. The husband/wife one-flesh relationship prefigured this very wonderful spiritual union the Church is offered with Christ. It is more than words on paper; it is life in Him, with Him.

Jesus declared, " . . . because I live, ye shall live also" (John 14:19). John wrote, "In him was life; and the life was the light of men" (John 1:4). Many of us have made a commitment to walk in the light, and this light is directly related to the life we are experiencing. Dullness of spiritual life means dimness of light. But remember, He came not just that we might have life, but that we might have it more abundantly. Abundant life is the key to abundant light.

I am convinced that the Church today needs further illumination of its divine revelation. But such illumination grows out of the richness of its union with Christ, the richness that each of us has with Him, the abundance of our life in Him, of our abiding in Him and of His abiding in us. This is the undergirding rock for His Church—"I . . . know my sheep, and am known of mine"—I know them, and they know me." It is interesting that the word translated here as "know" in the original language is the same word used by Mary when she said to the angel Gabriel, "How shall this be, seeing I know not a man?" (Luke 1:34). It is a term of intimate knowledge between a bride and bridegroom, or in the husband/wife relationship.

Such knowledge involves more than knowing what may be written in a book, it is more than knowing correctness of doctrine. It is intimate acquaintance, intimate union with a Person, whose presence is felt and loved. Yes, He is building His Church, and this special spiritual union with Him must undergird the entire building process. Otherwise, we will find ourselves involved in an attempt at building through intellectual procedures, through human rationalizations. Such intellectual building is fleshly. It is of the earth, earthy—it is building upon sand, an unstable, undependable and unworthy support for God's Church.

Jesus' words were, "I will build . . . ." God forbid that we try to take the building of His Church out of His hands. It is a glorious privilege just to be laborers with Him. We must remember that we are neither the architect nor the superintendent in charge of construction—we are only laborers. Laborers do not design the building, they only work at their assignments, in harmony with the one in charge.

No enduring building will be done that is done apart from Him. Some such building might appear as progress, but it will not stand the judgment of God. Ezekiel wrote of those who built with untempered mortar, and God's message through His prophet was, "So will I break down the wall that ye have daubed with untempered mortar, and bring it down to the ground, so that the foundation thereof shall be discovered, and it shall fall, and ye shall be consumed in the midst thereof: and ye shall know that I am the Lord" (Ezekiel 13:14). Dare we be so foolish as to try to build the Church of God apart from union with Him? God forbid!

To build God's Church is more than to build a religious organization. The Church is a living organism. Organizations can be built through human effort, through planning and programming, through setting goals and implementing strategies for their achievement.

The growth of an organism, however, comes through nurture, and is more unpredictable. Human effort is only indirectly involved. One plants, another waters, but it is God who gives the increase. It is God who causes an organism to grow. It makes a difference as to how one regards the Church. When viewed as an organization, strategies for growth are determined by measurable factors such as membership, buildings and finances. As an organism, the quality of the Church's life is expressed in attitudes and relationships. We speak often of perfection, and for the Church this is a comprehensive term, much of which begs for understanding. But I suppose it will be reflected more in attitudes and relationships than any other way.

When we speak of quality of life within the Church, we do not relate it to an organization which, though it may be growing and expanding, is unfeeling and uncaring. We think rather of a blessed fellowship, first with a loving

Saviour, then with one another. Organizations have a way of becoming impersonal, where people become expendable, if need be, for so-called progress. The Church of God, on the other hand, is a fellowship of loving and caring people. Infused with divine love through their union with Him who is the epitome of love, they care deeply for one another. At the same time they are one with their Lord in and concern toward those now outside the Church.

How can it be otherwise when we truly know Him? And I repeat, this kind of knowing Him is the rock upon which He is building His Church. There is so much supposed knowledge which falls far short of doing for a person what really knowing Jesus does in one's life. There is a knowledge that *puffeth up*. It gives people a feeling of spiritual superiority, and they become extremely judgmental in the treatment of others whom they consider less spiritual than themselves. Such people are to be pitied.

I am sensing some attitudes today that are somewhat troubling to me. Christ's Church is a fold, a place of safety, a place of fellowship for all Christians. All believers should be able to feel the warmth of Christian love and concern within this fold. Yet, I hear of some who evidently consider themselves superior in revelation and knowledge inviting others whom they regard as not having a pure enough vision of the Church to leave it. This judgmental attitude often seems harsh, and is the Church only a place for those who meet our sometimes very narrow definition of being "Church of God," or is it a place for all Christians? If it is a place for all Christians, then who am I to invite another Christian to "love it (like it is), or leave it"?

Such a spirit is not compatible with the spirit of Christ, the spirit of the strong bearing the infirmities of the weak. The spirit of Christ was prefigured in Moses' prayer for the Israelites as he prayed, "Yet now, if thou wilt forgive their sin—; and if not, blot me, I pray thee, out of thy book . . . " (Exodus 32:32). While God would not blot out Moses' name to forgive the sins of others, he was such a beautiful type of Christ who would become sin for us.

We must make sure at all times that we are allied with Christ, being built upon the rock that is unshakable—the rock of knowing Him, which brings us into intimate fellowship with Him and with other believers. We begin to assimilate His character, His principles, His love for people. It has been correctly stated that to know Him is to love Him, and to love Him is to love those whom He loves. To reflect accurately the name, the Church of God, we must become the Church of love.

How can we then be harsh toward a fellow Christian? This is Christ's Church, and none of us has a monopoly on membership in it. He has deemed that every one of His followers can be a part of it. There remain many who are yet to become one with us, and without them the Church will not be made perfect. They are required for its completion. They need the Church, and the Church needs them. Is there enough of Christ's encompassing love among us to facilitate the unity of all Christians for which He prayed?

We do not understand all the ways of God, and just how He will complete His Church. It is quite probable that many who will be prominent in leadership for the consummation of the work are, right now, outside the Church. Although the Church had its arise from the Dark Ages in the United States and was propelled forward during a period of great revival, from all indications there is a greater move of the Spirit, a greater evangelistic thrust now taking place outside the United States than within this country. And it may well be that this new growth in the kingdom will produce new spiritual leadership for the Church. We must remember that God is sovereign and will use whom He pleases. Certainly, He will use those who know Him, and any attitude of bigotry would disqualify a person for His use.

Paul wrote concerning those who were "puffed up" in their presumed knowledge and said, " . . . if any man think that he knoweth any thing, he knoweth nothing yet as he ought to know. But if any man love God, the same is known of him" (1 Corinthians 8:2, 3). John wrote, "He that loveth not knoweth not God; for God is love" (1 John 4:8). The writer of Hebrews referred to a prophecy of Jeremiah who wrote, "I will put my laws into their mind, and write them in their hearts: and I will be to them a God, and they shall be to me a people: And they shall not teach every man his neighbour, and every man his brother, saying, Know the Lord: for all shall know me, from the least to the greatest" (Hebrews 8:10, 11). This is the provision in the new covenant for Christ's Church which gives it its solid support. All shall know Him from the least to the greatest.

Divine revelation is precious, enabling us to know Him. It is reassuring, also, to know that He knows us. Just as Christ knew Peter, He knows each of us. And in His love He deals with us as individuals, never requiring more of us than is for our own good. To a rich young ruler He said, ". . . sell all that thou hast, and distribute unto the poor" (Luke 18:22). Jesus could see within this young man's heart, and He saw mammon enthroned there. The requirement seemed too great for this ruler, but obedience to the Master would have enriched his life.

Now Jesus has not made this same requirement for everyone. Many have been allowed to retain their possessions while following Him. But He knows each one of us. He declared, "I know my sheep." He knows when anything holds too high a priority in our lives, and His demands are always just and they are for our good. Some have testified to having been convicted of television, for example, being required to get rid of their sets. Perhaps it was an addiction which they could not handle. Instead, it handled them. There are those who have felt they had to get rid of luxury automobiles, while others have not. Yes, the Lord may require certain things of some which He does not require of others. But He will require each of us to give up whatever is a detriment to his spiritual well-being.

The desire among us for uniformity turns this into a problem. We find ourselves saying, "Whatever the Lord requires of one He requires of all." This is not always true. Certainly, it has not been true with regards to selling everything we possess and distributing it to the poor. Some who know how to handle their possessions properly have retained the stewardship of them. Others could not handle them, their riches handled them; so for these people the Lord has made a requirement not made of others.

I am convinced that we have over-emphasized uniformity, equating it with unity. Neither as Christians nor as members of the Church have we been made clones, exact reproductions of one another. God knows each of us and deals with us differently. In the spirit of Romans, chapter fourteen, we must allow freedom for individual growth and responsiveness to God. Paul wrote, "For one believeth that he may eat all things: another, who is weak, eateth herbs. Let not him that eateth despise him that eateth not; and let not him which eateth not judge him that eateth: for God hath received him. Who art thou that judgest another man's servant? to his own master he standeth or falleth. Yea, he shall be holden up: for God is able to make him stand. One man esteemeth one day above another: another esteemeth every day alike. Let every man be fully persuaded in his own mind" (vv. 2-5).

Through the years I have preached rather strongly from Philippians, chapter three, " . . . let us walk by the same rule, let us mind the same thing" (v. 16). In taking a further look at this verse of Scripture, I have become aware that it does not say, "the same rules," but "the same rule." Inasmuch as Paul was warning earlier in this chapter against trusting in righteousness by the law, may we not conclude that he was advocating walking by "the rule of faith," rather than by the works of the law? If this be the proper sense of this verse, it would not be in conflict with what he wrote in Romans 14. Of course, there are certain cardinal doctrines of the New Testament on which we must agree. At the same time there may be other things which are to be resolved between an individual and His God. And all of these will be resolved satisfactorily on the basis of "I . . . know my sheep, and am known of mine." On this rock He is building His Church!

This insatiable desire to know the Lord caused Paul to

count his own considerable knowledge of the law as nothing. He wrote, "Yea doubtless, and I count all things but loss for the excellency of the knowledge of Christ Jesus my Lord: for whom I have suffered the loss of all things, and do count them but dung, that I may win Christ . . . That I may know him . . . " (Philippians 3:8, 10).

There is within many of us the same burning desire to know Him, and God has put it there. Simon had much to learn about his revelation, and so do we. Had he spent his years boasting about his revelation which had been acknowledged by Christ, without a willingness for further illumination, he would have been destroyed by his ignorance. Thank God that this was not the case. Even so, we must not be content with present revelation. There is more to know. But we are on the way, and we will not stop until we have come to the knowledge of the Son of God, until our lives are reflecting His nature, His character, His love for people. Short of that, how can we be ready for presentation as a glorious Church?

Even now, however, He is building His Church. The stirring of hearts by His Spirit makes us know something divine is happening. The building He is doing will not come to naught, He is building upon a rock—"I know my sheep and they know me." For us to suppose we will confine what God is doing to narrow structures and forms devised by man is folly. Those who attempt to do so are fighting a losing battle. Why? Because they will find themselves fighting against God. When anyone fights against God, I know now who is going to win. May God help us to know Him and to know what He is doing.

A Vision

7

The Center for Biblical Leadership
Pastor's Conferences
Spring 1993

When speaking to the Church about a vision, one Scripture passage comes immediately to most everyone's mind: "Where there is no vision, the people perish" (Proverbs 29:18). But what is this vision that prevents perishing, about which the inspired writer spoke? The answer, I believe, is—a vision of God. The correctness of our vision, the quality of this vision, is the determinant of the relationship we will have with Him. Yes, the quality of our relationship with God is greatly affected by the correctness of our vision of Him. A low vision of God is causing many of the problems we are now experiencing.

Isaiah describes graphically the vision he had which shaped his prophetic ministry, "In the year that king Uzziah died," he wrote, "I saw also the Lord sitting upon a throne, high and lifted up, and his train filled the temple" (Isaiah 6:1). The effect upon Isaiah was powerful. In the light of God's power and glory, he saw his own wretchedness, declaring, "Woe is me! for I am undone; because I am a man of unclean lips . . . for mine eyes have seen the King, the Lord of hosts" (v. 5).

Probably, not many of us have had such a dramatic experience; yet, each of us who has been called to minister divine truth has had an encounter with God. And as it was with Isaiah, for each of us also it was and is a humbling experience. Though overwhelmed with a feeling of unworthiness, as divine fire touches us and purges us of self-will, we respond "Here am I; send me" (v. 8).

Such a vision must not be a one-time experience. The man or woman who follows faithfully the divine call must continually "see the Lord." We must look at Him and to Him. Looking at Him we see the greatness of His power, that He is indeed God, ruling sovereignly over all He has created. We can sing, "Our God Reigns!" as the sun stays in its place by the word of His power, as all other celestial bodies follow their prescribed courses. We see Him clothed with majesty, and there is the overpowering sensation to fall prostrate in His presence declaring, "Thou art worthy, O Lord, to receive glory and honour and power!" (Rev. 4:11). The vision which John the Revelator saw of the Lord sitting upon His throne, surrounded by twenty-four elders who fell down before the throne and cast their crowns at His feet, inspires us with a sense of awe. We can imagine that we would do the same thing. The fact is, we do not have to wait till we get to heaven. He is in our midst right now, and we must recognize Him, humbling ourselves before Him. Our vision should approximate the one seen by John in Revelation 1:13-18, "And in the midst of the seven candlesticks one like unto the Son of man, clothed with a garment down to the foot, and girt about the paps with a golden girdle. His head and his hairs were white like wool, as white as snow; and his eyes were as a flame of fire; And his feet like unto fine brass, as if they burned in a furnace; and his voice as the sound of many waters. And he had in his right hand seven stars: and out of his mouth went a sharp twoedged sword: and his countenance was as the sun shineth in his strength. And when I saw him, I fell at his feet as dead. And he laid his right hand upon me, saying unto me, Fear not; I am the first and the last: I am he that liveth, and was dead; and, behold, I am alive for evermore, Amen; and have the keys of hell and of death."

Then, for the work which we have been assigned, reaching out to a world in need, we look to Him for direction, for guidance. We never want to feel that we are working for Him so much as we are working with Him. He has not absented Himself from this earth, waiting for us in heaven, as it were, to finish our assigned task. A true vision will not allow such a concept, but will always see Him as the active Head of the Body.

We sense His presence, we go in the strength of His presence. O, but how sad it is when we allow ourselves to drift, to be pulled away from His presence by the mundane things of this world, still professing to be working for Him. We may wonder how much of this is going on right now as we faithfully pursue our religious duties, yet failing to impact our communities with the gospel.

Where does the power for divine performance really lie? The answer is simple. It lies in the strength of divine power, as Paul expressed it, "which worketh in me mightily " (Col. 1:29). To the Galatians this apostle wrote, "(For he that wrought effectually in Peter to the apostleship of the circumcision, the same was mighty in me toward the Gentiles:)" (Galatians 2:8).

Paul's charge was to penetrate the Gentile world with the gospel, the gospel which he described as "the power of God unto salvation to every one that believeth" (Romans 1:16). He knew it was "to the Jew first," but now the time had come for it to go to the Gentiles also. This apostle-servant was driven by a vision wherein he saw such an influx of Gentiles receiving the gospel that they would become the dominant membership of the Church. This vision dominated Paul's ministry.

During his Damascus-road experience, God had indicated the ministry He would assign this apostle-to-be. To Ananias the Lord said, "for he is a chosen vessel unto me, to bear my name before the Gentiles . . . " (Acts 9:15). As Paul recounted that experience to King Agrippa he said, "And [Jesus] said . . . rise, and stand upon thy feet: for I have appeared unto thee for this purpose, to make thee a minister and a witness both of these things which thou hast seen, and of those things in the which I will appear unto thee; Delivering thee from the people, and from the Gentiles, unto whom now I send thee, To open their eyes, and to turn them from darkness to light, and from the power of Satan unto God, that they may receive forgiveness of sins, and inheritance among them which are sanctified by faith that is in me " (Acts 2:15-18)."

What a vision this man had! It was a vision of a great harvest field which lay virtually untouched. He saw spiritual blindness descending upon Israel while there was going to be an opening of the eyes of the Gentiles, that they were going to turn from darkness unto light. He foresaw this blindness remaining in the Israelites until the fulness of the Gentiles be come in (cf. Romans 11:25). He understood his call to be for this specific ministry.

Hear his testimony to King Agrippa: "Whereupon, O king Agrippa, I was not disobedient unto the heavenly vision: But shewed first unto them of Damascus, and at Jerusalem, and throughout all the coasts of Judaea, and then to the Gentiles" (Acts 26: 19, 20).

To those of you who have been chosen and set apart for the ministry, is your call any less definite than was Paul's? Is God less serious at this time? Perhaps it was less dramatic, but surely no less definite. What was your dominating vision at the time of your call? Is that vision dominating you now? Was it a heavenly vision? That is, did it come to you from heaven?

Perhaps it came to you first as a crushing burden for those who are lost, who, without your ministry, you felt would spend their eternity in a lake of fire. For me, this was something I could not escape. It brought me to tears time after time.

My vision was not that I would be a leader—a pastor, an overseer. My vision was of a vast sea of humanity who needed a Saviour, and I was answering God's call to go into this great harvest; I wanted to be used by God to reach people who were lost.

Later, this vision acquired a leadership focus, to where I would be leading people into this harvest of souls. Most of you are at that place today. As God leads us from one functional role to another, it is proper that we adjust the focus of our vision. We must never lose sight, however, of our real mission—we are here to carry on what Jesus began. He came to seek and save the lost.

When He saw the multitudes, He was moved with compassion toward them. This is what made Him say, "Let us go into the next towns, that I may preach there also: for therefore came I forth" (Mark 1:38).

This undergirding vision must be there to support the more clearly defined focus of our particular ministries. At the same time, some of us may be living with no true vision of the specific function God has assigned us. It is possible to live "out of range" of God's voice. While making an initial commitment of surrender to God's will in order to enter the ministry, it is possible that a truly spiritual relationship has not been maintained to where we are right now being directed from heaven. This condition can be corrected by re-establishing a deep communion with God. To build and maintain this relationship requires time spent alone with God—quality prayer time.

With Paul it began in the Arabian desert. Would this apostle's vision have been so clearly defined without this communion he found in isolation with the One who had called him? I think not. O for a clear vision of our mission today, a vision that will give positive direction to our ministering.

Is your vision one of "serving" the church you are pastoring, or of leading the church you are pastoring into an aggressive outreach ministry? It is unlikely that you will go beyond your vision. I have known pastors whose "servicing" vision was reflected by statements which indicated that they felt they had an "ideal" church. It was small in membership, yet it paid the limit. Therefore, it did not require so much of them, time wise. They could take care of their visitation responsibilities, never having to feel "stressed out" like pastors whose congregations were larger. With that vision it is unlikely that they will ever become bothered with the challenges that a larger church presents.

I do not believe such a "servicing" vision is a proper one, however, and I believe we need to pray for a "leadership" vision. This is one wherein the pastor sees himself not just as a servicer of his membership, but leading these members in their communities. He will not be the sole minister but rather the leader of a growing number of people who have been inspired by his leadership to involve themselves in ministry. They will need direction, of course.

When we speak of "being the Body of Christ," what picture does this bring to your mind? Is it simply the Church of God of Prophecy as you have always known it? If this is our vision then we will probably remain as we have always been. I believe the scriptural vision is more far-reaching than we have realized.

Paul wrote of there being "many members" in one body, all having different functions, each ministering according to his peculiar giftedness. These individuals should be allowed to rise to the capacity God has given them. A pastor should never feel threatened by men and women whose abilities in many areas may exceed his own. These endowments of God's grace are to be respected and appreciated. What each of us is, we are only by the grace of God. If you have been set in the body to pastor, you will be endowed with the grace of pastoring. But this does not mean you have been given expertise in all fields superior to those whom you are pastoring. Just allow the grace of leadership to flow through your ministry.

At the same time, as a leader, you must respect the giftedness of others. Where the Holy Ghost is being given liberty to work we may expect to see all the grace gifts of Romans 12 being employed. God has designed a body ministry for His Church. Satan's business is to stop or hinder the flow of the Spirit throughout the body. It is your responsibility as pastor to see that this does not happen. It is only as the Holy Ghost has complete liberty to actuate each member of the body to fruitful service that the Church will be what God designed it to be.

Every pastor should have two churches. One is the church that now exists, the reality which is, the one with which he is very well acquainted. The other is the one which exists within his head and heart. It is visionary. It is a far greater and stronger church than the one he is now pastoring. Yet, it is what the real one can become by the grace of God. Without this vision to inspire and guide him, the church as it now exists is the church that will continue to be.

The pastor's leadership ability will be tested as he is able to communicate his vision to his congregation and to inspire them to join him in progressive steps towards its realization. For this purpose you have been called by God, the God who will empower you with the grace of leadership as you commune with Him. He called you and chose you for this purpose!

Our Commitment

8

CBL Conference
Elizabethtown, Kentucky
November 20, 1992

What is it to be the Church of God of the Bible? Jesus declared, "I will build my church." To be the Church of God of the Bible is to be the Church which Jesus is building—and that is our commitment!

He began it with twelve apostles. He acquainted them with the divine principles by which His Church would be guided, and gave these men the responsibility to convey these principles, for all time, to those who, in the future, would be a part of His Church. To assure that these principles would be preserved for the last days' Church, they were put into a Book—the Bible.

So, today, when we speak of being the Church of God of the Bible, we mean that we are to be faithful to what has been conveyed to us by the Holy Ghost through the Scriptures. This includes not just the letters the Apostles have written, but their lives and ministries as recorded in the Acts of the Apostles must also be considered, and it is for the Church today to follow faithfully what we observe in their history.

It is not as though Jesus would build two churches, one in the days of the Apostles and another in the last days. His principles, as set forth in His life and teachings, are constant. He is the same yesterday, today and forever. Therefore, we are safe to follow the pattern we find in the New Testament. The Apostles provide us a double assurance, somewhat. That is, they were eyewitnesses of the things Jesus did and they personally heard the things He said. In addition, Luke tells us that they were all filled with the Holy Ghost, the great Revealer of Christ, and it was the daily witness of the Spirit that provided assurance that they were still following what they had seen and heard of their Saviour.

It was Jesus' choice that they be the foundational pillars in His Church. We will do well to study the Acts of the Apostles as well as to study their writings, to make certain we are fulfilling our call to be the Church of God of the Bible. It is when people are able to see the same things in the history we are now making, as they read about in the history of the Early Church, that they will give credibility to our claims to being the same Church.

It is not enough to point to a certain mountain where our leader prayed and received a divine revelation, or to display a banner which we adopted in 1933, as important as these may be. We must demonstrate today the outworking of God's Word in our lives. We must bear witness of the same graces and gifts of the Spirit as were evident in the Acts of the Apostles. We may point to and boast of the events of sixty years ago, or of ninety years ago, with the hope that these may excuse our lack of a vital relationship with the Holy Ghost. Such will not satisfy searching hearts which have been newly quickened, awakened to the importance of divine power in today's Christians.

These people read in the Scriptures that Christ's kingdom is not in word but in power. They hear Paul saying that his gospel was not in word only but also in power. Then when they see within a group an exhibition, more of words than anything else, they have difficulty identifying that group as being the same Church they see ministering in the Bible.

It is very important that our doctrinal positions be correct, that we understand exactly what Jesus taught, that we are fully embracing His principles in daily living and ministry. Just to defend doctrinal positions theologically, however, does little to bring sinners to Jesus or to convince suffering people of our care and concern for them. People who are hurting need help—not just words.

The compassion for people which Jesus demonstrated must be exemplified in His Church. In that way it may be said that the Church is the Body of Christ, as it reaches out to touch people, to bring His healing power to them, to acquaint them with His forgiveness, and to teach them of His holiness, which can be done most effectively by example.

Of what benefit is it for us to look back to the revelation of 1903 unless the burden of that moment is being carried today. That burden then was to be the Church of God of the Bible, not just another denomination which would further divide God's people. We must retain this commitment! Then by a continuing careful and prayerful evaluation, we must make certain that what we see in the Scriptures is the same thing being reflected in the Church today—the same Word, the same power, the same miracles.

When the Church flag was introduced in the Assembly in 1933, and, as was said by the General Overseer, "dedicated by the Holy Ghost," it was viewed to be because of our commitment to TRUTH! Unless that same commitment exists now, some sixty years later, do we have the right to display this banner? This is a valid question. Truth doesn't change! Our perception or understanding may be heightened as God shines a brighter light upon His Word. In that case, we are committed to walk in the light. With the same resolve that men and women of God embraced the truth in 1933, we must do so today and continue walking in the light to the best of our knowledge and ability. Who knows but what there are some things we will understand yet better as we move forward in the greater brilliance of Heavenly light, as the Word unfolds to us with deeper and fuller meaning?

Shall such then be for further theological debating? God forbid! May it be rather for a deeper relationship with the

One who loves us so much! Knowing Him better to serve Him more effectively—that is our desire. A fuller knowledge of the Word is only to add richness to the relationship between Christ and the Church. And this is not to know Him solely for our own personal enrichment. It is the Church's purpose to manifest this wonderful Saviour to all mankind. This world needs to know Jesus. O to know Him better that we may be more effective in introducing Him to others!

Paul described the Church as "his body, the fulness of him that filleth all in all" (Ephesians 1:23). Then he wrote, "And to know the love of Christ, which passeth knowledge, that ye might be filled with all the fulness of God" (3:19). The full expression of Jesus Christ to this world is to come through His Church. And Paul called this "the fulness of God" in us, which would denote our perfection. How will this fulness of God be attained?

Let us read from Ephesians 3:16-19: "That he would grant you, according to the riches of his glory, to be strengthened with might by his Spirit in the inner man; that Christ may dwell in your hearts by faith; that ye, being rooted and grounded in love, May be able to comprehend with [not above] all saints what is the breadth, and length, and depth, and height; and to know the love of Christ, which passeth knowledge, that ye might be filled with all the fulness of God."

Knowing the love of Christ, that we might be filled with all God's fulness for us—that is the key! The love of Christ is the answer! This world needs to see and feel the love of Christ, and God has designed that they are to experience this amazing love through Christ's Body, the Church. This love is the key to the Church's reaching its fullness, its perfection.

R. G. Spurling, one of our early fathers in this century, called this divine love "the lost link." It is something that is being overlooked oftentimes as Christians go on with their debating, doing much too little to reach a lost world. But the Church of God of the Bible is the Church of love. It was begun by Christ, whose initiating command was to "love one another as I have loved you." He is still building His Church

Our Commitment

and His principles for its construction have never been changed. It is certain that He will finish what He began.

The Church we see in the Acts of the Apostles was a society of caring people. "And all that believed were together, and had all things common; And sold their possessions and goods, and parted them to all men, as every man had need. And they, continuing daily with one accord in the temple, and breaking bread from house to house, did eat their meat with gladness and singleness of heart" (Acts 2:44-46). It could not be denied that they were the Church of love. Christ's command that they love one another was being carried out in a very practical way. In Acts, chapter four, Luke wrote, "And the multitude of them that believed were of one heart and of one soul: neither said any of them that ought of the things which he possessed was his own; but they had all things common" (v. 32).

Not only must the Church Christ is building be a loving, caring fellowship, with the love of God being extended freely to each member of the Body, it must demonstrate this loving concern also for those who remain unsaved. As we emulate the Church we see in the Book of Acts, there must be a fervent zeal for spreading this glorious gospel of a Saviour for all mankind. Of them Luke writes, "And daily in the temple, and in every house, they ceased not to teach and preach Jesus Christ" (Acts 5:42). They gave evangelism top priority. Theirs could be called a fanatical zeal!

Anything that threatened to slow down their ministry to the lost had to be dealt with. They saw reaching and saving lost men and women to be their purpose. Disputes that arose among them had to be settled promptly so as not to interfere with their evangelizing. That is why in chapter six when there arose a murmuring of the Grecians against the Hebrews, they came together to resolve the problem. Seven men were selected to supervise the distribution of resources to the widows. The Apostles were determined that nothing hinder their ministry of the gospel.

The council at Jerusalem as recorded in Acts, chapter fifteen, was convened for the same purpose. They wanted nothing to hinder the spreading of the gospel. The dissension caused by the Judaizers had to cease if the Word of God was to have free course in the Church's ongoing ministry of evangelization. So the problem was dealt with decisively.

The Church at this time must be an evangelistic Church. That must be our commitment. Otherwise, how could we properly lay claim to being the Church of God of the Bible? We must recapture the fervor with which they proclaimed the message of Jesus Christ, being propelled by a deep compassion for those who are lost.

In our early history in this century, when the need for having an Assembly of the churches was recognized, it was decided that January would be a good month for such a meeting. Their reasoning was that the weather at that time was less suitable for evangelistic work. They did not want even an Assembly, as important as they viewed this to be, to interfere with their evangelistic endeavors.

With the passing of time this zeal for reaching the lost was superseded by the interest in a General Assembly, and what had been considered as prime time for evangelizing became Assembly time. To look honestly at the Church in the New Testament, there is no indication that they felt it necessary to have annual Assemblies which we have had now for some 85 years.

When the Apostles called for the selection of seven men who would oversee the distribution of goods, it was that they might give themselves "continually to prayer, and to the ministry of the word" (Acts 6:4). They did not want to be distracted from their praying by such administrative work. Nor was this administrative work so secular that carnal men could have done it. The requirement for this was "seven men of honest report, full of the Holy Ghost and wisdom" (v. 3). But they knew they had to have ample prayer time if the ministry of the Word was to be effective.

They had observed their Master and they knew the priority He had given prayer—at times praying all night. At other times, He would arise a great while before day to spend time alone with God, on those days when He knew the people would be seeking Him. He had to pray, and they knew they had to pray. They would allow nothing—not even good and worthy things—to rob them of their prayer time. Preaching without prayer would be just words without power. Great preachers are great prayers. This is the way it was in the Early Church, and that is the way it must be in the last days Church.

The wisdom of the Apostles' decision may be seen in verse seven: "And the word of God increased; and the number of the disciples multiplied in Jerusalem greatly." They prayed, they preached and God gave increase! Some have excused their failure to affect people with the gospel by such statements as, "Our group is small, but we prefer quality to quantity" We should ask, "Quality—by whose standard?" It seems that if the group is measuring to God's standard of quality there will be fruitfulness, to where there can be quality and quantity.

As long as the Church of God which we see in the Bible kept first things first they increased, they grew. This is attested to by such statements as, "Then they that gladly received his word were baptized: and the same day there were added unto them about three thousand souls" (Acts 2:41); "Howbeit many of them which heard the word believed; and the number of the men was about five thousand" (4:4); "And believers were the more added to the Lord, multitudes both of men and women" (5:14).

Our commitment then must be to keep first things first. We must have a ministry that is given, first of all, to prayer, then to the ministry of the Word. This must be a ministering by Holy Ghost anointing, a ministry that comes from a deep-felt burden for people who need the Lord. The Church must have a ministry that refuses to become bogged down in secondary things—even though these things be good and worthy. There must be a total involvement by the entire membership according to their giftedness, a membership full of the Holy Ghost. No less commitment will suffice for the Church of God of the Bible.

Form And Substance

9

North American Leadership Conference
Cleveland, Tennessee
January 5-10, 1993

Where there is substance it will take some kind of form, but it is possible to have form which is empty of substance. Paul wrote of a people who would have a form of godliness without its accompanying power. This is form without substance. Godliness is indeed substantive, and has the power to touch and influence lives.

Forms of religion abound today, but the Body of Christ is much more than form. It has form all right, recognizable form, but its substance is the thing that gives it its value to mankind. Form without substance is like clouds without water. Such clouds may appear in the sky and bring false hope for awhile to the farmer who is praying for rain that will water his parched ground. His disappointment comes because they were clouds without water. This is the way Jude described certain people (Jude 12).

To what extent are our local churches exhibiting visible form while being void of the substance demanded to meet the needs of this generation in their communities? Soon after a church is organized, the people usually feel the need for a building. This will provide them a place to assemble, plus give them some identity in the community. Then, in most places a piano, organ or other musical instruments are viewed as a necessity. Regular worship times are established. A Sunday school is organized, along with a youth group or women's auxiliary.

It doesn't take long for an organizer to get things going to where no one can deny that an organization exists. The form has taken shape. Why is it that in far too many places this form continues to exist, but ten, twenty, thirty or forty years later that church has failed to impact its community. It is still there—they still have a building, a piano, their regular worship times. They still have Sunday school, a youth group, a women' s auxiliary—the organization is still intact, but true ministry is missing. Where is the substance?

The substance of the Body of Christ is of divine origin. According to Paul it is "the power that worketh in (us) mightily." It is that which was missing in the old order among God's Israel. The form was there, great was the form! But the substance which provides life and power was missing. The congregation of Israel under the old covenant prefigured or foreshadowed the New Testament congregation of God—the ecclesia, the Church. "For the law having a shadow of good things to come" (Hebrews 10:1). A shadow has a form without substance, but the Body of Christ has life from the direct relationship it has with its Head, Jesus Christ. John wrote, "In him was life; and the life was the light of men." (John 1:4). It is this life which gives substance and power to the Body. This is what was missing under the law. Even though they took great pride in their dead forms, these could not produce life for the Israelites. These two covenants, the covenant of law and the covenant of grace, are represented well by the terms "form" and "substance."

The distinction between the two must be held forth clearly. One brought death, the other life. It was the new covenant that brought an end to Satan's power in an individual's life. It assures destruction of the flesh to where a person can walk in the Spirit, enjoying newness of life. The old covenant could not do that. We can see why Satan never gives up in his attempt to superimpose the old upon the new. This was his strategy in the apostolic Church, and he still schemes toward this end today.

Paul contended strongly against this ploy of Satan. He knew it would negate the benefits of the cross of our Saviour. It would be returning to the acceptance of the form for substance.

In his letter to the Galatians he was bold to cry out against this very thing by which they were being victimized. They were being drawn back to what they felt security in, the forms of the law. The grace walk is a walk of relationship, a relationship which must be maintained daily by prayer and communion with Jesus. The old covenant consisted of rules to follow, containing many prohibitions. Observing prohibitions can never create life. On the other hand, when a person is alive in Christ and walks in fellowship with Him, that person will observe scriptural prohibitions. Freedom in Christ does not mean freedom to sin or freedom to offend a brother or sister. It rather means walking as Jesus walked. He literally laid down His life for others. There was no self-interest or self-centeredness in Him.

To the Galatians it no doubt seemed simpler to have a set of rules they could follow, which the law had offered them, and for so doing to consider themselves righteous. In the new order established by Jesus, however, no one can outline a list of rules of which the keeping will assure righteousness. Righteousness is established and maintained in one's relationship to Jesus. It will only exist as His lordship is recognized and respected. He may ask more of you than others would. He might ask you to sell all you have and distribute it to the poor. He has the right to do so. He might ask you to get rid of your television set. He has the right to do so. He might ask you to give up your job and work full time for Him. He has the right to do so. Whatever He requires of anyone, however, is for the good of that person. His perfect love for every individual assures that.

Relationship with Jesus Christ is costly. Therefore, many would prefer just a list of do's and don'ts, the same list for everybody. This would eliminate times of agonizing prayer when Christ's demands are such that the human will desires an easier path. At the same time a list would provide the means to criticize others who are not "measuring up." This always feeds a self-righteous spirit.

Paul made it clear to those who were being tempted to revert to keeping the law instead of paying the price of the "grace walk," that to take this route simply meant they were fallen from grace (cf. Galatians 5:4). It is impossible to follow the walk of grace while living with the spirit of the law. This is to frustrate the grace of God (cf. Galatians 2:21).

"Then said he, Lo, I come to do thy will, O God. He taketh away the first, that he may establish the second" (Hebrews 10:9). He took away the first covenant that He might establish the second covenant. The spirit of the law and the spirit of grace could not co-exist in the Church Jesus came to build. "For finding fault with them, he saith, Behold, the days come, saith the Lord, when I will make a new covenant with the house of Israel and with the house of Judah: Not according to the covenant that I made with their fathers in the day when I took them by the hand to lead them out of the land of Egypt. . . . For this is the covenant that I will make with the house of Israel after those days, saith the Lord; I will put my laws into their mind, and write them in their hearts: and I will be to them a God, and they shall be to me a people" (Hebrews 8:8-10).

From a strictly human standpoint, living by the spirit of the law is more desirable than to walk the grace walk. The individual retains control in the former, while surrender is required in the latter. A feeling of independence appeals to the flesh. To be the Body of Christ, however, demands that we recognize the headship of Jesus, that we are indeed only the body, that He is the Head. The body does not control itself. It has not the capacity for so doing. Because the desire for independence and self-assertion is so strong in the human psyche, it is easy to drift back into the spirit of the law, but this must be avoided!

To these Galatians Paul wrote, "Tell me, ye that desire to be under the law, do ye not hear the law? For it is written, that Abraham had two sons, the one by a bondmaid, the other by a freewoman" (Galatians 4:21, 22). He refers them to Genesis, the first book of the law, and draws their attention to the account of Abraham, Ishmael and Isaac. "But he who was born of the bondwoman was born after the flesh; but he of the freewoman was by promise. Which things are an allegory: for these are the two covenants; the one from the mount Sinai, which gendereth [bears children] to bondage, which is [Hagar]" (vv. 23, 24). Paul emphasized that Hagar represented the covenant of the law which was received at mount Sinai and corresponded with Jerusalem of that day which, having rejected Christ, remained in bondage with her children.

To the saints of Galatia he declared, "Now we, brethren, as Isaac was, are the children of promise. But as then he that was born after the flesh persecuted him that was born after the Spirit, even so it is now." Drawing from this analogy this brave apostle quoted from Genesis 21:10, "Cast out this bondwoman and her son: for the son of this bondwoman shall not be heir with [Isaac]." He reminded them that they were "not children of the bondwoman, but of the free" (v. 31). Then he wrote "Stand fast therefore in the liberty wherewith Christ hath made us free, and be not entangled again with the yoke of bondage" (Galatians 5:1).

Paul treasured what he knew had been provided through Jesus. He saw its beauty and the power and health that it was offering to the Body of Christ. But he saw also Satan's attempt to pull them away from this blessedness in order to impose upon Christ's Church a substitute of form for real substance. So, he took them back to the Book of Genesis to show them in type what God was truly desiring. This new covenant of grace could be firmly established only by a replacement of the Sinai covenant. The bondwoman and her son had to be cast out. This corresponds with Hebrews 10:9, "He taketh away the first, that he may establish the second."

"For what the law could not do, in that it was weak through the flesh, God sending his own Son in the likeness of sinful flesh, and for sin, condemned sin in the flesh: That the righteousness of the law might be fulfilled in us, who walk not after the flesh, but after the Spirit" (Romans 8:3, 4).

This is a point that must be emphasized. To revert to the spirit of the law would assure our walking in the flesh. There can be no proper function of the Body of Christ apart from walking in the Spirit. It is time for an honest and frank assessment as to whether we are truly free from the spirit of the law and fully walking in the Spirit.

The Church which Jesus instituted, and which today He is building, is radically different from the world in which it functions. We require frequent reminders of Jesus' prayer in John, chapter seventeen where He said, "they are not of the world, even as I am not of the world" (John 17:14). It is only by walking in the Spirit, in the grace of the new covenant, that we will be saved from trends of worldliness. A test of whether we are indeed walking in the Spirit is to determine whether we are displaying worldly attitudes.

It was easy for people to see that Jesus was "not of the world." His view of people was different. The poor felt His concern for them. Lepers did not have to keep their distance from Him. As a leader, Jesus set new standards of leadership. He contrasted the worldly style with the style of leadership that was from God. When strife developed among His disciples as they desired rank or position within His Church, Jesus' reminder to them was as follows:

> "The kings of the Gentiles [the nations of this world] exercise lordship over them; and they that exercise authority upon them are called benefactors. But ye shall not be so: but he that is greatest among you, let him be as the younger; and he that is chief, as he that doth serve. For whether is greater, he that sitteth at meat, or he that serveth? is not he that sitteth at meat? but I am among you as he that serveth" (Luke 22:25-27).

It is significant that Jesus said, "I am among you as one that serveth"—not above you, but among you. In the world it is usual for a leader to be placed conspicuously above others. This may be seen in the size of his office, the plushness of its carpet and other trappings designed to show he is above those he is leading. We must ask whether this is proper for those of us who identify with Jesus.

With the deference given by the Church to those who are "over them in the Lord," a leader must be careful lest he begins to feel that somehow he deserves the special treatment he receives. This temptation is fed both by our natural inclinations and by the world's model of authoritarian leadership. Charles Colson, in his book, *The Body, Being Light In Darkness*, (page 310), writes about a pastor of one of America's fastest growing churches who so far seems to have resisted this temptation. He practices conscious awareness of the little things that would inflate his ego. For example, his congregation has outgrown its parking facilities and has been forced to use a satellite area about a mile away for the overflow. Instead of reserving a "senior pastor" parking slot next to the church, this pastor has chosen to park in the overflow lot and ride a shuttle bus to the church. This may seem a bit extreme to some of us, but he has probably seen what special favors can do to a leader.

In the Body of Christ, where we emphasize substance above form, should it not be the spiritual authority, the divine giftedness, rather than worldly trappings that distinguish leaders? I do not believe it was difficult to know who the Leader was among those thirteen men who walked together in Galilee.

It is so easy to drift into worldliness, where the leader's house must be larger, his car and clothing more expensive, etc., than those to whom he has been designated by Jesus as a servant. There was no doubt about Jesus' leader-servant role. He just did not give in to the ways of the world. Not only did He wash His disciples' feet, which definitely was a servant's function; Jesus, even after taking on immortality following His crucifixion, cooked breakfast on the seashore for those He had led. He was still "among them as one that serveth."

The two covenants of law and grace, form and substance, were so different. Under the first covenant men were elevated by position. When we read of Aaron in the priest's office, his clothing had to be more magnificent than others.

He wore a breastplate, an ephod, a robe, a broidered coat, a mitre, and a girdle. These were not garments associated with a servant. Later, when Israel desired a king and received a line of kings, they lived in palaces. They knew regal splendor, not at all like servants. Even the prophets had servants to serve them (cf. 1 Kings 18:43; 1 Kings 4:12).

When Jesus came, He was Prophet, Priest and King, but He was a king without a palace—He had nowhere to lay His head. He was a priest, but one would not have been able to detect it by His clothing. He was a prophet, but not a prophet with servants—He Himself was the servant to others. He was born in a stable and buried in a borrowed tomb, and when He needed a donkey to ride on, to fulfill prophecy, He had to borrow one. Isaiah wrote, ". . . he hath no form nor comeliness; and when we shall see him, there is no beauty that we should desire him" (Isaiah 53:2). No form, but what substance!

It was substance of divine origin. He was anointed with the Holy Ghost and power! It was an anointing that left no doubt about His leadership. Jesus was not the greatest Leader this world has ever known simply because He was born in a stable with no place to lay His head, having to borrow a donkey. Each of us could take a vow of poverty which would immediately make us stand out in sharp contrast to worldly leadership styles, but this alone would not make us great spiritual leaders. The one thing that is most important for this is heavenly anointing! Without this we may possess good management skills, but for the Body of Christ to fulfill its purpose, more than managers are required. We need spiritual leaders! The Church needs leaders who, recognizably, are in touch with God.

Will the Church rise above its leadership? I think not. The leadership that will inspire the Church for the ministering that is so much needed right now must be functional, not just positional. "The anointing goes with the office" is not necessarily true. History teaches us that there have been men appointed to offices who never were anointed men. Their rule was authoritarian. Instead of providing spiritual leadership, they simply managed, and that poorly. There is a difference between management and leadership.

The power of a leader's effectiveness will be in his relationship with Jesus, the Church's Supreme Leader. In this "new and living way" which He ushered in we have the privilege of being filled with the Holy Ghost. This provision which Jesus made for us cannot be overlooked or neglected if we are to provide anointed leadership to the Church.

This designation, "filled with the Holy Ghost," or, "full of the Holy Ghost," is used frequently to describe the Church which we see functioning in the Book of Acts.

On the Day of Pentecost we read, "And they were all filled with the Holy Ghost" (Acts 2:4). Jesus commanded the Apostles "not to depart from Jerusalem, but wait for the promise of the Father" (1:4). "But ye shall receive power," He said, "after that the Holy Ghost is come upon you" (v. 8).

Upon the leadership of the Church in the New Testament this power was evident. We may well ask what their success would have been apart from this empowering. But under the new covenant it was never intended that they function apart from this power. That's why we read, "Then Peter, filled with the Holy Ghost, said unto them." (4:8). Later in this chapter we read, "And when they had prayed, the place was shaken where they were assembled together; and they were all filled with the Holy Ghost, and they spake the word of God with boldness" (v. 31).

When the apostles felt it necessary, in order to give themselves continually to prayer, and to the ministry of the word, they appointed seven men to oversee the distribution of food among the needy. A requirement for these seven men was that they be "full of the Holy Ghost and wisdom" (6:3). One of these, Stephen, was specifically described as being "full of faith and of the Holy Ghost" (v. 5). In verse eight we read, "And Stephen, full of faith and power, did great wonders and miracles among the people." In verse ten, "And they were not able to resist the wisdom and the spirit by which he spake." In chapter seven, verse fifty-five, we read, "But he, being full of the Holy Ghost, looked up stedfastly into heaven, and saw the glory of God, and Jesus standing on the right hand of God."

These were the kind of men the Apostles appointed to administrative work so they could give themselves "continually to prayer, and to the ministry of the word" (6:4)—in that order. First, prayer; then, to the ministry of the word. They would not allow administrative work to keep them from what was primary. In prayer, they could cultivate their relationship with Jesus. Through prayer, they could keep themselves emptied of themselves and filled with the Holy Ghost, something that was absolutely necessary if they were to minister, not with form but with substance.

Several years later, after Saul had been converted and was ministering in Cyprus, we find that the nature of the Apostles' ministry had not changed. "Then Saul, (who also is called Paul,) filled with the Holy Ghost, set his eyes on him [Elymas], And said, O full of all subtlety and all mischief, thou child of the devil, thou enemy of all righteousness, wilt thou not cease to pervert the right ways of the Lord? And now, behold, the hand of the Lord is upon thee, and thou shalt be blind, not seeing the sun for a season. And immediately there fell on him a mist and a darkness; and he went about seeking some to lead him by the hand" (13:9-11).

The emphasis upon this type of New Testament ministering was that these men were "filled with the Holy Ghost." I must add that this was not just a one-time occurrence. It is easy for us to assume that this happened to the Apostles on the Day of Pentecost. It is true that on that particular day they were filled with the Holy Ghost, but it was a continuing experience. A person who receives this blessed Gift does not automatically remain full of the Holy Ghost. This is a divine relationship that must be maintained and nurtured. Being the Body of Christ involves being an extension of the revelation of God in Christ to this world. Jesus had form all right—He could be seen and touched, but what gave power to His ministry was substance. Peter told about this at the house of Cornelius when he said, "How God anointed Jesus of Nazareth with the Holy Ghost and with power" (Acts 10:38).

The Body of Christ is not something mystical to which we belong. It is something which we are. It takes its form in groups of people joined together in a strong commitment to be the Church under the headship of Christ. It has its form in local congregations who see themselves as functioning units of the larger congregation of God. The strength of the Body is seen in those local congregations where spiritually gifted people, full of the Holy Ghost, touch and minister to a needy world.

The attention of the leadership assembled in this conference must be focused upon these functioning units of the larger congregation. It is at these local churches that lives will be changed, that nurturing will be done, that maturing will take place, that preparations will be made for the Rapture. These things will not be going on so much at our central offices, but in local congregations where liberty and freedom is given for the Spirit to take charge. We must have churches full of the Holy Ghost. The leadership within these churches must be men and women who are filled with the Holy Ghost.

In too many places we have struggling churches where there is form without this divine substance. And many times there is genuine dedication to preserve the form. They struggle hard to make payments on buildings, to pay utility bills, etc. Many faithful people, at great personal sacrifices, have seen to it that the form remains intact where they are. At the same time, you will find discouragement and frustration there. This will continue until these local congregations become filled with the Holy Ghost.

Many local churches have been set in order which are too weak to function. Only God knows the motivations behind these organizations. In many instances the motives were entirely worthy. In some cases, it simply should not have been done. In many cases, inadequate leadership assures a continuing form but without substance.

What is the solution to this problem? Some would suggest mergers of many of these small churches into larger ones that would be strong enough to function. Some of this is going on now and I am not opposed to this being done where it improves ministering. At the same time, I see the possibility of simply creating some larger forms, still without substance! The success of the new formations will hinge, to a great degree, upon the quality of leadership that is provided. We need leaders (to borrow from some of the phrases in Acts, chapter 6) "full of the Holy Ghost and wisdom," "full of faith and the Holy Ghost," "full of faith and power." It is for the development of such leaders that the Center for Biblical Leadership is dedicated. I know nothing more important than the development within the Church of strong, spiritual leadership. For this to occur, there is a price to be paid, and it will not be done by a half-dozen men working out of Cleveland. A mobilization of all our resources, dedicated to this end, will be required.

The full cooperation of our Overseers is a "must." I am aware that many of you have a full calendar of events. You are not spending your time in idleness. In fact, some of you are going at a pace that is a peril to your health. A cursory review of our records, however, reveals that we are not doing too well as the Body of Christ. Too many of our local congregations are at a standstill, or in some cases, regressing. We are not impacting our communities to the extent that God is pleased. So, some change in our manner of operating seems in order.

First of all, I want to encourage you to spend more time alone with God. We want to make sure that we ourselves are "full of the Holy Ghost." This may require that you spend less of your time in administrative work. Pastors are going to have to be taught to look more to the Holy Ghost than to their Overseers. I want you Overseers to look less to my office and more to the Holy Ghost. God's Church must become a "spiritual house." Those to whom we minister must recognize that we are in touch with Heaven. The authority with which we govern must be recognizable spiritual authority.

Then, it is important that you devote more of your time to spiritual leadership development. The Center for Biblical Leadership will be a resource center for you, but, as I said, a half-dozen men from Cleveland cannot fill all the needs. It will be largely up to you to seek God for the initiatives you need to take. Let me emphasize that, yes, we do need education in the truest sense of the word, but first our ministers need to be led into the certainty that they are "full of the Holy Ghost." Become a teacher, a "discipler." This means pouring your life into the lives of your pastors and ministers. Do you desire the ministers under your supervision to become what you are?

More will be required than a few sessions which do little more than inspire ministers with the desire to learn. These are helpful and necessary, all right, but such must be followed up with substantive teaching. You, yourself, may not be the best classroom teacher, but you should find someone whom God has gifted to teach. I believe God will make provision for what He requires and inspires. The Church needs leadership which knows the Word and which knows its Author.

The theme of this conference is "Being the Body of Christ." Our claims mean little unless they are marked by reality. To a needy world, unless we are truly being the Body of Christ, it is just form without substance, clouds without water. As we read of the Church in the New Testament we find Jesus saying to them, "Ye are the light of the world," and "Ye are the salt of the earth." And Paul could write, "Now ye are the body of Christ." They were made so by God, not by inherent abilities, but by divine impartation.

When our fathers, in the early part of this century, made their commitment to be the Church of God of the Bible, they were not wanting to simply start another group to further divide the children of God. They were dissatisfied with forms without substance. They saw in the Scriptures something different from what they were seeing in the denominational structures that were abounding. It surely was not their desire or intent to start another one of these. They were committed to be that same Church which they read about in the Book of Acts, having the same spiritual power and authority over the powers of Satan. That remains our commitment today— to be the Church of God of the Bible, to be the Body of Christ.

This power and authority is available only in the life of the new covenant. It is held in our relationship with Jesus, the Saviour of the Body. The Early Church eventually drifted from this relationship to the point of their being rejected by God. In 1984, in the spirit of repentance, we confessed that we also had drifted from this vital relationship. This admission, though somewhat painful to the self-righteous among us, was necessary as a first step toward reestablishing ourselves as a truly spiritual house.

This repentance requires more than just a formal Assembly resolution. Except it be from the heart, God does not accept it. It is my prayer that this group be resolved to rediscover and reaffirm this divine relationship in our commitment to be the Body of Christ. The times demand it; God requires it, and we must not fail!

The Body of Christ cannot be refreshed from "hewed-out cisterns" of stagnant water. Our life is from the *fountain of living water* springing up within us. Many of our congregations are in a state of stagnation right now, having no vitality of the Spirit. They are trying to survive off the inspiration of the past. Stagnant water often becomes contaminated to where it is a risk to the health of the body. In my judgment, this is the cause of many of the problems we are experiencing, having forsaken the *fountain of living water,* attempting to live from *cisterns* of stored water.

We need to give heed to the voice of the One who stood one day in Jerusalem in the midst of a group who prided themselves in their stored water, water which was stagnant and producing death. This One who had descended from heaven cried, "If any man thirst, let him come unto me, and drink. He that believeth on me, as the scripture hath said, out of his belly shall flow rivers of living water" (John 7:37, 38).

That One stands among us today with the same cry.

Text: John 4:31-38

10

North American Leadership Conference
January 3-8, 1994
Cleveland, Tennessee

The theme, "Turning to the Harvest" has been carefully chosen and is meant to be taken very seriously. As we reflect upon, "turning to," the implication is clear that this involves "turning from." We must ask what it is that we must "turn from" in order that we may "turn to" our God-given directives.

It was almost ten years ago, in the 1984 Assembly, that we were called upon to repent, and many have continually asked, "For What?" May we review exactly what was said: "This Committee knows of no greater need to bring to this Assembly's attention than the need for repentance—the need to fall on our faces before God, confessing that we have drifted in many ways from a vital relationship with the Holy Ghost, confessing a self-centeredness lacking in deep compassion for a world of people who are living now under the judgment of God to eternal damnation, rededicating ourselves to being the Church of God of the Bible. God's message to the Church in this Assembly has been a call to repent, and we must not ignore His voice. We cannot afford to continue the pursuit of our mission without convincing evidence of His presence and approval. There is no acceptable substitute for repentance when that is what God is calling us to do."

"A self-centeredness lacking in deep compassion [for the lost]"—that was our confession ten years ago. Have we changed? Have we truly repented? To what degree have we been self-centered or egotistical? Have we really thought too highly of ourselves? Have we been guilty of egotistical pride? And is such still existing? These are questions we must face in this conference.

Genesis, chapter eleven, gives the account of a people who wanted to make for themselves a name. They purposed to build a city and a tower, but it was for the wrong purpose. It was to draw attention to themselves—to make for themselves a name. That which feeds human pride dishonors God. His alone is the name to be exalted. We exist only for His glory.

It has not been our intent, I'm sure, to dishonor God in our zeal to promote the Church, as we see it in the Scriptures; yet, we may be guilty of this. I remember some time ago when we would sing the chorus, "Heavenly Father, I Appreciate You," then we would continue with "Son of God, I appreciate you," and "Holy Ghost, I appreciate you." Then we somehow felt the need to sing "Church of God, I appreciate you." The chorus would continue, "I love you, adore you, I bow down before you; Church of God, I appreciate you." Strangely, we did not seem to feel we were doing anything wrong by giving this degree of worship to the Church. However, we know that God will not share with any of His creation the right to be worshiped. The Church had become in our minds something more than just a fellowship of believers. Divinely planned and originated—yes, but the Church is not an intangible, ethereal entity which somehow exists above and beyond real people—humans bonded together. The Church is people. No human or group of humans deserves to be worshiped.

While God may wink at ignorance for awhile, knowing the sincerity of hearts, the time comes as He foresees the disastrous results our ignorance is leading us to that He, in

Text: John 4:31-38

His mercy, convicts and calls for repentance. I believe this is what happened in 1984, and that we cannot afford to go further without giving serious heed to His call.

We had our beginning in this century amidst blazing evangelistic fervor which resulted in amazing growth from some 20 members in 1903 to 20,000 in less than 20 years. The Assembly Minutes in 1906 state the following: "After the consideration of the ripened fields and open doors for evangelism this year, strong men wept and said they were not only willing but really anxious to go. It is, therefore, the sense of this meeting that we do our best to press into every open door this year and work with greater zeal and energy for the spread of the glorious gospel of the Son of God than ever before."

This evangelistic zeal that caused such growth in our early history was not backed up by a financial system. Their trust was in God, not in a system. Evangelism was still occupying our minds in the 1930's and 40's as hearts were burdened to reach the lost.

Eventually, we began to lose our outward focus, looking inward instead. We gave much attention to what we called "perfecting the Church," concentrating upon what we felt was our uniqueness. It soon began to be expressed among us that evangelism was not our main business, that our work was to "get the ark ready" in order to receive those sheep which others were rescuing from sin. The consequences of this misconception are still being suffered. Only God knows how many souls are lost forever because we have erred in this matter. He knows also the degree of our accountability for this error.

Christ's commission to His Church has never changed. It still is, "Go ye into all the world, and preach the gospel to every creature. He that believeth and is baptized shall be saved; but he that believeth not shall be damned" (Mark 16:15, 16). How could we possibly have been led to the conclusion that this command of Jesus was to someone else, that our business was to turn inward and "get the ark ready," while others went into the harvest, rescuing from sin those who were lost? It is very plain that Jesus was speaking to His Church.

I thought surely that such a view no longer existed among us, but recently I have been assured that this feeling is still strong in many places. Does this faulty perception not signify the lack of a deep relationship with our Saviour, to see things from His perspective, whose will remains that none should perish?

As for the Church's perfection, more is involved than making certain the soundness of our doctrine. Can the Church claim perfection while stopping short of fulfilling its mission? In fact, perfection may be more directly related to the Church's relationship with its Head, Jesus Christ, than anything else. We will do well to keep our focus in harmony with that of Jesus, the Author and Finisher of our faith. Shall we continue to focus inward or shall we turn to the harvest?

Can we not learn from Christ's dealings with the Jewish church? By the covenant of circumcision they considered themselves exclusively His. In addition to this covenant of circumcision, they had received the Law at Mt. Sinai, pledging themselves to be faithful to "all that the Lord hath spoken" (Exodus 19:8). Reflecting upon their miraculous deliverance from Egypt, the parting of the Red Sea, being fed manna from heaven, being led by a pillar of cloud by day and of fire by night, seeing the Jordan River roll back, how could they not consider themselves unique and exclusive?

Yet, we find Jesus saying to these Jews in John 10:16, "And other sheep I have, which are not of this fold: them also I must bring, and they shall hear my voice; and there shall be one fold, and one shepherd." The view held by these high-minded people to whom He spoke was very restrictive, but the view of Jesus was not restrictive. It was an encompassing vision wherein He saw vast numbers of Gentiles who would hear His voice, people who were not of that Jewish fold. For Jesus, who could foresee the future as clearly as He saw the past, it was easy to refer to us Gentiles as "other sheep I have." These Gentiles had not subscribed to the covenant of

Text: John 4:31-38

circumcision, nor would He require this of them, but as Paul wrote, Jesus would "make in himself of twain one new man, [body] so making peace" (Ephesians 2:15).

Let's read what Paul wrote about this in Ephesians 2:11-22, "Wherefore remember, that ye being in time past Gentiles in the flesh, who are called Uncircumcision by that which is called the Circumcision in the flesh made by hands; That at that time ye were without Christ, being aliens from the commonwealth of Israel, and strangers from the covenants of promise, having no hope, and without God in the world: But now in Christ Jesus ye who sometimes were far off are made nigh by the blood of Christ. For he is our peace, who hath made both one, and hath broken down the middle wall of partition between us; Having abolished in his flesh the enmity, even the law of commandments contained in ordinances; for to make in himself of twain one new man, so making peace; And that he might reconcile both unto God in one body by the cross, having slain the enmity thereby: And came and preached peace to you which were afar off, and to them that were nigh. For through him we both have access by one Spirit unto the Father. Now therefore ye are no more strangers and foreigners, but fellowcitizens with the saints, and of the household of God; And are built upon the foundation of the apostles and prophets, Jesus Christ himself being the chief corner stone; In whom all the building fitly framed together groweth unto an holy temple in the Lord: In whom ye also are builded together for an habitation of God through the Spirit."

The institutional pride held by the Jewish nation, a pride which was carried over to become a strong influence in the apostolic church would not die easily. Jesus, while on earth with His Church, attempted to show them both by word and by example the broader picture. Not just in His "other sheep" discourse, but in our beginning text in John, chapter four, where He exhorted His disciples to lift up their eyes and look on the fields that were white already to harvest. He was in Samaria. It was here that He shared "living water" with a woman, an adulterous woman, a Samaritan woman at that. Then we find her sharing what she had found with many other Samaritans who believed on Jesus as the result of her testimony. As Jesus tarried there for two days, many more believed on Him, not because of the woman's testimony, but they heard Him themselves. This was one of the fields He wanted His disciples to see, which was white unto harvest.

Then there was His healing of the Syro-Phoenician woman's daughter and of the ten lepers. He inspired Luke to mention that the one leper who returned to give thanks for his healing was a Samaritan. Jesus asked, "Were there not ten cleansed? but where are the nine? There are not found that returned to give glory to God, save this stranger" (Luke 17:17, 18).

Was it not the display of a sectarian spirit which caused the disciples, when they found one casting out devils in Jesus' Name, who they said, "followeth not with us," to forbid him? Jesus rebuked them, saying, "Forbid him not: for he that is not against us is for us" (Luke 9:50). As if to give emphasis to this account God inspired both Luke and Mark to record it (cf. Mark 9:39).

If we could only see things from heaven's perspective, no doubt, some of our attitudes would change. Jesus spoke of the "joy in the presence of the angels of God over one sinner that repenteth" (Luke 15:10). Does this rejoicing occur only when it is someone saved in the Church of God of Prophecy? I believe heaven rejoices whenever and wherever a sinner is set free by the power of God. I further believe that when our hearts are in tune with heaven we will likewise rejoice. A sectarian spirit would probably prevent an exuberant rejoicing unless it happened among us.

O that we could become burdened for those who are lost without the desire for recognition when results occur! As our hearts unite with the heart of our Saviour, this burden will become more intense. In fact, herein lies the key to our present dilemma, I believe—our failure to spend enough time with Him to where we are truly one with Him. To be

Text: John 4:31-38

truly one with Jesus, to where His concerns are our concerns, to where His heart is our heart, requires more than verbalizing a covenant formula. In saying this, I find no fault with our membership covenant. It is a good covenant—well stated, one to which any Christian should be willing to subscribe. It is just that oneness with Jesus is not automatically attained by reciting certain words contained in a certain formula.

Notice Jesus' prayer as recorded in John, chapter seventeen: " . . . as thou, Father, art in me, and I in thee, that they also may be one in us . . . " (v. 21). He prayed further, "I in them, and thou in me, that they may be made perfect in one" (v. 23). I said earlier that the Church's perfection may be more directly related to its relationship with Jesus than anything else. I believe this is true. It is as Paul wrote to the Colossians in chapter one, verse twenty-seven: "To whom God would make known what is the riches of the glory of this mystery among the Gentiles; which is Christ in you, the hope of glory."

I believe all our ills can be traced to one cause—the lack of a deep, abiding relationship with Jesus Christ. Our trust has been too much in other things—the institution, the appointment we have received, the covenant of membership, as though these things would suffice. It is time that our trust be placed completely, totally in Jesus. "On Christ, the solid Rock, I stand; all other ground is sinking sand," and to give emphasis the songwriter repeated, "all other ground is sinking sand."

It is not a far-fetched idea, an unreasonable goal that we become one with Jesus. Jesus' words were "I in them;" Paul expressed the same thought, "Christ in you, the hope of glory." In this union we can "know the love of Christ, which [surpasses] knowledge, that [we] might be filled with all the fulness of God" (Ephesians 3:19).

Jesus said, "If any man serve me, let him follow me; and where I am, there shall also my servant be" (John 12:26). I have pondered this statement, trying to plumb its depth. What does it mean to be with Him where He is? We sometimes say to someone who has said something which required some extra thought in order to comprehend, "O I'm with you now," or, "I see where you are coming from," or, "Go ahead, I'm with you." Is this the essence of what Jesus was saying, "If any man serve me, let him follow me; and where I am, there shall also my servant be"?

For sure, we do not want to be void of understanding as to what Jesus is saying and doing right now at the beginning of 1994. We want to make certain we are with Him, that we are with Him where He is, listening to Him. Our paramount desire is to know Jesus, not just to know about Him, not just to know the truth He teaches, but to have an intimate relationship with our blessed Saviour. Paul was willing to discard everything else for such knowledge. That's why he could say, "Yea doubtless, and I count all things but loss for the excellency of the knowledge of Christ Jesus my Lord: for whom I have suffered the loss of all things, and do count them but dung, that I may win Christ" (Philippians 3:8).

Being circumcised when he was eight days old, he became a valid part of the Jewish church. (Later, he would write concerning the circumcision, "For in Christ Jesus neither circumcision availeth any thing, nor uncircumcision, but a new creature" [Galatians 6:15].) As touching the righteousness which came by keeping God's Word, he testified that he was blameless. He lived by the Word of God; yet, Paul did not know the Lord of the Word. The righteousness he knew was the product of his own strivings—it, therefore, was a self-righteousness. Paul had to give this all up if he was to trust fully in Jesus, if he was to be, as the songwriter expressed, "clothed in His righteousness alone, faultless to stand before the throne." What is that throne? It is a throne of grace. As we approach this throne of grace in prayer, it can never be through any merit of our own; our hope rests always in His mercy and grace. Jesus is our hope, our only hope.

If we are to fulfill our mission we must take on a new sense of mission, developing a relationship with Jesus that surpasses anything we have heretofore known. Unless we follow

Text: John 4:31-38

Him to be with Him where He is, our ministering will continue to bear the marks of human weaknesses and failures.

Realistically, we must know we cannot continue as we are. Following a program of maintenance, polishing machinery, waiting for the inflow is an unscriptural approach. It has not worked and it will not work! To pursue such an approach sends a clear signal that we have not followed Jesus to be with Him where He is.

Right now, where He is, He is looking at the harvest fields; He sees the fields as being white unto harvest. If we are with Him where He is we are sensing the same thing. O to be with Him where He is.

Paul's rule-keeping could never have made him to become the spiritual giant which he became. It was rather his relationship with his risen Saviour. Likewise, we cannot rise to God's demands for us in this, the Church's most demanding hour, by being simply, as we term it, faithful to the Church. There must be a power that possesses us which literally compels us to minister to people who will be lost forever unless they are brought to Jesus. It caused Paul to "have great heaviness and continual sorrow in [his] heart." He wrote, "For I could wish that myself were accursed from Christ for my brethren, my kinsmen according to the flesh" (Romans 9:2).

Mark wrote in his account of Jesus' wilderness experience, where Christ defeated Satan's attempts to pull Him away from His mission, as follows: "And immediately the Spirit driveth him into the wilderness" (Mark 1:12). We speak often of being Spirit directed, or being Spirit-led, but Mark uses a more forceful description of being Spirit-driven. I believe this was what Paul felt, that he was literally driven by the Spirit. To read carefully the account of this pioneer missionary, we must conclude that he was, indeed, driven. And is this not the compelling urge that we are feeling today? To be driven by the Spirit denotes a divine urgency.

As we really turn to the harvest sacrifices are going to be demanded. The harvest field is truly a battlefield. We must remember that Jesus did not come to this earth on a pleasure trip. He came to be sacrificed. Though we can now call Him King of kings, Jesus was not born in a palace. He was born in a stable. A stable was the appropriate place for sacrifices to be born. When John the Baptist introduced Him as the Lamb of God, Jesus knew the full implication of this term. He was to be offered as our sacrifice.

While there will be no more such sacrifice for sin, we are called upon to present our bodies as living sacrifices, "holy, acceptable unto God, which is [our] reasonable service" (Romans 12:1). Was it reasonable for Paul to suffer for this gospel as he did? Listen to his testimony: "Of the Jews five times received I forty stripes save one. Thrice was I beaten with rods, once was I stoned, thrice I suffered shipwreck, a night and a day I have been in the deep; In journeyings often, in perils of waters, in perils of robbers, in perils by mine own countrymen, in perils by the heathen, in perils in the city, in perils in the wilderness, in perils in the sea, in perils among false brethren; In weariness and painfulness, in watchings often, in hunger and thirst, in fastings often, in cold and nakedness. Beside those things that are without, that which cometh upon me daily, the care of all the churches" (2 Corinthians 11:24-28). Was this reasonable service?

Was it reasonable for Paul and thousands of others to go to their martyrdom by pursuing their God-given ministries? Was it reasonable for Livingstone to give his life in Africa, or Hudson in China? If all of these could speak to us now they would assure us that what they did was not unreasonable at all. Many today continue to offer themselves as living sacrifices. As I travel and see people who have chosen to leave families and friends to go thousands of miles from home to labor in God's great harvest, my spirit is stirred, and I feel enriched to be in fellowship with them. Thank God for their sacrificial spirits!

I have lived through a time to which I have no desire to return. A spirit of materialistic competition within the Church's leadership became very prominent in the 1950's and 60's. It had no identification with the One who came as a lamb of sacrifice. Their claims to represent Him repelled

Text: John 4:31-38

many young people of that generation. In fact, some of these young people left us, being attracted by what they felt to be truer models of Christianity elsewhere. A fascination with materialism has nothing in common with fasting, praying, weeping for the lost. The success of those so fascinated rather means to them fine buildings, parsonages, offices, fine cars and financial assets. In these things there has been progress.

Our people have prospered, bringing more tithes into our churches, providing us a greater financial capacity for evangelism to penetrate ripened harvest fields. Instead, we have felt the need for purchasing, upgrading and improving properties, and, in some cases, building large cash reserves. Right now, our members in the United States are paying around sixty million dollars annually into our churches. About six million of that is being sent to the state offices. Another six million to the general headquarters, with a sizeable amount of this being returned to state offices which are not as strong financially as larger states.

This sixty million dollars which God has provided, we have used principally for maintenance, and our records show that our growth over the past year here in this nation has been less than zero, in fact, a minus of 95 members. Is this any clue for God's call to repentance?

Some may argue that this condition did not develop overnight and that it will not be corrected suddenly. May we counter that argument with this thought? The Church is comprised of individual members. The nature of the Church is reflected in the nature of the individual. An individual, we admit, does not backslide overnight. Failures begin to show up gradually in different areas of his relationship with the Lord and his spiritual weakness becomes more apparent all the while.

That same person, however, when convicted by the Holy Ghost, can have an immediate turnaround. It does not require months wherein his relationship with the Lord is gradually restored. It is not a self-improvement plan that will do this. It is a work of the Spirit.

An individual is born again, not gradually over a period of months or years, but it is an instantaneous experience. I do not believe the Church will turn to the harvest until it experiences a new birth. This new birth will occur only through Holy Ghost conviction.

My prayer is that this conviction will seize our hearts in this conference to where we will experience a real change. I believe where there is a core group that experiences a real change, that group can travail before God until Holy Ghost conviction will seize others, and then for them there can be immediate repentance and change. The process can spread throughout the Church.

There is hope for us! There can be change, not gradually, but suddenly! This change will cause us to return to the harvest. That's where Jesus' heart is, and that's where ours will be.

Where Is The Passion?

Center for Biblical Leadership
Instructor's Intensive
May 19, 1994

From the Minutes of the First Assembly we read, "Strong men wept, and said they were not only willing but really anxious to go."

Their spirits had been ignited with a passion which we can observe in the earliest history of that same Church they now had committed themselves to be, the Church Jesus declared He would build. What was it that had made the Apostles go, in obedience to their Master's command, as Mark recorded that, ". . . they went forth, and preached every where, the Lord working with them, and confirming the word with signs following" (Mark 16:20). Whatever it was, this small group of humble men felt it, as they were gathered in the mountain home of J. C. Murphy during a January snow storm in North Carolina in 1906. A fire burned in their hearts.

This passion had inflamed Peter's preaching on the Day of Pentecost. He and the other Apostles had seen their Master arrested, arraigned before Pilate, taken to Golgotha and crucified. They knew their lives were in jeopardy likewise. They had gone into hiding. John wrote, "the doors were shut where the disciples were assembled for fear of the Jews" (John 20:19). With the fire of the Holy Ghost burning in his heart, however, Peter, now with boldness, faced these murderers and preached a message that would resound through the ages.

"Ye men of Israel, hear these words; Jesus of Nazareth, a man approved of God among you by miracles and wonders and signs, which God did by him in the midst of you, as ye yourselves also know: Him, being delivered by the determinate counsel and foreknowledge of God, ye have taken, and by wicked hands have crucified and slain: Whom God hath raised up, having loosed the pains of death: because it was not possible that he should be holden of it" (Acts 2:22-24).

This gospel message, anointed by the power of His risen Lord, marked by passion from a newly emboldened preacher, who just a few weeks earlier had denied knowing Jesus with cursing and swearing, had its effect. Before that day ended, the church there grew by the addition of three thousand souls (cf. v. 41). And this was only the beginning. Daily new converts were added to their number as they with "great power" gave witness of their Lord's resurrection. Luke records in Acts 4:4, "Howbeit many of them which heard the word believed; and the number of the men was about five thousand." Then, in chapter five, verse 14, he wrote, "And believers were the more added to the Lord, multitudes both of men and women."

The realities of being imprisoned, of being beaten, of being beheaded—none of these things could cool their fervor. As Paul would say later, "None of these things move me." The successes they were experiencing, seeing souls set free from Satan's bondage, lives being changed by the gospel's power, fueled the fire that was already burning within their hearts. They knew they were following the dictates of Jesus' heart as they sensed His presence with them. He had told them to go, and they were going. He had told them to preach, and they were preaching. He had told them to lift up their eyes and to look on the ripened harvest, and that was their focus.

These men were not proceeding from a program of evangelism they had designed, their impetus was from the fire

Where Is The Passion?

of evangelism within their hearts. It was not program, but passion. Programs are designed by the mind while passion is of the heart; it sets the spirit aflame.

We have had our programs in the Church—the "Big Business Program" of 1928, the "On to Perfection" program of the 1940's, the Honor Stone program, the Airplane program—all of these with good intentions, no doubt. We were designing programs that were going to impact the world, we thought, and we were sincere. Furthermore, we must conclude that some good came out of these programs. At the same time they became substitutes, crutches upon which we leaned, to excuse an aggressive pursuit of reaching perishing people for whom Jesus died with the gospel. The gospel is the power of God unto salvation—salvation is its aim.

The "Big Business Program" initiated some fund-raising which continues today to be vital for the continuance of missions, for printing literature and other general ministries of evangelism. For many people, however, this fund-raising became a substitute for personal involvement in reaching out to people. Instead, we became expert in fund-raising—soliciting, selling doughnuts, chicken dinners, fried pies, etc.

As a follow-up of the "Big Business Program" we created rivalries among churches and states, awarding trophies, banners and other prizes to those who excelled in fund-raising. Much of this was done without real compassion for people by whom our churches were surrounded. In our minds we were getting the gospel to the world.

The "On to Perfection" program, which included the Honor Stone program, caused us to turn our eyes not to the harvest fields but upon ourselves, focusing inward. We became more interested in "perfecting our churches" than in reaching people. To make an honest appraisal of many of our churches today after all the "perfecting" we did, we can see the failure of this program. It proved again that programs do not produce passion for true ministry.

The "airplane program" created a degree of excitement among many. Flying over a city and throwing out handfuls of tracts, most of which probably were never found or read, created the illusion that we were impacting this world with the gospel without the necessity for any great degree of personal involvement. I recall our General V.L.B. Secretary, in a burst of enthusiasm, declaring that we were going to sow this world down knee-deep with Church of God literature. Somehow that would be our response to the Great Commission. Zeal without knowledge! Aren't you glad that when you leave this campus you will not have to attempt to drive home through knee-deep literature on the highways?

I believe we will admit that we have relied too heavily in the past upon programs, without that vital element we call passion. It is my prayer that what we are attempting through C.B.L. will not become just another program. If we succeed in the particular ministries each of us has been given, or as a corporate body, it will not be because we have designed the right program. It will rather be because our spirits have been ignited with holy fire, that our hearts are aflame with the fire of the Holy Ghost.

Jesus' words were, "But ye shall receive power, after that the Holy Ghost is come upon you" (Acts 1:8). He described this as being "baptized with the Holy Ghost and with fire." Where is the fire? Where is the passion? Passion is defined as "extreme, compelling emotion; intense emotional drive or excitement."

The passion being called for by God is not just a "pumped up" emotion, one that rises and falls in proportion to someone's ability to excite or arouse feelings in a meeting such as this. It is rather the passion which our Saviour exhibited while He was "tabernacled" among us. It will be felt in our hearts in proportion to our relationship with Him—indeed, as we become one with Him!

Luke gives us the account of the day Jesus came to Jerusalem about five days prior to His crucifixion. We term this as His "triumphal entry." The Scripture says, "he beheld the city, and wept over it" (Luke 19:41). He had created everything in it. He had created the ground upon which it sat. He had made the stones with which the build-

Where Is The Passion?

ings had been built, including the Temple of which the people were so proud. He had created every individual who inhabited the city. Those men who even then were plotting His death were His creation.

As Jesus stood there beholding all of this, knowing that here were those who would seize Him and crucify Him, with one word He could have destroyed them all. Instead, He wept. His love for them held Him to His course. Jesus knew of God's impending judgment upon this beloved city. He foresaw its coming destruction which would not leave one stone upon another. He foresaw the defenseless people fleeing in terror from their murderers. O how He wanted to gather them unto Himself, even as a mother hen would protect her chicks from their destruction, but they had rejected Him, they had rejected His love—and He wept.

He is the same yesterday, today and forever—His love has never changed. As He views God's impending judgment upon this world, with all the horror that awaits the people, people whom He loves with perfect love, not willing that any of them perish, is His feeling not the same for them as when He looked down upon Jerusalem and wept? I believe it is.

And as we become one with Him will not that kind of compassion fill our hearts? We read that Jesus was moved with compassion because He saw them as sheep having no shepherd, He saw them as being bewildered with no true sense of direction, headed toward their destruction. Is it any different today? What is their hope? Apart from this gospel we have been commissioned to take to them, they have no hope.

If I had the power to reach into hell and pull one person out to set before you tonight, to allow you to look upon him, be it that rich man about whom Jesus spoke who has been suffering now for thousands of years, begging for water, or perhaps another who has been there only ten years—it might be someone with whom you were personally acquainted—if that pitiful creature could be suspended here in our view, we would, no doubt, leave this place with a new passion for evangelism.

Jesus sees all that, and weeps. Can we become one with Him in His compassion for those who are lost, that we can weep with Him? Do we really carry a crushing burden for them? Some of them are your sons and daughters, your brothers and sisters, headed for hell while, too often, we carry on with our programs. We should be and we must be, instead, driven with a consuming passion.

It has been easier for us to focus upon the doctrine of eternal punishment for the wicked than to focus upon the reality that thousands are dropping into that horrible pit called hell every day. Yes, we will memorize the Scripture verses to support and defend this teaching of the Church, and we call it being established in the doctrine. But we can do that while having little real passion to rescue the perishing. We take great pride in having correctly interpreted biblical doctrine and we will argue to defend it while souls continue to drop into hell, lost forever.

Do you think it bothers Satan for us to spend our time disputing about doctrine instead of being driven by a burden for the lost? I rather think he delights in it. He would much prefer that we memorize Scriptures and take a stand defending "Signs Following Believers" than for us to go forth and preach everywhere, having God working with us confirming His Word, with signs following. We can embrace and defend the doctrine of His second coming, and still miss the Rapture. It is unto those who are looking for Him that He will appear, not necessarily to those defending this doctrine.

Where is the soul-burden? Where is the passion? How can it be recovered? I believe it is in finding relationship with the One who wept over Jerusalem, to become one with Heaven—that Heaven's interest and our interest will be the same. There is rejoicing in heaven over one sinner that repents more than over ninety-nine just persons who, dispassionately, are "abiding in the faith."

Recapturing this passion, we will be viewed by those who enjoy a comfortable religion as being radical. I suppose those religionists who were enjoying a profitable business as they carried on their merchandising in the Temple felt that Jesus was radical when He disrupted their gainful activity. With divine authority He walked in among them with a whip in His hand. He overturned the tables of the moneychangers and drove from the Temple all these men with their oxen and sheep and doves. "And his disciples remembered that it was written, The zeal of thine house hath eaten me up" (John 2:17). Yes, they surely had to view Jesus as radical.

Was it not radical to curse a barren fig tree so that the next morning the disciples would see it "dried up from the roots" (Mark 11:20)? Was it not radical for Him to stop a funeral procession and present to his mother alive her son who was being carried as a corpse?

Was not Paul radical when with great heaviness of heart he could say, "For I could wish that myself were accursed from Christ for my brethren, my kinsmen according to the flesh" (Romans 9:3). It would be difficult to view Paul as a conventional preacher. To the Corinthians he confessed that he was with them "in weakness, and in fear, and in much trembling." His preaching to them therefore was not the formulation of a well-prepared sermon which would bespeak his eloquence. Rather, it was in demonstration of the Spirit and of power (cf. 1 Corinthians 2:3, 4).

This apostle was somewhat an enigma to those who observed him. He could withstand to the face a senior apostle who had walked with Jesus when he felt it to be in order. While he could rebuke with authority, he could also be tender. To the saints at Thessalonica he wrote, "But we were gentle among you, even as a nurse cherisheth her children" (1 Thessalonians 2:7). Rebuking—then tender; was this not a mark of his relationship with Jesus?

Paul reminded the Ephesian elders of his ministry among them: "Serving the Lord with all humility of mind, and with many tears" (Acts 20:19). He said, ". . . by the space of three years I ceased not to warn every one night and day with tears" (v. 31). He was a weeping preacher, and was this not also a mark of his relationship with his weeping Saviour?

Paul had paid a price to have this special relationship with Jesus. He had learned the meaning of being crucified with Him. He had to renounce his trust in everything else—only in Jesus did he trust. To the Philippians he wrote that he had suffered the loss of all things and counted them but dung that he might gain Christ and be found in Him. Paul counted himself dead and his life hid with Christ in God.

Thereby, he could exhibit Christ's love, Christ's compassion for people, Christ's authority over Satan's power. Yes, Paul had died with Him and now he lived in the power of Christ's resurrection. The passion by which Christ was driven is the passion which drove this apostle. And it will be no different for us.

The key, then, is to abandon our trust in any program we have designed, to abandon our trust in all traditions which are purely our own, to count them all but loss that we might reach that place which Paul called being "found in him." Then Jesus' love will flow through us, His compassion will be felt from us, His power will propel us. His passion will be our passion. The time for finding this relationship is not in the future; it is now!

In the International Conference for Itinerant Evangelists in July of 1983, fifteen affirmations were made by over four thousand evangelists. One of these affirmations is very fitting that those who are gathered here should make: "We affirm our commitment to the Great Commission of our Lord, and we declare our willingness to go anywhere, do anything, and sacrifice anything God requires of us in the fulfillment of that Commission."

When this affirmation comes from the heart, it will reflect a passion that is essential for reaching people, a passion which again causes strong men to weep.

"And Sinners Shall Be Converted Unto Thee"

North American
Evangelism Conferences
1995

"Create in me a clean heart, O God; and renew a right [steadfast] spirit within me. Cast me not away from thy presence; and take not thy holy spirit from me. Restore unto me the joy of thy salvation; and uphold me with thy free spirit. Then will I teach transgressors thy ways; and sinners shall be converted unto thee" (Psalms 51:10-13).

David, the man after God's own heart, had failed miserably—no doubt surprising himself. He had known and experienced God's power in his life, meeting and slaying Goliath when everyone else was afraid of this giant. He had lived through persecution, fleeing from Saul who was seeking to kill him. On an occasion when he was given the opportunity to avenge himself, being told by Abishai, "God hath delivered thine enemy into thine hand this day" (1 Samuel 26:8), David's reply was, "The Lord forbid that I should stretch forth mine hand against the Lord's anointed" (v. 11). David feared God more than he feared Saul.

After rising to a position of prominence, however, his relationship with the Lord suffered. Being drawn away from this relationship by his own lust, this one-time good man committed adultery. Then to cover his sin, he had a faithful husband, an innocent man, killed.

How many times have we seen this example repeated? A righteous man, one who loves God with all his heart, in his total dedication to the Lord would not do anything that he feels would displease his Saviour in any way. As time goes on, however, becoming more experienced, as he rises to a position of prominence that same man may seduce and destroy spiritually one he was assigned to protect and lead into Christ's fullness. Such has brought reproach upon the name of our Lord and has greatly hindered the propagation of the gospel.

How blessed a person should feel who has been singled out by God for divine leadership! He has an obligation to be an example to other believers. It is sad when a Christian fails his Saviour, but it is far worse when that person who has been divinely chosen to be a leader of God's people betrays that trust he was given.

May I suggest that there are more ways to fail the Lord in the trust He has given us than by committing adultery or by murdering, as David did. The fact is, in answering God's call, all of us submitted to the lordship of Jesus Christ. Our response was a relinquishment of any claims upon our own lives and of the direction our lives would take. It was a rejection of self-preservation or self-assertion. It was surrender—complete surrender, placing ourselves at His disposal.

Yet, how many of us have failed Him in that wholehearted surrender, which involves a crucifixion of the flesh with its affections and lusts (desires)? When we offer ourselves as living sacrifices, we really have no more claims upon our lives. For many of us our lives have been a series of failures, which were followed by godly sorrow and repentance. I stand here tonight only by His abundant mercy and grace, as each of you do. We thank God that all failure is not fatal.

Sometimes we are not cognizant of our failures until we experience conviction by the Holy Ghost. This was evidenced very clearly when we were arrested by a call to repentance in 1984, and the question was raised many times, "What do we have to repent of?" This question was raised even though we were charged with "having drifted from a vital relationship with the Holy Ghost, lacking in a deep compassion for a world of lost people who even now are under the judgment of God to eternal damnation." Is not that drift something to repent of? Why has it been so difficult for some to accept this reprimand? Would David have somehow excused himself if Nathan the prophet had not confronted him? We cannot know, but we should all be thankful for whatever means God chooses to bring us to repentance when we have failed Him. The execution of God's judgments is not pleasant. We may smart under His conviction and chastening, but we know that "afterward it yieldeth the peaceable fruit of righteousness" (Hebrews 12:11).

There are lessons for us in David's prayer of penitence. Notice the purpose of his praying for forgiveness and for a restoration of "the joy of thy salvation." "Then will I teach transgressors thy ways; and sinners shall be converted unto thee." While we are calling this an Evangelism Conference, we must observe that restoration or revival always precedes evangelism, that evangelism is the product of revival. Penitent praying as a result of Holy Ghost conviction is a part of revival. We do not pray from our hearts until our hearts are stirred, which is a work of the Holy Ghost. This stirring to pray which many are feeling right now is from God. It is a necessary part of revival. There is no doubt in my mind that this spirit of prayer that is now being experienced by many is going to become more intense. Great prayer movements have preceded and been a major part of every great revival movement.

Notice that David's prayer was personal: "Create in me a clean heart, O God; and renew a right [steadfast] spirit within me. Cast me not away from thy presence; and take not thy holy spirit from me. Restore unto me the joy of thy salvation; and uphold me with thy free spirit. Then will I teach transgressors thy ways; and sinners shall be converted unto thee." Gypsy Smith's formula for revival was a good one; that was to draw a circle, put yourself in that circle, and then pray for revival within that circle.

Recently while praying, I did just that in my mind. I was praying "Send revival to me, to Billy Murray." It was a prayer for restoration, for renewal, as I have felt so very ill-prepared and ill-equipped for the ministry to which I am called. I know that it started out well. My salvation experience was real. My baptism with the Holy Ghost was real and powerful. My call into the ministry was real, something I have never doubted.

It is in changing into His image, from glory to glory, that I seem to have fallen short and thereby to have a ministry of power which I sense to be so much needed. I remember Paul's testimony that his gospel was not in word but in power. Some of us are quite powerful with words, but that is not enough to reach this lost generation. Paul's reminder to the Romans was that "Through mighty signs and wonders, by the power of the Spirit of God . . . I have fully preached the gospel of Christ" (Romans 15:19). I cannot feel that Jesus' charge was just to the Twelve when He said, "As ye go, preach, saying, The kingdom of heaven is at hand. Heal the sick, cleanse the lepers, raise the dead, cast out devils: freely ye have received, freely give" (Matthew 10: 7, 8). If the Great Commission of Matthew 28:19, 20 was to the Church of today, why would we suppose this charge of Matthew 10:7, 8 was not also for us to take seriously?

In that imaginary circle, as I pray for revival, it is for a spiritual refreshing and renewal that will send me forth with new power, a power that is recognizable. The gospel that convicts sinners is much more than well-prepared intellectual discourses. The gospel of power bears the marks of divine anointing and inspiration. This anointing will most likely come to the one who secludes himself to pray, "Send revival to me, O Lord."

How easy it is to pray for revival for the Church, but it is time now to pray for revival to come to you. This kind of praying will proceed from a broken heart, broken by realization of failures before God. Most likely, this will stem from an encounter with God, an encounter such as Isaiah had which caused him to cry, "Woe is me! for I am undone" (Isaiah 6:5). Until one meets God he may feel pretty secure in his own self-righteousness. He may be performing his Christian duties of regular church attendance, tithing and giving, carrying out assigned functions, etc., all the while being deficient in the kind of relationship with God to which he has been called. Coming into God's presence, then living in relationship with Him, will change all that feeling of self-righteousness.

In the conclusion of Psalm 51, David wrote (beginning with verse 16), "For thou desirest not sacrifice; else would I give it: thou delightest not in burnt offering. The sacrifices of God are a broken spirit: a broken and a contrite heart, O God, thou wilt not despise. . . . Then shalt thou be pleased with the sacrifices of righteousness, with burnt offering and whole burnt offering: then shall they offer bullocks upon thine altar" (v. 16-19). To carry out prescribed duties would not suffice as acceptable worship until first there was the sacrifice of a broken spirit. We may wonder how much so-called "service for the Lord" is being done today by people whose hearts are not broken.

In many of our churches there is much activity, and our state/national calendars are filled with activities, while bringing sinners to Jesus remains at a low ebb among us. David said, "Then shall I teach transgressors thy ways; and sinners shall be converted unto thee." "If my people, which are called by my name, shall humble themselves, and pray, and seek my face, and turn from their wicked ways; then will I hear from heaven, and will forgive their sin, and will heal their land" (2 Chronicles 7:14).

It is not because God has lost interest in sinners. He cares to the degree He always has cared. It remains His will that none perish; yet they are perishing daily. The question is, "How much do we care?" Do we sense daily how awful it is to be lost? How strong is our belief in an endless hell? Do you really believe there is such a place? Whether or not any of us believes does not alter its reality.

Our lack of a convinced belief which grips our hearts may well be the cause of sinners entering hell who otherwise could have been saved.

If we could be suspended over hell for just five minutes to view its horrors, it would no doubt change us for the rest of our lives. No longer would our motives for evangelism be just to build larger congregations, which would generate more financial revenues, which would enable us to have multiple ministries and expanded facilities. The underlying motive for all we are doing would be to save souls, lest they, too, shall go to that awful place. With such a vision we would decry our lukewarmness, begging God's forgiveness for the lack of compassion we have had for lost souls. With this vision we would be praying fervently, "Will thou not revive us again?" All our efforts, then, would be emptied of any pride of accomplishments for which we might take credit, giving honor and glory to God for his abundant mercies.

Paul wrote, "Knowing therefore the terror of the Lord, we persuade men" (2 Corinthians 5:11). Can we not be more effective in persuading men? Their choice is the pleasures of sin for a season or the joys of heaven forever. When one enters hell, all pleasure is gone for eternity. Even the simple pleasure of seeing a sunrise, or gazing into the sunset, or beholding a star-studded sky, or hearing a bird sing, or watching a child play will be no more. Never again will that person experience the beauty of a snow-covered landscape, or feel a spring breeze—no more trees, no more green grass, no more sparkling streams, no, not even a drop of water. Never again shall he hear music or singing—no laughter, no joy, no peace—do we really believe in hell?

If so, our evangelistic endeavors should proceed with these things in mind. How can we be apathetic about the thousands who drop into that terrible place every day? The need for revival is urgent, a revival of prayer that will produce evangelistic fervor. There is a world of people to be harvested. Many of them live in the communities where you live, where your churches are located. As many of you are aware, many of these churches have not reported a single salvation experience this year, or in the past two years. You do not have to be told that something is wrong. God cares for these people who are lost as much as He ever has cared. Then the fault has to be in our relationship with Him, to where His concerns are indeed our concerns. It is for this lack of relationship that we have been called upon to repent. Can we afford to wait longer?

I don't believe any of us doubt that this is the period of the latter rain about which Hosea prophesied (cf. 6:3). Now we know that the rain which produces harvest is not the harvest itself. The rain and the harvest are two different things. The rain must precede the harvest. In Zechariah 10:1 the prophet wrote, "Ask ye of the Lord rain in the time of the latter rain." It is time to pray for rain—a rain, a revival, that will lead to a harvest. It was when Daniel was convinced that it was time for Judah's deliverance from Babylon that he set himself to pray. He understood Jeremiah's prophecy that after seventy years of captivity Jerusalem's desolation would be ended and the Jews would go back home. (cf. Jeremiah 15:11, 12). Daniel said, "And I set my face unto the Lord God, to seek by prayer and supplications, with fasting, and sackcloth, and ashes: And I prayed unto the Lord my God, and made my confession. . . We have sinned, and have committed iniquity, and have done wickedly, and have rebelled" (Daniel 9:3-5).

Daniel could have read the prophecy and then have just declared that it was bound to happen, that divine prophecy could not fail, but this was not God's way of working. God directed his attention to the prophecy, then He stirred Daniel's heart to pray.

And now as we read Hosea's prophecy of the latter rain, and Joel's corroboration of that prophecy (Joel 2:23), God is stirring our hearts to pray for rain in this time of the latter rain. The harvest will follow the revival. O for a revival of prayer, a conviction to pray, that we would be taken over by the Holy Ghost, finding that place where the Spirit prays for us with groanings that cannot be uttered!

As we study the history of the great revival movements throughout the world, all of them began with an urgency to pray which would begin to grip the hearts of God's people. This would begin with a small group, then expand as others would feel the same urge. Eventually thousands would be praying. This praying would be accompanied by repentance, confession and restitution. Then came the conversion of sinners in large numbers.

This kind of evangelistic success has at times occurred without great preaching or without singing, or great choirs. It has happened without great planning or strategizing, but never has it happened without great praying!

Thank God that He is even now instigating a revival of prayer. Prayer meetings are springing up on college campuses in this nation. In many towns and cities, ministers of different denominations are coming together to pray with one another, something they would not have done a few years ago. Local churches are praying. On May 2, we closed our International Offices at noon to spend the afternoon together in prayer. Then the General Overseer's appointees, along with the CBL staff, had a further time of prayer from midnight to 6:00 a.m. This was unprecedented in our history. Yet, it was not done just to set a precedent, but because our hearts were stirred to do it. I share this information only to let you know what God is doing and how serious we are about our response to Him to do whatever is necessary to focus upon the harvest of souls.

This is an exciting time and a fearful time. It is exciting to witness what God is doing in setting the stage for what is probably the last great revival in preparation for the Rapture. It is a fearful time if we should fail to make the proper response to what He is initiating. The manner of our response is of eternal consequences, the consequences of heaven or hell, both for us and for those who at this moment are still lost. We just must not fail!

In 1748, Jonathan Edwards wrote a book on the prayer movement of his day. He predicted that movements of prayer would accelerate in succeeding generations, climaxing with the greatest one around the year 2000.

Edwards was right on several points. First, he emphasized that the movement is God's creation, not ours. Then he said the movement would express itself corporately. Third, the overriding agenda and concern for these prayer movements would be for revival.

I find it interesting that he believed the dawn of the 21st Century will experience a prayer wave that surpasses anything seen before. With that in view, I want to respond to what God right now is initiating. O we must pray!

Before Elijah ascended to the top of Mt. Carmel, before he prayed until there appeared a little cloud like a man's hand, he had already declared, ". . . there is a sound of abundance of rain" (1 Kings 18:41). He had acted at God's command, and now he approached this time of prayer for rain in full assurance of God's promise.

As we have gathered here in this conference, can you say with me, in the assurance of God's promise, "There is the sound of abundance of rain"? Can you hear that sound?

Vibrant Local Churches

13

January Overseers Meeting
January 1996
Cleveland, Tennessee

Reaching people, ministering to people is our business. We have a heavy responsibility to those who are lost, those who will be lost eternally unless they are reached with the gospel, the good news that Jesus purchased their salvation at Calvary. All those who have accepted Him as their Saviour, along with all those who shall accept Him, need also to be nurtured. They need to be equipped for service in helping to reap this end-time harvest.

What is your vision for this accomplishment? (We seldom exceed our vision.) What is the role of the local church in fulfilling the Great Commission? Every member of the Church (universal) is a member of a local church, with every member having a pastor/shepherd. Certainly, this design is for a purpose, a purpose that God has set forth—the local church as a body of believers extending themselves in ministry.

God speaks to local churches. It is local churches to whom Paul addresses his letters. In the Book of Revelation, it is seven local churches to which Jesus expresses His concerns through John. When God purposed to send Paul and Barnabas on their missionary journey, He visited their local church to initiate that action. Within the local church at Antioch there was strong leadership, gifted ministers. "Now there were in the church that was at Antioch certain prophets and teachers. . . . As they ministered to the Lord, and fasted, the Holy Ghost said, Separate me Barnabas and Saul for the work whereunto I have called them. And when they had fasted and prayed, and laid their hands on them, they sent them away. So they, being sent forth by the Holy Ghost, departed unto Seleucia; and from thence they sailed to Cyprus" (Acts 13:1-4).

While Paul and Barnabas had what might be called trans-local ministries, wherever they went, they established local churches. Subsequent visits were to strengthen those churches. Paul's letters were for aiding, strengthening, edifying these local churches.

Assembled here today are those of us who have trans-local ministries, yet we must recognize the responsibilities we have to local churches. Few of us, for example, are multi-gifted, but God's design for the local church is that it be a multi-gifted body of believers, thereby being the functioning Body of Christ. It was to the local church at Corinth that Paul wrote, "Now ye are the body of Christ, and members in particular" (1 Corinthians 12:27). Obviously, he did not mean that local church was the exclusive, entire Body of Christ. They were just one local body, but his instructions to them concerning the manifestations of nine spiritual gifts seem to indicate that all of these gifts should be evidenced among them. Then he makes the comparison of the foot, the hand, the ear, the eye to the different members of the Body of Christ, which he says, "Ye are."

In our zeal to report churches organized in the past, we may not have fully recognized the proper composition of a church. I have even heard of so-called churches being organized with one member. I really don't see how one member could be properly called a church. It might well be necessary at this time for some of our so-called churches to be consolidated before a truly functioning body could appear in a given area.

The purpose of existence for any local church, such as the one at Corinth, is to do the work of Christ. It is to the Corinthian church that Paul writes, "And all things are of God, who hath reconciled us to himself by Jesus Christ, and hath given to us the ministry of reconciliation" (2 Corinthians 5:18).

Just as no one who is called by God to minister satisfies that call by being licensed and placing his license in a conspicuous place, even so no church satisfies the reason for its existence by putting up their church sign to announce that they have been organized there. Just as the preacher has a ministry to perform, so does a local church. Theirs is a ministry of reconciliation— reconciling their community to God, bringing people to the knowledge of Jesus Christ. It is only when they have a correct assessment of themselves, a proper vision of the reason for which they exist, that this is likely to happen. Even then that vision must be accompanied by a divinely-imposed burden, a burden for people who are lost.

It evidently is of the Lord's design that we have VIBRANT LOCAL CHURCHES, churches that are actively engaged within their communities, their towns, their cities—engaged in reaching out to people, touching lives, bringing people to Jesus. These churches will be comprised of people who have been divinely gifted as members of the Body of Christ and who are being exercised by the Holy Ghost to make an impact upon someone who will be eternally lost unless he/she is introduced to the Saviour.

This thought of VIBRANT LOCAL CHURCHES came forcefully to my mind about three months ago while I was praying. At the same time, I was impressed with the thought of each church doubling its membership by the year 2000 A.D. This came so strongly that I felt the need to share it with the others who were praying with me. To some, this goal might seem to be too ambitious. It probably would have seemed that way to me if I had not felt it was from the Lord.

In reality, is it too much to expect that a 20-member church could become a 40-member church by that time, or a 40-member church could grow by another 40 members? I believe it to be highly realistic. It is important, of course, that our motive for growth be proper. If it is just that we could boast of a larger membership, that would be an unworthy motive—one for which we should repent. We must see these to whom we will be reaching out as people who are lost, on their way to a burning hell, people whose only hope is Jesus Christ, and that we have been commissioned by our Lord to go to them.

As we approach the end of a millennium, this time of harvest demands an aggressive approach. In fact, the urgency I'm feeling causes me more and more to restate this goal as for each church to at least double its membership by 2000 A.D. While that calendar date draws our attention to the closing of a century and a millennium, perhaps we should be reminded that 1996 really marks the end of 2000 years since the birth of Jesus. To correct a miscalculation in our present Gregorian calendar, we mark the birth of Jesus by our calendar to have occurred in 4 B.C. While not attempting to tie Christ's second coming to a specific calendar year, we all may be assured that our time is short to prepare for His coming. The verse of Scripture, "Looking for and hasting unto the coming of the day of God" (2 Peter 3:12), seems particularly relevant.

As we view the great harvest fields which now are waiting for reapers, we are reminded of Jesus' command for us to pray for harvesting laborers. The dynamic of the gospel is that as souls are reaped, they can immediately become reapers, joining those who reached them in reaching others. So, as we pray and work toward an increase in church membership, we are in effect praying for more harvesting laborers.

We know this increase in membership does not occur in the Church in general, but specifically in the local churches. More harvesting laborers, therefore, must be enlisted in the local churches. Some of our churches are involved in vibrant witness. They are impacting their communities with the gospel. For this, we praise the Lord! We will quickly agree,

Vibrant Local Churches

however, that this is the case in too few of our churches.

Inasmuch as harvesting is to occur by local churches, it becomes apparent that we need more VIBRANT LOCAL CHURCHES! As you Overseers here today reflect upon the local churches in your region, with their strengths and weaknesses, there is an acute awareness that a powerful awakening is needed, and in many cases, a real transformation, before each of your congregations can become a VIBRANT LOCAL CHURCH.

In the brochures that have been distributed, we listed several things that seem essential toward any church fulfilling our vision of what a VIBRANT LOCAL CHURCH should be. Different churches may be strategically placed for different types of ministries. A church should evaluate its mission and ministry. Some will never do all that others may be doing. An initial step in such an evaluation would be to take the matter to the Lord in earnest prayer, waiting on the Lord in intensive prayer, waiting on the Lord for direction of ministry. It is important that we become a praying and listening people:

A high priority for becoming a VIBRANT LOCAL CHURCH is a worshiping congregation. Heartfelt, spirited worship not only pleases the Lord but it fills a basic spiritual need, also. People will not be drawn to a church where there is no excitement in celebrating the Lord's presence. In fact, where there is no fervency of spirit, people are likely to be repelled.

Where people are fervent worshipers, there will almost always be manifestations of Holy Ghost power. It is this Pentecostal power that will produce physical as well as spiritual healing. We may wonder how the Book of Acts would read without the power that came at Pentecost. We should thank God that the same power with which the Apostles ministered is available today, and it will produce a VIBRANT LOCAL CHURCH.

Earlier, I spoke about multi-giftedness in the Body of Christ. The pastor is important, but he is only one person. Paul writes, " . . . according to the effectual working in the measure of every part, maketh increase of the body . . ." (Ephesians 4:16). Elsewhere he writes about "having then gifts differing according to the grace that is given to us" (Romans 12:6). God has designed the local church to be a ministering unit with each member exercising his or her spiritual giftedness. The pastor, being only one person, one member, cannot do alone what the church is designed and gifted by God to do.

It becomes the pastor's responsibility to give direction to gifted people and to assist them in developing their ministries. Leadership development in the church he is pastoring should be one of his prime concerns. For this to become a reality, he himself may need assistance toward his development as the key leader of his congregation. This help can be provided by his Overseer.

All spiritual leadership development must be pursued from the basis of one's union with Christ. Apart from this, all academic achievement will probably serve only to elevate one's self-esteem. Paul reminds us that "knowledge puffeth up [breeds conceit]" (1 Corinthians 8:1). A proper union with Jesus, however, will prevent this and will assure a proper union and fellowship with one another. Spiritual formation should be high on the agenda for leadership development.

The fellowship that existed in the Early Church caused Luke to write that they "were of one heart and of one soul" (Acts 4:32). Abiding in Christ, abiding in divine love, a love that extends both vertically and horizontally, will foster an observable, close fellowship. Where members bear one another's burdens, suffering together, then rejoicing together, in that church there is a magnetism for the unsaved, who have an inner longing for such sweet relatedness. Did this not add power to the witness of the church at Jerusalem in its infancy? I believe it did.

In the United States, we speak of living in a post-Christian nation. It is true that Satan has won victories in many areas. We live in a corrupted society where much immorality exists. At the same time, there is a move of God underway, and many people are being stirred to search for something better than what they are experiencing. They want something better for their children. As they turn, in a spiritual search for a local church, one of the first questions asked will be, "What does your church offer my children?"

Children and youth are that segment of the population that is most receptive to the gospel. A church that is to be vibrant and growing must give them their attention. This is a ministry that will require extra planning and much hard work, but it must be done.

How about Christian schools! Where facilities and personnel are available, a valuable service could be offered. Many parents no longer feel comfortable sending their children to public schools because of the unfavorable conditions existing in so many of them. Not only would this afford the opportunity for the children to be taught in a wholesome environment, but every unchurched parent would be at least indirectly exposed to that local church which teaches their children. If a church is to become a VIBRANT LOCAL CHURCH, there must be aggressive leadership, unwilling to just follow all the traditional approaches which have led to little or no growth in the past. One of the major Pentecostal denominations has over 1,000 Christian schools with more than 150,000 students right now.

A local church's vision should encompass also the utilization of senior power. We are told that in the United States, for example, the people over 65 years old exceed the number of those under 18 years of age. This may well be our greatest reservoir of prayer power. For sure, the ministry of prayer is one of our greatest ministries, which for some reason is undeveloped among us. Of course, there is the need for people to be ministered unto in order for them to have more effective ministry.

While focusing upon the development of a VIBRANT LOCAL CHURCH, there is the danger of our vision becoming myopic (nearsighted, to where distant objects become blurred). There is the temptation to be self-centered, while souls in neighboring cities and throughout the world continue to go into eternity unprepared to meet God. Each church should be a mission-minded church. We must continue to establish new outposts in our warfare against Satan, planting and nurturing new churches for spreading this glorious gospel. A burden for the lost will also prompt generous mission giving.

This, in fact, seems to be the key to success in all our labors of outreach—hearts that are burdened for the lost. The awfulness of being lost too often fades from the Christian's mind with the passing of time. The best prevention for this, I believe, is earnest, fervent prayer. Such prayer can assure our fellowship with Jesus, to where His concerns are our concerns. He loves people, and when our relationship with Him is maintained, so will we.

VIBRANT LOCAL CHURCHES which at least double their membership by the Assembly of the year 2000—not only is it a realistic possibility, but a very real probability!

A Spirit Of Reconciliation

14

Annual Address to the 85th Annual Assembly, 1990

"And all things are of God, who hath reconciled us to himself by Jesus Christ, and hath given to us the ministry of reconciliation" (2 Corinthians 5:18).

There was a gulf which seemed impassable. Man, in his sinfulness, had no way to approach unto God. God, in His holiness, could have no part with that which was sinful. The Incarnation was the only answer, and it was the perfect solution, the product of Perfect Wisdom. Thank God for the Incarnation! Where would we be otherwise?

Paul wrote, "To wit, that God was in Christ, reconciling the world unto himself" (v. 19). God became man, without accepting man's accompanying sinfulness, never surrendering His divinity, and by this means, which is totally incomprehensible to us, He bridged the gulf between sinful man and Holy God. And now, He has committed to us, His Church, the ministry of reconciliation. Jesus said, "As thou hast sent me into the world, even so have I also sent them into the world" (John 17:18). We have been redeemed unto God, called out and separated from the world, but our business is reaching back toward those who are still lost, extending the invitation to them, saying, "Come!"

We want them to know they can be delivered from the dark dominion of sin, that they can cross over this gulf of separation from God. Jesus remains the Bridge by which they must cross. Pointing out and bringing people to Him is our part in the ongoing ministry of reconciliation.

We must never tolerate the feeling that we belong to some kind of exclusive club. This is not the nature of God's Church. We would more accurately be compared to beggars who have found bread and are wanting to share it with other beggars who even now are perishing. Our concern for them must be manifested by the kind of effort which Jesus demonstrated as He allowed nothing to distract Him from His primary purpose to seek and to save the lost.

Also, in our commitment to Christian unity we must identify and tear down those things that are unnecessarily keeping us apart from fellow Christians. Pious, self-righteous attitudes are repugnant to sincere worshipers and they will repel rather than draw Christians together. It is not difficult for kindred hearts to unite in true fellowship. Nearly two hundred years ago, John Fawcett wrote: "Blest be the tie that binds our hearts in Christian love; the fellowship of kindred minds is like to that above." Where the Spirit is in control the natural tendency is for believers to come together, not to stay apart. It is when the flesh asserts itself that divisions occur. Sincere Christians will never be repelled or driven away from where their Blessed Saviour is being exalted. He is the only means of anyone's reconciliation with God, and it is in Him that the reconciliation of differences between His followers will be found. The Church's ministry is one of reconciliation.

Instead of building walls, it should be our determination to build bridges, to extend ourselves in true fellowship to every believer. There are no second-rate Christians. The only legitimate claim to salvation for any of us is the precious blood of Jesus. His blood does not make one person any holier than another. When we manifest a spirit of aloofness from another of His lambs or sheep it displeases our Lord, who prayed that we all would be one. And God will see to it that His children become one, in answer to Christ's prayer. It is not an unachievable goal. If He could take some forty men and have them write sixty-six books over a period of sixteen hundred years, embracing all kinds of theological subjects, then have all these books put together and they be totally without contradiction, He can surely, by the same Spirit which directed these authors, make us one.

In this final decade of the second millennium of Christianity, the limited time that remains demands that blood-bought Christians unite as one under the lordship of Christ in order to convince an unbelieving world that God sent His Son for their salvation. This is the prayer that Christ prayed, "That they all may be one . . . that the world may believe that thou hast sent me" (John 17:21). If we are to finish the work given us by Christ, we must somehow lay aside petty differences that divide Christians and concentrate upon the basics of preaching the gospel of the kingdom to every creature. May the Holy Ghost give us the resolve and spiritual strength to do this at this most critical period of the end time!

Some of our best leaders for the days ahead are, no doubt, right now outside the Church. When God needed a leader in the Early Church for a special ministry, for a leadership role that would explore new horizons, new frontiers, He went outside the Church for His man. He found him on the road to Damascus. Without consulting the apostles at Jerusalem, God chose this apostle. In a manner with which the leadership of the Church was not familiar, the Lord communicated with this new leader-to-be. They had spent years walking the dusty roads with Jesus of Nazareth, watching, listening and learning. This new apostle was caught up miraculously into the third heaven, into paradise, "And heard unspeakable words . . . not lawful for a man to utter" (2 Corinthians 12:4).

When finally he presented himself at Jerusalem and "assayed to join himself to the disciples . . . they were all afraid of him" (Acts 9:26). We know that Paul's relationship with the Lord was sound, his having been divinely chosen to be the apostle to the Gentiles, but the Church did not trust him. It was at this point that Barnabas became a "bridge builder." "But Barnabas took him, and brought him to the apostles, and declared unto them how he had seen the Lord in the way, and that [the Lord] had spoken to him, and how he had preached boldly at Damascus in the name of Jesus" (v. 27).

Paul's experience of having been caught up into paradise was different from the other apostles, and that most always creates apprehensions. That which is different we seem prone to distrust. We must remember, however, that God is sovereign and can work with anyone in whatever manner He chooses to do so. We cannot confine His working with people to a method which we ourselves have approved. He does not require our approval. He need not consult with anyone.

God never intended for His children to live in isolation from one another. It is His desire that they be joined together and compacted together. The scriptural injunction is, " . . . that there be no divisions among you; but that ye be perfectly joined together in the same mind and in the same judgment" (1 Corinthians 1:10). To bring Paul into this fellowship that he needed, in face of the distrust that was existing, someone was needed who could build a bridge of trust, and Barnabas was that man.

Satan seeks to bring divisions among brothers and sisters, and whenever he succeeds in creating any gap, he persists in his efforts to immediately make that gap wider and wider. He does this by exploiting any human traits, any feelings, any unscriptural traditions that are conducive to division.

Within the Church he even would have you dwelling upon your faithfulness in comparison to another Christian's unfaithfulness or carelessness. In fact, he might have you glorying over your own steadfastness. We must remember that it is only by God's grace that we possess any steadfastness; therefore, we have nothing of ourselves of which to glory. When we glory, let us glory in the marvel of

His grace. Such glorying will exalt His majesty and place us, at the same time, in a position of humility.

In the account of the Prodigal Son, a gap was created between the elder son and the younger, a gap that continued even when the younger son returned home from his waywardness. The elder son prided himself upon his faithfulness in his father's house: "Lo, these many years do I serve thee, neither transgressed I at any time thy commandment" (Luke 15:29). These were his words as he pouted jealously at the royal welcome being given his prodigal brother. The father's reasoning was, "Son, thou art ever with me, and all that I have is thine. It was meet that we should make merry, and be glad: for this thy brother was dead, and is alive again; and was lost, and is found" (vv. 31, 32).

The attitude displayed by the father is the one that we must possess in this time of restoration and reconciliation. "But when he was yet a great way off, his father saw him, and had compassion, and ran, and fell on his neck, and kissed him" (v. 20). He did not sit in the comfort of his home, waiting for his son to come knocking on the door, begging for admittance. He kept looking in the direction he knew his son had gone, so that when he was yet a great way off he saw him. Then he ran toward him—he was willing to go out to meet him and escort him home.

Oh, the greatness of the love of God! And as this divine love abides in us it will manifest itself in loving concern for others. This love is not passive; it is actively seeking opportunities to manifest itself. In Paul's life it was the domination of divine love that made him say: "For though I be free from all men, yet have I made myself servant unto all, that I might gain the more . . . . I am made all things to all men, that I might by all means save some. And this I do for the gospel's sake" (1 Corinthians 9:19, 22, 23).

Can we feel that we are pleasing the Lord today while at the same time we are ignoring all those who once rejoiced with us in the bounties of our Father's table, but who now are separated from our fellowship with Him? When we display a nonchalant attitude of "Am I my brother's keeper?"

it is evident that our love has grown cold and that our spiritual status is lukewarm, at best. I believe it is time for us to make a concerted effort to restore fellowships that have been broken. How many precious brothers and sisters who once walked with us into the house of God, whose testimonies blessed and encouraged us, are now cut off from that precious fellowship? The scriptural injunction still stands: " . . . ye which are spiritual, restore such an one in the spirit of meekness; considering thyself, lest thou also be tempted" (Galatians 6:1) or, "considering yourself; it could happen to you."

I want to introduce to you this morning an endeavor I am entitling, "A Time for Restoration." Following this Assembly I am urging each pastor to go back to his church and call the members together in a special meeting. From the church records, from memory, or from whatever source, compile the names of those who once rejoiced with us but who now are separated from our fellowship. Then go before the Lord in repentance for any past carelessness concerning genuine, compassionate efforts to restore them. At the same time pray for a burden from the Lord to seize your hearts, which will enable you to go to these people in a spirit of meekness and heartfelt compassion. Pray until you can weep in concern for these precious souls. After this burden has come upon you, you should review once more the names of these whom you want to see restored. Then, pray again, this time for a burden for specific individuals to settle upon those praying. After this, call for volunteers who will go two by two on a mission of love, to manifest to each one who has become separated from us the genuine concern and burden God has placed on our hearts.

You may then conclude this special meeting with a mighty prayer as each pair of volunteers kneels consecutively for the rest of the group to lay hands on them to pray for a special empowering by God to make their efforts fruitful. They may be admonished that the Lord will be going with them, and that He wants them to succeed. Before adjourning, announce another special meeting, perhaps one week later. This will be a time for reporting and enlisting additional prayer support where it is needed. This is not a one-week operation, nor just a program, but the beginning of a battle campaign to break the bands by which precious people are being held in captivity, in isolation from the Body of Christ. Know that it will be a battle, but it is a battle about which the Almighty God is deeply concerned, and in His strength we will win this battle! Then, we will rejoice together, even as Heaven rejoices, when those we love come back to the warmth of Christian love and fellowship in the Father's House.

One Thing Thou Lackest

"Then Jesus beholding him loved him, and said unto him, One thing thou lackest: go thy way, sell whatsoever thou hast, and give to the poor, and thou shalt have treasure in heaven: and come, take up the cross, and follow me" (Mark 10:21).

"Jesus said unto him, Thou shalt love the Lord thy God with all thy heart, and with all thy soul, and with all thy mind. This is the first and great commandment. And the second is like unto it, Thou shalt love thy neighbour as thyself" (Matthew 22:37-39).

The first of these commandments deals specifically with one's vertical relationship — his relationship with God, while the second deals with the horizontal — his relationship with his fellow man. The young man in our text seemed to pass the horizontal test as Jesus enumerated that category of commands: "Thou knowest the commandments, Do not commit adultery, Do not kill, Do not steal, Do not bear false witness, Defraud not, Honour thy father and mother" (Mark 10:19). His reply to Jesus was, "Master, all these have I [kept] from my youth" (Mark 10:20).

Had Jesus chosen to enumerate the other four commandments which dealt with man's relationship with God, the young man might have given the same affirmative answer concerning them. However, instead of reminding him of the commandment to have no other gods before God Jehovah, Jesus, discerning that mammon, the god of riches, was enthroned in the young man's heart, simply said, " . . . go thy way, sell whatsoever thou hast, and give to the poor, and thou shalt have treasure in heaven" (v. 21). At this point he faltered and ". . . went away grieved: for he had great possessions" (v. 82).

The young man must have felt Jesus was asking too much of him; but the Lord never asks too much from any of us. He loves us too much to do so. And when one loves Him with all his heart, soul and mind, he will obey whatever the Lord requires, and He does not always require the same actions from each of us.

As we come face to face with the Lord today, in these times of perplexity, I feel He is saying to us, "One thing thou lackest." That one thing is the same that was lacking in the life of the young ruler. It was that which was and is the fulfilling of all the law of God. As Paul wrote, "For all the law is fulfilled in one word" (Galatians 5:14). That one word is LOVE. This love is not some mere sentimental emotion. It is rather a bestowal of what is divine. The very nature of God is love. When that one element is missing, all our efforts for building the Church, all our efforts for extending Christ's kingdom, all our efforts to glorify God are unacceptable. Though we give our bodies to be burned, though we give our goods to feed the poor — having all knowledge, understanding all mysteries, having faith to remove mountains — apart from love all this, from a spiritual standpoint, is an exercise in futility.

This is the "missing link" about which R. G. Spurling wrote as he and A. J. Tomlinson were trying to understand God's plan for His Church. James called it "the royal law" (James 2:8). When that "royal law" is missing from the heart we may write a thousand other laws and seek to enforce them for the perfecting of the Church, but it will all be to no avail. The testimony of Moses verifies this, as we look at the great number of laws and ordinances he wrote to govern a people whose hearts were not attuned to God. The writer of

Hebrews referred to the "disannulling" of these laws because of "the weakness and unprofitableness thereof" (Hebrews 7:18). He went on to say, " For the law made nothing perfect, but the bringing in of a better hope did; by the which we draw nigh unto God" (v. 19).

This better hope came to us in Jesus Christ, who is forever the epitome, the perfect personification of divine love. None of us can doubt His love for us. And this Blessed Saviour said, "This is my commandment, That ye love one another, as I have loved you" (John 15:12). This is the "royal law" in which all the commandments are fulfilled.

I want to reiterate that this divine love is more than a sentimental emotion. It perseveres under tough circumstances. It reflects always the character of the One from whom it is received. We receive it as an impartation of His very nature and this immediately sets us apart as being "not of this world." His lordship of our lives becomes apparent. This love is the enabler for faithfulness to our Lord's commands. "For this is the love of God, that we keep his commandments: and his commandments are not grievous"(1 John 5:3). Jesus' words to us are, "Love your enemies, bless them that curse you, do good to them that hate you, and pray for them which despitefully use you, and persecute you; That ye may be the children of your Father which is in heaven. . . . For if ye love them which love you, what reward have ye? do not even the publicans the same? And if ye salute your brethren only, what do ye more than others? do not even the publicans so? Be ye therefore perfect, even as your Father which is in heaven is perfect" (Matthew 5:44-48).

What is this perfection of which Jesus speaks here? Is it not related to the love about which He is talking? We know that Paul calls charity the "bond of perfectness" (Colossians 3:14). Is the perfectness about which Jesus speaks a state to strive for, or is it reflected by an attitude we may now possess through our relationship with Him, wherein the "royal law of love" finds its fulfillment and lives in us?

We have been pursuing a vision of becoming a perfect church. Paul describes it as a glorious church without spot or wrinkle or any such thing, holy and without blemish. We believe this will consist of all the children of God among whom now there is an evident lack of divine unity and perfection. Doctrinal differences and traditions continue to divide believers into sectarian camps. These divisions dishonor Christ who prayed that we all would be one.

But where is the solution to this problem? Will it be in our coming together to debate issues and doctrines with the resultant formulation of still more articles of faith or rules for perfection? The need exists, all right, for brethren to counsel together, and I hope to see a forum developed where we can gather together in an Assembly like this for more substantive counseling, but dialogue alone is not enough. After putting forth our best effort, I believe we might hear our Lord saying, "One thing thou lackest."

How is it that we have overlooked that which is so basic, so essential? This "royal law" stands out so prominently in the Scriptures. Peter said, " . . . see that ye love one another with a pure heart fervently"(l Peter 1:22). John wrote, "And this is his commandment, That we should believe on the name of his Son Jesus Christ, and love one another, as he gave us commandment" (1 John 3:23). Jesus said, "As the Father hath loved me, so have I loved you: continue ye in my love" (John 15:9). Love is the key!

I do not mean to over-simplify, but we must put first things first and make certain we are keeping this "royal law." God is not going to bless our substitutes for this one command no matter how sacred they may seem to us.

Love is patient and kind. It is never arrogant or haughty. It never looks down on people, but sees them as a creation of God. It never belittles a fellow believer who is struggling against our common enemy. It is understanding and it extends a helping hand, reaching out in genuine compassion and concern. Love builds bridges, not walls. The maxim, "Good fences make good neighbors" may have some merit in the world where Satan is prince, but not in the family of God where we are to love as brethren and all be as one.

A Spirit Of Reconciliation

Our witness to a world which is suffering, which needs so much the ministry we have been commissioned to exercise, will be effective only when it is bearing the evidence of divine love. To tell them about Jesus, about His selfless love for them, to where He was willing to be crucified for their sins so that they could stand justified before a righteous God, having no condemnation—this is a beautiful story. But for this gospel to have credence they must see this same love in us. Jesus said, "A new commandment I give unto you, That ye love one another; as I have loved you, that ye also love one another. By this shall all men know that ye are my disciples, if ye have love one to another" (John 13:34, 35). This love will give us the identity they are needing to see, and it will not let us rest until we are moving out in ministry to them. "For the love of Christ constraineth us" (2 Corinthians 5:14).

To what may we attribute, then, our lack of evangelistic fervor? "One thing thou lackest." Why is the Church of God and the family of God marked by divisions and contentions? "One thing thou lackest." Oh, for a revival, a new baptism of the love of God to be "shed abroad in our hearts by the Holy Ghost."

This is such a serious matter that I am calling for the beginning of a twenty-four-hour prayer chain to begin October 1. For the restoration effort which I introduced in an earlier section to succeed, for the rebuilding of which I spoke to become more than mere rhetoric, and for us to experience a new baptism of divine love will call for earnest supplication to God. We just must pray! There is no reason we cannot have unceasing prayer ascending to the throne of God day and night all year long. This will not be just one individual praying each hour, but thousands of our members praying each hour. We have prepared commitment forms which each pastor will be receiving very soon, whereby he will secure commitments from his membership to a specific hour to pray every day. Some may want to choose an hour that will require an extra sacrifice on their part.

Pray for a fresh baptism of divine love; pray for God's blessings upon our efforts to restore those members and former members who have been overcome by Satan; and pray for a spirit to take hold of all our people which will cause them to say "Let us rise up and build."

This must be an ambitious and aggressive prayer endeavor, and I am requesting every department of the Church to become involved in its promotion. Some may be able to begin it prior to October 1. If so, please do. The need is urgent. We must pray! Let each one know that he will not be praying alone. Thousands will be joining him at his hour of prayer. We know God will hear!

Let Us Rise Up and Build

Just as Nehemiah returned from Babylon with a burden to rebuild the walls of Jerusalem which were in shambles, God is laying upon hearts today the burden of restoration, repairing the damages that have been done by our adversary—restoring relationships, both with God and with one another. It was not Nehemiah, but the hand of the Lord that was upon him, that rallied the people and caused them to say, "Let us rise up and build" (Nehemiah 2:18). I am sensing in many hearts this same spirit. There can be and there will be restoration! Together, by God's grace, we can build the Church of God!

Yes, there must be a restoration of our relationship with God and with one another. A restoration of relationship with God will come through the restoration of fervent praying among us. It is when the spirit of prayer takes hold of us that it becomes easy to pray, and this is the kind of praying that refreshes the soul. In such times of praying we can thank God for what He is doing within us and through us.

In my experience I have found this to occur most often when I have a regular time each day to meet and spend time with God. Each day will be different, and some days you will feel defeated. But God is observing your steadfastness, your consistency, and in His love for you, He will visit you again and see that you sense His presence in a most blessed way. These times of His special visitations make all the other times of praying worthwhile. They surely strengthen our relationship with Him. When our relationship with Him becomes what it should be, it will not be difficult to have good relationships with one another.

May there be also a restoration of the joy of corporate worship. David said, "I was glad when they said unto me, Let us go into the house of the Lord" (Psalms 122:1). It is not enough to pray, to read the Word and to worship privately, we need the blessings which come also through worshiping with other saints. I don't think I could have survived through my years of Christian living apart from the fellowship of my local church, as I joined them in singing, in praising, in receiving the Word. We must have a restoration of joyous worship in our churches. If you are too busy to assemble regularly with the saints of God for worshiping together, you are too busy, and you are the only one who can make the needed adjustments in your schedule.

A restoration of the close fellowship we are needing in the Church right now can be heightened through the proper function of care groups which meet in homes and in activities outside the walls of our churches. I want to challenge our pastors to give their attention to the formulation and proper function of these groups which not only will strengthen fellowship but will channel energies for ministering within our communities. This is a proven means for growth and outreach.

While dwelling upon the theme of restoration and rebuilding, I consider two more aspects to be very timely. One is a restoration of holy living. "Thy testimonies are very sure: holiness becometh thine house, O Lord, for ever" (Psalms 93:5). God's command to us is, "Be ye holy, for I am holy." The holiness of God deserves our highest respect. Because of the fallen nature of man through Adam's transgression, there is a separation between men, who were born in sin, and God, who is altogether holy. And today, only through the sanctifying blood of our Saviour can we claim any degree of holiness.

Many have attempted to become holy through their own efforts—by self-denial, by abstinence from smoking and drinking and immoral behavior, or by stringent dress codes, but none of this adds one iota of holiness. Holiness can be known only in relationship with Him who is holy, the One to which the seraphims cry, "Holy, holy, holy."

Yet, when one enters into and maintains this relationship, there will be a noticeable difference in his lifestyle and behavior. It will be a lifestyle marked by a spirit of humility and servanthood, revealing one's identification with the greatest Servant of all time, "Who, being in the form of God, thought it not robbery to be equal with God: but made himself of no reputation, and took upon him the form of a servant" (Philippians 2:6, 7). Serving God by faithfully and effectually serving people becomes the Christian's delight.

Whatever impairs this relationship with God, or the effectiveness of his service, he will want to lay aside—so, there goes his drinking, use of tobacco and other drugs and his immoral behavior. Quitting those things did not make him holy, but his relationship with the One who is holy caused him to quit whatever impaired his effectiveness as a servant, and I repeat—WHATEVER IT IS! The idea of setting forth a set of rules as a standard for holiness has its weaknesses. There is the tendency to lay claim to holiness whenever the rules are being faithfully kept, while the individual making the claim may be totally devoid of a real, vital relationship with God. And whenever this relationship is missing, there is no holiness, no matter how acceptable his behavior may be to others.

When this right relationship with God is existing, however, there will be a humble spirit. Any arrogant, judgmental spirit, or spirit of rebellion, is a telltale sign of low spirituality or carnality. "Becoming all things to all men" in order to serve more effectively requires a renouncement of pride and self-will. This caused Paul to forego some things that were perfectly legitimate for him in God's sight.

This may be seen in his declaration, "Wherefore, if meat make my brother to offend, I will eat no meat while the world standeth, lest I make my brother to offend" (1 Corinthians 8:13). This spirit of servanthood can be seen further in the circumcision of Timothy who was a Greek, when Paul wanted to take him with him on his missionary journey. We read in Acts 16:3, "Him would Paul have to go forth with him; and took and circumcised him because of the Jews which were in those quarters." Timothy was not a Jew, and he could have rebelled against this tradition of the Jews being imposed upon him, especially since God was not requiring this even of the Jews any more. That he submitted to this rite gives indication of his desire, like Paul, of becoming "all things to all men, that [he] might by all means save some" (1 Corinthians 9:22). Our identity with Christ will be shown by a selfless love for people. Some of our Christian liberties we will forego if we find that the taking of these liberties destroys our fellowship with other brothers and sisters in the Lord or impairs our effectiveness in reaching people. I am praying for a restoration of holy living—living in a pure relationship with Him who is holy.

I believe also that in rebuilding we need a restoration of Church loyalty. The Christian's highest loyalty, always, is to Jesus Christ, and many today, with a sense of high idealism, are professing their loyalty to Him and Him alone. While this may sound good, when such people, through this kind of idealism, deny their need for loyalty to the Church, they are rejecting what Jesus has ordered for them. The Church is of His design and it was designed for a purpose. It brings believers into a close-knit fellowship where relationships are developed and tested.

These relationships within the Body of Christ are designed to help us mature spiritually. Some have opted to separate themselves, to where they do not have to be concerned about the effect their choices and actions have on others. But God never willed that His children live in alienation from their brothers and sisters. The Church is one body with members being mutually dependent upon and supportive of one another. The lessons to be learned from living together and, through love, making lifestyle adjustments for the edifying of another brother or sister are necessary for maturing spiritually.

The spirit of independence which some are getting caught up in is not of God, and it is dangerous. His word is, "that ye be perfectly joined together." This same spirit of independence is the cause of many marriages now being broken up by divorce, where immature people choose to live for themselves and their own pleasure, rather than to submit and make adjustments, and through the lessons to be learned in the relationship of husband and wife arrive at a greater maturity.

God designed marriage for the good of the individuals involved, to help them mature. It is a divine institution, even as the Church is. For a marriage to remain intact requires more than romantic fantasy. It requires a commitment to marriage, not just a commitment to another individual, but commitment to marriage as an institution that is divinely ordained.

How many of you expect loyalty from your companions? It is reasonable to expect such loyalty, also to give it. The same is true concerning Church loyalty. Your companion is not always going to please you, neither is he/she always going to agree with you. There will be differences to be resolved. This requires some "give and take." So it is within the Church.

I made a commitment to marriage 40 years ago, and I made a commitment to the Church 48 years ago, and I fully intend to remain loyal to both. There has been some "give and take" in both, and I consider myself to have gained much in each of these relationships.

There is a growing number who do not want to make the commitment to marriage, so they choose an arrangement of their own making rather than to pursue God's way. This arrangement which provides for fleshly gratification not only displeases God, it denies people the benefits that God intended marriage to bring.

In the same sense we are witnessing a growing unwillingness on the part of many to commit themselves to the Church. The demands that membership imposes seem to many to be too restrictive, and they would rather be free and independent. This is the spirit of the age, but this is not God's way, and it does not please Him for His children to pursue such a course. People need to be taught the value of Church membership, even as they need to be taught the value of marriage.

Don't teach your children that all that matters is that they love each other, that then they can live together without making the commitment to holy matrimony. It is important that they love each other, all right, and it is important that people have a genuine love relationship with the Lord, but the Church has been designed by God for the joining together of believers in one body, even as marriage has been divinely instituted for the joining together of lovers in a one-flesh union. Let there be a restoration of Church loyalty!

There are conflicts still to be faced and resolved among us, but I do not want us to spend all our time in conflict with one another. It is a sign of our immaturity when we pick at small differences. We must become more tolerant of one another. Charity, according to the Scriptures, is the bond of perfectness. And this charity must abound within the Body of Christ. Its importance was emphasized by Peter as he wrote, "And above all things have fervent charity among yourselves: for charity shall cover the multitude of sins" (1 Peter 4:8).

Living together with a satisfactory degree of harmony and peace, as important as that is, is not our main task; it is to reach a perishing world. This we must not forget! And I believe as our focus becomes more outward we will have fewer difficulties within. Our assault must be upon the gates of hell, in an attempt to free souls from Satan's dominion. We are engaged in a war of liberation, and the price of failure is just too great. We must not fail!

The Captain of the Lord's Host

"And it came to pass, when Joshua was by Jericho, that he lifted up his eyes and looked, and, behold, there stood a man over against him with his sword drawn in his hand:

and Joshua went unto him, and said unto him, Art thou for us, or for our adversaries? And he said, Nay; but as captain of the host of the LORD am I now come. And Joshua fell on his face to the earth, and did worship, and said unto him, What saith my lord unto his servant? And the captain of the LORD'S host said unto Joshua, Loose thy shoe from off thy foot; for the place whereon thou standest is holy. And Joshua did so" (Joshua 5:13-15).

Joshua was a great leader, second to none among the Israelites, but here we find him falling on his face before this One who called Himself "captain of the Lord's host." Inasmuch as this stranger did not forbid Joshua's prostrated worship, we must presume that He was more than an ordinary man or angel. In fact, we may be assured that He remains even today "captain of the Lord's host."

Having crossed over Jordan, Israel's wandering in the wilderness was now history, but here they were, facing the challenge of possessing their promised possession. It was a land filled with a people from whom their hearts had shrunk in fear some forty years earlier. It was a land inhabited by giants to whom they had compared themselves as grasshoppers. No wonder then when Joshua beheld this stranger standing with a drawn sword that he inquired, "Art thou for us, or for our adversaries?"

His reply to Joshua is interesting even to this day as it is given current application: "Nay; but as captain of the host of the Lord am I now come." Perhaps Joshua needed a reminder that this was not his battle. Perhaps he thought that he himself was captain of the Lord's host. Then, as now, however, the battle is the Lord's, and as a contemporary chorus goes, "The Captain of the host is Jesus." As He stood before Joshua on that day, even now He is not among us to take sides. He is in charge, and it is up to us as to whether we will align ourselves with Him in this warfare against Satan, the enemy of God and all mankind.

In our unaided strength we are no match for this deceiver, this enemy of all that is good and decent and pure. But we have no fear of failure as we march into battle with the One who has all power in heaven and earth. What blessed assurance His presence provides us as we go forward to possess our possessions, to claim as our own all the eternal promises for the people of God, and to pursue this battle of liberation for those who are being held captive by this cruel enemy.

Because of his deceptive tactics we must be reminded occasionally of who the enemy really is. He would have us warring among ourselves. But we who are following the "captain of the host of the Lord" are all on the same side. We are not enemies of one another. I am not your enemy; you are not my enemy—we are on the same side in this battle against Satan.

Our business parallels the mission of Jesus who came to seek and to save that which was lost. There is a world of hurting people—people who have been victimized by sin's power, whose hope now lies in our faithfulness to our commission. What hope do they have when we allow Satan to divert our attention from our appointed task and engage in internal disputes and bickering?

Some occasional introspection seems necessary; however, when our focus becomes totally inward you may be sure the enemy of souls has succeeded in turning us away from our primary task of reaching out to people who are lost, people who need to feel our love and concern in sharing with them the message of a loving Saviour. That the enemy has succeeded to an intolerable degree in diverting us from our mission to the unsaved is hardly debatable. This is clearly reflected in our statistics of outreach and growth.

There are some areas of the world where our people are working compassionately to reach the lost and we thank God for the number of salvation experiences they are reporting. In too many areas, however, attention has been diverted to other things of lesser importance and the record speaks for itself.

Are we truly aligned with the Captain of the Lord's host? The ministry of Jesus, who remains the same yesterday, today and forever, was marked by His concern for people. There were those of the religious establishment who were totally devoid of compassionate caring for people who would have loved to engage Him in theological debating, but Jesus would not allow this to happen. His disdain for such was clearly demonstrated. He loved sinners, and they felt His love and responded. They meant much more to Him than doctrinal disputes.

Sinners, indeed, were attracted to Jesus. Luke wrote in chapter fifteen, verse one, "Then drew near unto him all the publicans and sinners for to hear him." This was something the Pharisees and scribes did not have to be concerned about. Sinners left them alone. In many churches today, we might look around and ask, "Where are the sinners?" Why did the sinners draw near to Jesus while avoiding the religious leaders? They sensed that here was Someone who cared about them. Jesus never forgot His mission. He came to seek and to save the lost.

His love for them eventually took Him to Calvary, and even there, in the midst of His dying He reached out to another one, and Satan met another defeat. This is the Captain of the Lord's host. Does this same kind of love for people mark us as being identified with Him? Oh, that we could become consumed with the love of Jesus!

May we presume that the Master cares any less today for the victims of sin than when He walked in Galilee? Would His ministry be directed in a different way if He should return in the same form in which He appeared then? Would He become bogged down altogether in seminars and conferences? Would He spend His time totally in administrative work, analyzing statistics on a computer, getting caught up in the paralysis of analysis? Or would He be out among the people—opening blinded eyes, healing the sick, forgiving sins? I believe the answer is clear—"Jesus Christ the same yesterday, and today, and forever."

Can we not envision Him among us now saying, "I am not here to take sides, but to lead you out into a sick society where you can show them a better way." Would He not be saying, "Put away from among yourselves your petty bickering and arguments. There is a world of hurting people out there for whom I suffered beyond measure on a cruel cross. My love for them is just as great as My love for you, and it is not My will that any of them perish, but that they be brought to repentance." Is this not what the unchanging Christ would say?

Then He might remind us, "As Captain of the host of the Lord am I now come. I am asking you to join Me in that which is dearest to My heart—that for which I paid the supreme sacrifice. Dispense with your analyzing and criticizing and follow Me into the harvest fields. The time is short and there remain yet many souls to be harvested." I believe this is the message from our Captain today.

The Joy of the Lord Is Your Strength

"Then he said unto them, Go your way, eat the fat, and drink the sweet, and send portions unto them for whom nothing is prepared: for this day is holy unto our Lord: neither be ye sorry; for the joy of the Lord is your strength" (Nehemiah 8:10).

To create feelings of hopelessness and despair is Satan's delight. This enemy of our souls would have us continually focusing our attention on the victories he has achieved within God's creation, all the sorrows which the curse of sin has fostered in this world. We admit that it was his victory in the Garden of Eden that caused all of us to be born in sin. Mankind has suffered and is continuing to suffer the terrible consequences of the Fall. But that is not the end of the story.

The good news is that our Blessed Saviour came and bruised this enemy's head at Calvary. And now millions can testify that Satan's dominion over them is broken. He has no authority over their lives, as they now live by faith in the Son of God. This is cause for rejoicing. And those who have experienced this exhilarating freedom from sin's power can rejoice with joy unspeakable and full of glory. We exult with John Newton as we sing, "I once was lost but now am found, was blind but now I see." At the beginning of His ministry Jesus met Satan in the wilderness and was subjected to his temptations. Satan was the loser in this encounter, and as Christ returned to Nazareth He stood in the synagogue and read from the prophecy penned by Isaiah and declared its fulfillment that day. Isaiah's words were, "The Spirit of the Lord God is upon me; because the Lord hath anointed me to preach good tidings unto the meek; he hath sent me to bind up the brokenhearted, to proclaim liberty to the captives, and the opening of the prison to them that are bound; To proclaim the acceptable year of the Lord, and the day of vengeance of our God; to comfort all that mourn; To appoint unto them that mourn in Zion, to give unto them beauty for ashes, the oil of joy for mourning, the garment of praise for the spirit of heaviness; that they might be called trees of righteousness, the planting of the Lord, that he might be glorified" (Isaiah 61:1-3).

What better cause for rejoicing could we have? We were being held captive by Satan. There was no way that we could liberate ourselves from sin's prison, but what we could not do, Jesus did for us.

We must not lose sight of the wonder of being saved, of being a child of God. What a treasure we have been given! Jesus made this a point of emphasis when His disciples were rejoicing over their ministerial successes. " . . . Rejoice not, that the spirits are subject unto you," He cautioned them, "but rather rejoice, because your names are written in heaven" (Luke 10:20). It is much better to rejoice in what He has done for us than in what we are doing for Him. Infectious joy is an accelerant to the spread of the gospel. This was true in the Early Church and it has the same effect today. We read in Acts 13:52, "And the disciples were filled with joy, and with the Holy Ghost." The records of their success in the spread of the gospel is indisputable. They had their problems, even as we have, but something within provided them a joyful witness. Paul and Silas, with backs throbbing from the stripes they had received, and with their feet secured in stocks, in the midnight darkness of a dungeon sang praises unto God. This same Paul could later write the Corinthian church and declare, "I am filled with comfort, I am exceeding joyful in all our tribulation" (2 Corinthians 7:4). What gave this apostle the exceeding joyfulness of which he spoke, a joyfulness which circumstances could not affect? At this time he was more than just a missionary, he was an administrator, who, in his words, had "the care of all the churches" (2 Corinthians 11:28). And this Corinthian church to which he was writing had about as many problems as any of our churches do today. Yet, he could say, "I am exceeding joyful." Church problems did not affect his joy.

The fact is, the joy of the Lord is not predicated upon circumstances. Joy is the fruit of the Spirit, and when you are indwelt by the Spirit you will have joy. How otherwise could one be joyful in tribulation? But, thousands can attest to the reality of Paul's testimony, and the joy of the Lord is their strength.

How can we today affect a troubled, tormented world while exhibiting the same kind of worry and frustrations they are feeling? They surely will not desire more of the same. To turn from lives of sin they must be given the hope of something better. It is our business to point them to Him who is all of mankind's Blessed Hope. Thank God for the joy of salvation! Thank God for the joy of living in His presence, drawing strength and assurance from His Spirit.

The Psalmist wrote, "There is a river, the streams whereof shall make glad the city of God" (Psalms 46:4). Are you being refreshed today by the streams of this river? Are you viewed by those who know you as a joyful Christian? Only by this means will your witness be effective in turning the eyes of the unsaved to Jesus.

To the Philippian church Paul wrote, "Rejoice in the Lord alway: and again I say, Rejoice" (Philippians 4:4). His admonition to the Thessalonians was, "Rejoice evermore" (1 Thessalonians 5:16). The life of continual rejoicing can be lived only as we focus upon God's graciousness—the joy of sins forgiven, the joy of living in divine fellowship, knowing that our brief mortal limitations will soon be ended and we will move into the unrestricted fulness of heavenly joy!

Satan seeks to distract us, diverting our focus to the troubles, the distresses, the cares of this life, but we can resist all such diversions. We cannot prevent these troubles from coming—we live in a world where Satan is the prince; this is his domain and it bears all the marks of depravity. It is filled with suffering, with heartache, with sorrow. But in the midst of such we can boldly lift our heads and declare that our citizenship is in heaven, and that our redemption from this earth is drawing near.

Thank God that this world is not our home. It is only the place of a brief pilgrimage, and even while traveling through this land in which we are strangers our fellowship is with the One who has triumphed over this world, and we have entered into His victory. We sense His nearness and His presence is cause for rejoicing. The Psalmist stated it well when he wrote, " . . . in thy presence is fulness of joy" (Psalms 16:11).

No, we are not alone. Thank God for His presence. Thank God for joy. Let there be joy in the Church, as Jeremiah wrote, "The voice of joy, and the voice of gladness, the voice of the bridegroom, and the voice of the bride, the voice of them that shall say, Praise the Lord of hosts: for the Lord is good; for his mercy endureth for ever" (Jeremiah 33:11).

I feel like saying with Isaiah, "I will greatly rejoice in the Lord, my soul shall be joyful in my God; for he hath clothed me with the garments of salvation, he hath covered me with the robe of righteousness" (Isaiah 61:10). Oh, the wonder of it all!

Jesus, Take Charge!

15

This message was part of the General Overseer's presentation to the 86th Assembly, 1991

" . . . And upon this rock I will build my church" (Matthew 16:18).

God had a people whom He had chosen long ago. They were the seed of Abraham, descending from Jacob and his twelve sons. They had been sovereignly chosen to be unto God a peculiar treasure, a kingdom of priests, and a holy nation, and God had worked wonders among them, showing Himself strong in their behalf.

No other people in history experienced such manifestations of divine intervention as did these people. A sea opened up so that six hundred thousand men, besides women and children, could march across it on dry ground, only for those waters to come together again to drown their pursuers. God's presence was among them as a cloud by day and a pillar of fire by night. At Mount Sinai the Lord descended in fire and the smoke of a furnace and the whole mountain quaked greatly, causing fear and trembling among all the people who were camped nearby.

What other people ever experienced bread from heaven to be given them daily for forty years, or water for them to drink to gush out from a flinty rock, or the sun to stand still so that a battle could be fought to its conclusion?

They had been divinely chosen to be the special people of God as a witness among the nations. This was God's sovereign choice, but over and over again they failed the One who chose them. The people who constituted this nation were of a certain lineage. The family into which one was born determined, for the most part, whether he would be a part of God's chosen nation. A requirement as a member of this covenanted nation was that every man child was to be circumcised when he was eight days old, but here again this was not a decision on his part. It was a decision that was made for him. So, a true heart commitment was lacking among this chosen people.

They were reminded by their parents of how special they were among the nations, but this seems only to have created arrogant attitudes instead of causing them to cultivate a deeper relationship with their God. Their continual failings to fulfill God's purposes did not cause Him to love them any less, however. His love for them was perfect.

God's love was demonstrated to perfection when He condescended to come to them as a man, and He was born and lived among them as Jesus of Nazareth. What a wonder! This was the ultimate visitation that God could visit upon them. However, He found a people whose hearts were hardened by the deceitfulness of sin. They were proud of their godly heritage, but they did not know the God of their heritage. Nor did they want to know Him, especially those in leadership. They had forms set up which would preserve and perpetuate their positions and their institutional bigotry and they wanted no interference from God. They were in control, a control which they had no intention to surrender; no, not even to God!

So, in our text we hear the pronouncement of Jesus that He would build His Church, a new creation—not a revamping or restructuring of the Jewish institution, but a new entity, which Paul later would identify as the Body of Christ. Furthermore, it would not be just for those of a certain lineage.

God's love did not embrace just the Jews. He loves everybody in every nation, and His love for them is perfect, also. Thus, came His declaration, "I will build my church." It was to be an inclusive body for all men everywhere.

This must have been in Jesus' mind when He said to the Pharisees, "And other sheep I have, which are not of this fold: them also I must bring, and they shall hear my voice; and there shall be one fold, and one shepherd" (John 10:16). This one fold, which He predicted here, to be led by "one shepherd," would not be the exclusive Jewish fold, however. It would be the Church He promised He would build. Paul addressed this subject to the Gentile members in Ephesus.

> "That at that time ye were without Christ, being aliens from the commonwealth of Israel, and strangers from the covenants of promise, having no hope, and without God in the world:
>
> "But now in Christ Jesus ye who sometimes were far off are made nigh by the blood of Christ.
>
> "For he is our peace, who hath made both one, and hath broken down the middle wall of partition between us;
>
> "Having abolished in his flesh the enmity, even the law of commandments contained in ordinances; for to make in himself of twain one new man, so making peace;
>
> "And that he might reconcile both unto God in one body by the cross, having slain the enmity thereby" (Ephesians 2:12-16).

Only in Jesus could the twain of Jew and Gentile become one new man—one new creation, one new body. The middle wall of partition was an allusion to the partition in the temple, which separated the court of the Gentiles from that into which the Jews had liberty to enter. But then even for the Jews there was a heavier barrier, the veil of the temple, which shielded the holy of holies. Their sinfulness, which was manifested by the law of commandments, made them to be at enmity with God, and they could not approach His presence in the holy of holies.

Paul wrote that Jesus had abolished in His flesh the enmity, even the law of commandments contained in ordinances. By His death on Calvary He took away the binding power of the ceremonial law so that neither the Jews, nor the Gentiles, would any longer have to be at enmity with God. Rather, He died to reconcile both unto God, that they could dwell without enmity toward one another, in one body. Paul stated it well when he said, "For he is our peace."

When Jesus said, "I will build my church," He knew it would have to be purchased with His own blood, that only His death could bring mankind into harmony with God and with one another. It is significant that He did not say, "My church will be built," but rather, "I will build my church." No one else could do it.

The building of His Church is not so much something which He did as it is something which He is doing. He is still building His Church. It is an ongoing process. The Church is not a static institution but a growing, developing organism. That we who are present in this Assembly today are now a part of the Church attests to this fact. We must never attempt to calcify a Church that must be alive and growing, reaching out in dynamic witness to bring others into this glorious fellowship we are experiencing with our Saviour. We have taken our places in the Church's ongoing development. And we are enjoying this privilege because of what Jesus is still doing. He is building His Church. And He views thousands of others, perhaps millions, as a part of His Church, not yet in place. But they will be, and His prayer will be answered, "That they [all] may be made perfect in one" (John 17:23).

Problems arise when men become architects and designers, when they become the builders of what Jesus has reserved unto Himself. I believe it is time that we truly pray a prayer of relinquishment from the heart, "Jesus, take charge!" We do not know how to build His Church. He never intended that we should build it. It is of divine design and it will be constructed divinely. True, we are called to be laborers with Him, but He let us know that we are laborers with Him rather than for Him. It will be done His way!

Judge Not

In the Sermon on the Mount, which may be referred to as Jesus' inaugural sermon to His Church following its establishment on Mount Hittin, our Lord said, "Judge not, that ye be not judged." Very early He was condemning all judgmental attitudes within this new creation which He called "My Church." He would be its Owner and its Judge, quickly warning against "mote-hunting" in a neighbor's eye while ignoring a beam in one's own eye.

Why did Jesus include this as one of the cardinal teachings for His Church? There were many other things He could have included instead of, "Judge not, that ye be not judged." And if some of us had been delivering this sermon it is very probable that this teaching would have been preempted by something else more in keeping with our views of what is right and wrong; indeed, we might have included something as a teaching which could even have accommodated a judgmental attitude which Jesus was here condemning.

It is interesting that in compiling a list of important truths which have come to be known as prominent teachings of the Church that this teaching did not make the list. The closest thing to it that we have is a teaching entitled, "On Meats and Drinks." The emphasis of this teaching is that we are not to judge one another as to the sinfulness of eating certain types of meats or of drinking non-alcoholic drinks. To my knowledge we do very little judging or condemning one another in these matters, but there are other areas where judgmental attitudes are rampant.

For years many of our sisters were condemned for what many considered improper hair grooming. For curling, straightening or trimming their hair they were censured and some were even excluded from membership in the

Church as the teaching by Jesus to "judge not" was ignored. Some of the brothers felt so strongly about women's hair until they introduced, and finally obtained its approval by the Assembly (where the women could not speak), a recommendation advising against the cutting of the hair. I remember leaving that Assembly with a heavy heart, as did many others, feeling that as the Church of God of the Bible we had gone too far, that this was a matter to be left to individual conscience.

As was the case with some of the ceremonial laws which lived for awhile in the Early Church and then died, I lived to see this Assembly recommendation wither and die, and, after some thirty years, to be given an honorable burial in the Assembly of 1986. To have allowed our sisters earlier to have curled, or straightened, or to have trimmed their hair, following their conscience, would have been termed by some as the Church's lowering its standard of holiness. But is it really lowering the standard for us to remove extra-biblical requirements and to stop judging one another in purely personal matters where Christian conscience should be the determinant? We would do well to continually ask whether it is our standard or God's standard. To bring all of our practices into harmony with God's standards would actually be raising the standards of the Church.

It seems sad that we should spend so much time judging and criticizing one another while a world of lost people continue their spiraling plunge toward an endless hell from which there is no deliverance. Why can we not see what is important to Jesus? If the greatest commandment is to love God and to love one another, would not the greatest sin be the failure to love? Is this not why we are instructed to "above all things have fervent charity among [ourselves]"? Something is needed to put an end to a harsh, judgmental spirit among us, and I believe this is it—loving one another with pure hearts fervently. Some have established an arbitrary standard as to what a proper vision of the Church of God is and they are quick to judge who is Church of God and who is not Church of God.

I feel like asking with Paul, "Who art thou that judgest another man's servant? To his own master he standeth or falleth. . . . But why dost thou judge thy brother? or why dost thou set at nought thy brother? for we shall all stand before the judgment seat of Christ. For it is written, As I live, saith the Lord, every knee shall bow to me, and every tongue shall confess to God. So then every one of us shall give an account of himself to God. Let us not therefore judge one another any more: but judge this rather, that no man put a stumblingblock or an occasion to fall in his brother's way" (Romans 14:4, 10-13).

The instruction of James is much like this as he wrote, "Speak not evil one of another, brethren. He that speaketh evil of his brother, and judgeth his brother, speaketh evil of the law, and judgeth the law: but if thou judge the law, thou art not a doer of the law, but a judge. There is one lawgiver, who is able to save and to destroy: who art thou that judgest another? (James 4:11, 12). James goes on to say, "But now ye rejoice in your boastings: all such rejoicing is evil" (v. 16). Some of us may boast that we are conservatives; others of us may boast that we are moderates; and generally, such boasting is against those brothers who do not share our views. Often we seem to take pride in and rejoice in our boastings that we are not like those other brethren. "All such rejoicing is evil."

What do we truly have to boast of or to glory in, but in the cross of our dear Saviour. Apart from His shed blood we are all sinners doomed for hell. We should be rejoicing that by His death we are saved, and we should be rejoicing over every other soul who, by the same grace, has been saved. We have become brothers, not by any merit of our own—we did not deserve this great salvation. It came to each of us by God's mercy.

We have brothers and sisters all over the world, all of whom have been saved by the same marvelous grace of God, and it is God's will that we all be united in Him. He does not want us to be separated by carnal divisions, criticizing and attacking one another. This year we have been in contact with many Christians in Eastern Europe who desire closer fellowship with us. Some of these have endured much suffering and hardship because of their Pentecostal testimony. Many have spent time in prison. They truly love the Lord.

Many of these people feel that they should not wear gold for ornament; however some of them wear their wedding bands, which they do not consider as an ornament but as a symbol of their being married. I hope as they are brought into closer contact with us they will not be too critical or judgmental of all the pins and other jewelry which our people are wearing for ornament. It would be hard for us to argue "symbolism" for our pins while calling their wedding bands "ornament."

Somewhere along the way we made the arbitrary determination that is was wrong to wear a wedding band, that that would be "gold for ornament," but that it was all right to wear gold pins if they were not "large and showy." However, the size of the pin was left to the conscience of the individual. So we have adopted a policy that a person who is wearing a wedding band may not be accepted into the fellowship of Church membership. However, they might take a half dozen of those rings and have them put together to form some kind of a pin to be worn on a dress, and that would be no barrier to their joining the Church. How can we justify such judging of people's eligibility for membership in the Church Jesus is building?

Is not the criteria for membership in God's Church "such as should be saved"? Are not all God's children eligible for membership in His Church? Can we refuse those whom He accepts? Is it right for us to say, "Lord, you may be able to fellowship them, but we cannot"? Is our standard of holiness higher than His? Do we consider ourselves holier than He to whom the angels sing, "Holy, Holy, Holy"? Have we been too judgmental of some of His children? If so, would we not stand condemned before Him? For that would He not call us to repentance?

I am aware that the Church must make judgments against sin and exercise proper discipline. It would not be right to accept for membership those who, though professing salvation, are guilty of sins for which they would need to be excluded in the next business meeting. Paul names some works of the flesh in Galatians, chapter five, and declares that they which do such things shall not inherit the kingdom of God. He names "adultery, fornication, uncleanness, lasciviousness, idolatry, witchcraft, hatred, variance, emulations, wrath, strife, seditions, heresies, envyings, murders, drunkenness, revellings, and such like" (vv. 19-21). Those whom the Scriptures declare ineligible for the kingdom of God are, understandably, ineligible for membership in the Church of God.

Paul instructed the church at Corinth to put away from among them a fornicator. He said, "if any man that is called a brother be a fornicator, or covetous, or an idolater, or a railer, or a drunkard, or an extortioner; with such an one no not to eat" (1 Corinthians 5:11).

Sin and holiness are not compatible, and the Church must remain firm in its stand against sin. Some things, however, are only marks of spiritual immaturity, and we must be able to distinguish the difference. To label as sin things that simply show evidence of immaturity is usually a mark of a judgmental spirit, or at best immaturity on the part of the critic.

When Peter wrote concerning the subjection of Christian wives to their husbands so that the unsaved husbands might become believers, he emphasized that the wives' adorning should be that of a meek and quiet spirit. In the absence of such a spirit substitutes of outward adorning would be vain. He said, "Whose adorning let it not be . . . of plaiting the hair, and of wearing of gold, or of putting on of apparel; But let it be the hidden man of the heart, in that which is not corruptible, even the ornament of a meek and quiet spirit, which is in the sight of God of great price" (1 Peter 3:3, 4).

Paul went a little further in his epistle to Timothy and suggested modest apparel for the women, and while Peter wrote that their adorning be not the putting on of apparel, Paul designated that it not be an adorning with "costly array" (1 Timothy 2:9). Now it seems easy for us to turn the emphasis of these verses away from the meek and quiet spirit that is being advocated to an emphasis against plaiting the hair, wearing of gold, and wearing expensive clothing.

It seems easier for us to judge externals than to judge the spirit a person has. There are some who specialize in externals, whose hair, dress and adornment seem quite in order but whose critical attitudes and judgmental spirits identify them with the Pharisees, whom Jesus compared to whited sepulchres, which outwardly appeared clean and white but inside were full of dead men's bones. Oh, that all of us could possess inward purity and fervent love for one another! Harsh, critical spirits then no longer would exist.

Our lives should be dedicated to reaching a world of lost people for the glory of God. Whatever we may be doing that hinders the effectiveness of our Christian testimony we should be willing to lay aside. Those members who are putting on their wedding bands in defiance of the Church's teaching do not have the General Overseer's approval. Why would anyone desire to wear excessive make-up or jewelry when it makes their testimony less effective? At the same time it seems unreasonable for a person who has no reticence about putting color on his/her hair to be critical of others who may put some color on their faces. How do we justify the condemnation of a wedding band on one's finger while allowing for five times that much metal to be worn as an ornament pinned on a garment or worn in the hair?

If we are going to condemn one, it seems reasonable to condemn all. But must we do that? We have seen neckties condemned, curling or straightening the hair condemned, luxury automobiles condemned, expensive clothing condemned, expensive homes condemned. Must the Church enter into such judgments? Are not these things better left to the conscience of the individual? The words of Jesus remain the same: "Judge not, that ye be not judged."

The 80th Assembly in 1985 endorsed a simple lifestyle as more in keeping with the example set for us by our Lord.

"What would Jesus do?" is still an appropriate question for each of us to ask in all matters of conduct. Can we not depend upon the grace of God to teach us to deny ungodliness and worldly lusts and to live soberly, righteously and godly in this present world?

Grace is a great teacher. Grace does not condone sin, it is not even tolerant of sin; it gives us the victory over sin. At the same time it is tolerant of immaturity in the Christian walk. It allows time for spiritual growth, a time of forbearing one another in love while we are coming into the unity of the faith.

To live in the grace of God is not to lower the standard for God's Church. It is the raising of the standard from the legalistic spirit of the old covenant to the beauty of the covenant that has its power in the relationship one has with Jesus Christ, wherein His Word, by the power of His blood, is written in the hearts of His children. In this grace we will love one another with pure hearts, fervently, not judging, not condemning, but rather "endeavoring to keep the unity of the spirit in the bond of peace."

The teaching against wearing gold for ornament first appeared in the Assembly Minutes in 1914. Then in 1922, a book was published by our publishing house titled *Book of Doctrines* which elaborated on the prominent teachings of the Church. On this teaching the following was written:

> Gold serves a real purpose in the world—but not as an ornament, worn for the sole purpose of saying—"Look, I am wealthy, I can afford to spend my money for something that serves no purpose." This is true of all jewelry, such as pins, rings, broaches, etc. of great cost.
>
> There is considerable feeling about the wedding ring, a little inexpensive ring that tells the story of wedlock to all. In New York City, as in most northern states, people look askance at the girl who is acting like a married woman, and even has children, but they do not see the wedding ring. In that case the wedding ring serves a very important purpose. There may be

sections of the country where so much honor is not given the wedding ring. The wedding ring is not worn for ornament. It should not be expensive, not over five dollars. But Church of God people do not feel disposed to be controlled by custom in wearing wedding rings. (Pp. 124, 125.)

So far as I am able to determine, this remained as the Church's position on this teaching until 1944, at which time the Assembly took a much harder position in its elaboration upon this teaching. That year the following statement was approved: "If people are wearing gold for ornament, ninety-nine times out of one hundred, you will find some other sins in their lives."

So in a little over twenty years we went from the position of saying that the wedding ring serves a very important purpose, making an exception for it, to a rather dogmatic position, making no exception, and labeling anyone who wears one as a sinner.

Now I am not necessarily advocating a return to our earlier position which made an exception for the wedding band, but I do feel the statement approved by the Assembly in 1944 was extreme in labeling anyone who wears gold for ornament as a sinner. No distinction is made in this statement as to whether reference is made only to those who are members of the Church. I can see where Christians who are non-members could be offended by this statement whereby they feel we are judging them as sinners just because they are wearing a wedding band.

I do not believe we should make that judgment.

Even if we are speaking only of Church members, I consider this to be an extremely harsh statement. Since it labels the wearing of gold for ornament a sin, does that classify those ministers who are wearing tie pins and cuff links as sinners? If they are sinners, they would need to surrender their licenses. Then how about those bishops' and deacons' wives who are wearing jewelry on their clothing or in their hair? Are we saying they are sinners? If so these bishops and deacons may have to surrender their licenses until their wives repent and get saved. One may say, "O we allow for gold pins and broaches and cuff links, etc." Wherein is our power for such arbitrary allowances?

It seems to me that this statement needs to be reviewed and revised. I have asked the Questions and Subjects Committee to review this ruling of 1944 for a possible revision by the Assembly. This judgment just seems too severe.

It concerns me deeply and it grieves my spirit that we are allowing such small things to claim so much of our attention and to cause so much biting and devouring of one another. Satan must surely be enjoying some of our attitudes. As we prepared to come to this Assembly, I wonder what occupied our minds the most, what our chief concern was. Was it to find greater effectiveness in reaching people who are dropping daily into hell? Or was it to see that "our side wins" in some of these issues Satan is exploiting to divide us and to distract us from our real mission?

That we could get stirred about reaching people! If we were allowed one glimpse into hell and to see in advance those who are going to be dropping into that horrible pit this year, many of whom may be our own children, surely we could see the folly of judging one another, devouring one another over rings and pins. We must return our focus to our mission!

"And Ye Are Complete In Him"

As the Church continues to take form in its progressive development it will reflect more and more the nature of its Builder or of its builders. If we fail to relinquish control to Jesus it will look more and more worldly. But if He builds His Church it will increasingly reflect His nature and His character. To be what God has purposed is for us to grow up into Jesus Christ in all things. He is the express image of God, and it is the Church's privilege to be the expression of her Saviour to the world. Jesus said of His primitive Church, "They are not of the world, even as I am not of the world" (John 17:16). To the church at Ephesus Paul wrote, "In whom [in Jesus] all the building fitly framed together groweth unto an holy temple in the Lord" (Ephesians 2:21).

Holiness is the hallmark of Christ's Church. It most assuredly identifies us with Him. In fact, there is no holiness apart from Him and for us to be a Church of holiness means that our relationship with Him must be genuine. Holiness can be held only in a true relationship with Jesus Christ. He is our holiness. This is the essence of Paul's saying to the church at Corinth, "But of him are ye in Christ Jesus, who of God is made unto us wisdom, and righteousness, and sanctification [holiness], and redemption" (1 Corinthians 1:30).

To abide in Him is to abide in God's holiness. Oh, how wonderful! Man initially was created holy, made in the image of God, but Adam's sin separated him from God, and all of us were born with Adam's mark. We seemed hopelessly estranged, but thanks be to God for the second Adam, the Lord from heaven, who came to this earth and walked among men as the epitome of holiness. He faced all the world's pollution but was not contaminated. He faced Satan head-on and defeated him, and in His death He won the victory over sin for each of us. God's command, "Be ye holy; for I am holy," seemed impossible for us, but Jesus made it possible.

Holiness is the antithesis of worldliness. One cannot be worldly and holy at the same time. Worldly attitudes indicate that one is no longer abiding in Him who is holy. A holy church and a worldly church are a contradiction of terms. Either we are holy or we are worldly. Which is it?

This world needs to see in God's Church an expression of His holiness. It will be little affected by anything less. We know for sure that the Church which Jesus presents unto Himself will be "holy and without blemish" (Ephesians 5:27). But we must never suppose this can be possible apart from Jesus. He is what we need and He is all we need. Jesus, take charge!

To the Colossians Paul wrote, "Beware lest any man spoil you through philosophy and vain deceit, after the tradition of men, after the rudiments of the world, and not after Christ. For in him dwelleth all the fulness of the Godhead bodily. And ye are complete in him . . . " (Colossians 2:8-10). Substitutes abound and are offered continually to pull us away from the sufficiency of Jesus Christ. Some of these substitutes may appear to be good and wholesome, being carried on in the name of Christianity. There are religious activities which can keep us very busy and they may seem commendable and praiseworthy.

The Church which Christ is building, however, is much more than a religious club which does good works. Indeed, it is ". . . his body, the fulness of him that filleth all . . ." (Ephesians 1:23). It is the bodily expression of Christ's love, of His power, of His judgment against sin. It is where Christ reaches out through us to convince the world of God's love for them and of His power to deliver them from sin's enslavement.

Some members seem to feel secure in merely maintaining membership in the Church; others find assurance in abiding by certain aspects of its Advice to Members. Some seem to feel a sense of safety by refraining from the evils of alcohol and drugs, from cursing, swearing, cheating and other vices.

We should thank God for fellowship with one another, and should be thankful for wise counsel and advice. To refrain from sinful indulgences is commendable, but these things can be practiced without having a deep personal relationship with Jesus. We must remember that we are complete only in Him and it is the fulness of Christ being worked out in and through the Church by the Holy Ghost that will enable it to fulfill its purpose for being.

There are those also who view the Church as a kind of static repository for truth. They would spend their time refining and defending doctrinal positions. Discussing, debating, disputing, arguing appeals to them. Their counterparts in the days of Jesus were the Pharisees and Sadducees, men who tried to engage Jesus in quibbling over points of law. Jesus refused to become sidetracked by these who cared little for people but rather were obsessed with their debatings.

He never lost sight of His mission. He had come to seek and to save the lost. As we become one with Him, finding our completeness in Him, being His body, "the fulness of him that filleth all in all," we also will refuse to become bogged down by trivia. We will refuse all religious substitutes Satan would foist upon us which prevent true ministering to a hurting world.

Rather than being a so-called static repository the Church is to be a dynamic force, assaulting the strongholds of Satan, rescuing souls being held in his grasp. People need deliverance no less today than when Jesus walked on earth. It is for us to observe His manner of ministry and to know that we are His body on earth right now. As the Father sent Him into the world, even so He has sent us. We must not fail Him, or the world to which we have been sent. Satan would have us arguing with and attacking one another. May God help us to recognize this as a diversion planned by our enemy and to be steadfast in focusing upon our mission. We have a work to do!

Fervent Love From Pure Hearts

"Seeing ye have purified your souls in obeying the truth through the Spirit unto unfeigned love of the brethren, see that ye love one another with a pure heart fervently" (1 Peter 1:22).

Obedience to the truth as the Holy Ghost had visited them had brought a love among the brethren that did not have to be pretended. It was real; it was genuine. It was that love which Paul described as having been "shed abroad in our hearts by the Holy Ghost" (Romans 5:5). Now Peter is saying to the saints who had received this divine gift, " . . . see that ye love one another with a pure heart fervently."

The Church that honors God and which will be able to communicate the gospel of Christ effectively is a fellowship of loving, caring people. The degree to which they remain united in mission will be determined by the quality of their love. That is why Peter's charge to the saints nineteen centuries ago was included in the Holy Scriptures for us to read today, and at this crucial time through which we are now passing there is no more timely message for us to observe. Fervent love from pure hearts will defeat every attempt by Satan to divide the Church and thereby weaken its testimony to a perishing world which so desperately needs deliverance.

What hope does this world have if the Church fails? Is it any wonder that Satan is at work to create divisions? That is his most effective strategy. But Satan's power cannot succeed where there is fervent love from pure hearts. It is only when love wanes that our enemy is successful.

It pleased God that His Church be comprised of diverse personalities. Distinctive differences exist as its members come from different cultures and backgrounds, each one being influenced by the traditions which have shaped his own thinking. Now you might think that it would be wonderful if every other member thought just like you do, but that is not the fellowship of which God chose for you to be a part. He has placed you in the Church with me and thousands of others whose thinking has been influenced by traditions and cultures to which you may never have been subjected. We all have our differences.

Yet, we have been brought together in one body, according to the will of God. We do not agree on everything. We do not all see alike. But can we not all love alike? Peter said, "See that ye love one another with a pure heart fervently." Later in this letter he wrote, "And above all things have fervent charity among yourselves" (4:8). Paul called this charity "the bond of perfectness" (Colossians 3:14).

Someone has said, "Where love is thick, faults are thin." By the same token it may be said that where love is thin, faults are thick. In the absence of fervent charity we most often find critical, judgmental attitudes where there is fault-finding, mote-hunting and condemning one another. Not only are sinners whom we have been commissioned to reach repelled by such harsh attitudes, but we ourselves come under the judgment of God. Even now in His mercy His judgment lingers as He waits for our repentance, but we dare not wait longer before crying out to Him for a restoration of divine love, that "first love" restoration which He demanded of the church at Ephesus.

Need we be reminded that we are one body and all members one of another? But union does not automatically make unity. Yet, unity is the demand of God for His Church and something for which Christ earnestly prayed, but it is something for which a price is to be paid. It is a costly endeavor. It requires forbearance and longsuffering; it requires self-denial. Paul wrote, "With all lowliness and meekness, with longsuffering, forbearing one another in love; Endeavouring to keep the unity of the Spirit in the bond of peace" (Ephesians 4:2, 3).

Love is the strength of forbearance. Love is the power for longsuffering. It will cause us to forego personal pleasures, even legitimate pleasures, which we know might be offensive to a brother or sister.

"We then that are strong ought to bear the infirmities of the weak, and not to please ourselves. Let every one of us please his neighbour for his good to edification. For even Christ pleased not himself. . . . Now the God of patience and consolation grant you to be likeminded one toward another . . . that ye may with one mind and one mouth glorify God. . . . Wherefore receive ye one another, as Christ also received us to the glory of God" (Romans 15:1-3, 5-7). When Paul says, ". . . receive ye one another" is he not saying, "Accept one another"?

If you are my brother I must accept you even when I do not agree with you. Earlier, in the fourteenth chapter Paul wrote, "Him that is weak in the faith receive ye, but not to doubtful disputations" (v. 1). Accept the weaker brother, he says, but not to argue and dispute with him. Such disputing shows Christian immaturity. To accept him as a brother is to love him, and through mutual forbearance to grow together.

The Church at Rome was composed of both Jews and Gentiles. The Jewish members had grown up with the observance of ceremonial laws concerning meats and days, while the Gentile members did not consider these things as being relevant to their salvation. They felt that every creature was good and nothing to be refused if received with thanksgiving, that it was sanctified by the Word of God and prayer. Others disagreed, and felt they should refrain from certain meats, some being vegetarians.

Those members who felt obligated still to ceremonial laws esteemed certain days above others—the feast days, the new moons, the sabbaths—while some of their fellow members knew that these observances were abolished by Christ's coming and esteemed every day alike. Paul's plea was for tolerance and forbearance rather than for uniformity. He knew there could be unity without uniformity. His instruction was, "Let not him that eateth despise him that eateth not; and let not him which eateth not judge him that eateth: for God hath received him" (Romans 14:3). The apostle's reasoning was that if God has received or accepted a person we should also.

It would be presumptuous for us to say, "Well, God may accept you, but we can't." Do we presume ourselves to be holier than God? Are our standards higher than His?

Paul's message to the saints at Rome was that some differences could be tolerated within the Church. It was not so much the differences between the Jewish and the Gentile members that was destructive as it was the manner in which these differences were being handled. It was their attitudes toward one another. Those who were knowledgeable in the liberties Christ had brought were despising those who failed to understand. Fervent love would have prevented such feelings. Knowledge without love still causes members to be puffed up with feelings of superiority. At the same time the Jewish Christians judged and censured the others as breakers of the law and considered them as not being very consecrated. The need was for mutual forbearance through fervent love.

In verse six Paul wrote, "He that regardeth the day, regardeth it unto the Lord; and he that regardeth not the day, to the Lord he doth not regard it. He that eateth, eateth to the Lord, for he giveth God thanks; and he that eateth not, to the Lord he eateth not, and giveth God thanks." Instead of pushing for a verdict to which all would align themselves, the apostle seemed willing to let the ceremonial law wither by degrees, and to let it have an honorable burial. He did not take a stout stand against all further adherence to ceremonial laws. Today, some traditions may be continued as something we feel is right for us, but we should not seek to impose our traditions upon others. There are places where some of our sisters feel very strongly, for example, that they should not go into a worship service without a hat or other covering upon their heads. These people should not be condemned for this, because they are doing it unto the Lord. At the same time they must not condemn others who feel no necessity for covering their heads in this manner.

I believe we have pressed beyond its true application the verse of Scripture which says, " . . . let us walk by the same rule, let us mind the same thing" (Philippians 3:16). We may note that the apostle did not say "the same rules," but "the same rule." Was he not referring to the rule of faith as opposed to the works of the law?

I believe he was. Jesus purposed that His Church would be operated by grace through faith.

While advocating tolerance toward the brethren who felt obligated to keep the Jewish traditions, Paul stood firmly against any legalistic spirit which sought to preempt the spirit of grace. He would not tolerate any demeaning of the grace of God, which is the spirit of the new covenant. We have to admire Paul's vision of an all-nations Church, comprised of some people who would never be willing to subject themselves to the narrow views of a Jewish group whose numbers in the future would be decreasing in proportion to the great influx of Gentile members. These newcomers soon would constitute the larger membership of the Church.

Today we might profit from a similar broadness of vision. Although we had our beginning here in the Southeastern United States, we want to make certain that we do not seek to perpetuate traditions which an expanding, global

Church will find unacceptable among those by whom only biblical truth is respected. Courage was required, when other apostles were perpetuating narrowness, for Paul to withstand them, defending the principle of pure grace for Christ's Church. Such courage today will resist our being a Southeastern church, or a United States church, but stand strong in the commitment that we be the Church of God of the Bible. That is the Church which bows in submission to its Head, being willing to relinquish human control while praying, "Jesus, take charge!"

The Illustration Explained

(The following is taken from the tape of the General Overseer's presentation with a minimal amount of editing. The parenthetical explanations have been added to identify what was drawn to what was said—Assistant Editor.)

Introduction
I'd like a chalkboard if I may have. Oh, thank the Lord. I felt like using an illustration here and I didn't know how to do it with my hands, so I asked them if they would bring this chalkboard out. I hope to illustrate something here that I think is meaningful. I am searching, I am praying, and you can believe me brothers and sisters, I have been agonizing over some of these things that just ought not to be.

Picture 1
Now here is where we are, my friends. There is a spectrum here (the line), and some of us are off over here on this side (dot on line's left end), and some of us are off over here on this side (dot on line's right end). And both are wanting the other to come to them, but we are all members of the Church. We are all born by the same Spirit, saved by the same grace. Amen!

Picture 2
From time to time there will be a little movement (shaded area in line). This happens not just with us, it happens in

many organizations. There are other groups today that have division among themselves, trying to make attempts to get together, but it does not work because they are doing it all wrong. From time to time you will see a little movement over this direction (shaded area on line moving toward the other end) from those who are more firmly established on that side. And then you will see a little movement from this side (other shaded area). What everybody thinks is, maybe we will come together here (center dot on the line). That's not it. It's not going to work. But we think so. You see, so we try it. You see this side move for awhile and then move back (shaded area moves to center then back again). They don't feel comfortable out here; never have been out here before. "I am going back to where I feel comfortable" (back to dot on end of line). See, I'm not taking sides here; both of them work the same way. These try to make a movement (other shaded area). After awhile they get out here where they have never been. They don't like it out here (away from the end of the line) and want to get back to their camp. And so this is the problem we have. But, I want to say what I believe is the solution.

Picture 3
There is One right up here (dot on top). His name is JESUS CHRIST!

Picture 4
And the way for these folks here to move is not this way (along the base of the triangle) but to move this way (up the triangle's side). The solution for these is not to move this way (other dot on the end moving along base), but to move this way (up the triangle side).

Picture 5
Now, let me go a little further. What has happened in the past (it happens in other groups as well as here) is that every once in awhile there will be a little movement up here (one side moves up the triangle's side). We go along and the

other side moves up and sees that we are closer together than we once were. So we say, "Why don't we just come right here and get together?" (second horizontal line of triangle) But that's not going to work; that's not the place. It is going to be tempting, when we get closer together up here (small line at near top of triangle) to say, "Now we are surely close enough. Let's come together." That's not the place either, and you will find yourself pulling back over (to the sides of the triangle). But this is He! (the apex of the triangle). This is He—we have got to come together in Jesus Christ! He is the Head of the Church, He is the Sovereign Lord, He is the Saviour of the Body! And He alone can save the Body today! But to get there, we are going to have to be willing to leave here (the end-most points of the triangle's base). We are going to finally have to give up and say, "Jesus, we can't do it, please take charge!"

Picture 6

Let me add something; I believe there is something even more significant there. We may have Him in the wrong place right there (apex of triangle). It may be that He is here (dot at the bottom of chalkboard), which is going to take some humbling of ourselves from that position to come down here where He is (making the sides of the bottom triangle). We cannot be exalted above Him! We have got to come down to Jesus Christ! We have got to come down to the cross of Jesus Christ! Hallelujah! It is by the cross, by His death, that we are going to be one! There is no other way to do it, my friend. We are fighting a losing battle to try it another way. This has got to be the way. Hallelujah!

Strong Local Churches

"And so were the churches established in the faith, and increased in number daily" (Acts 16:5). God's Church has its existence and its growth in local congregations. This is where members assemble regularly for fellowship and instruction in the Word of God. There these members are instrumental in bringing others to Christ as their lives reflect God's love and demonstrate Christ's power over sin. It is in the nurture of a local fellowship that members are strengthened spiritually as they engage in a relentless battle with their adversary, both to resist Satan's attempts to destroy them, and to rescue others from his grasp. As Jesus builds His Church it will be built in local congregations. In our text Luke records that it was local churches which were increasing in number daily. That is where sinners were being led to Jesus, that is where members were being added to the Body of Christ. And today, that is still where growth occurs and where members find food for their souls.

Most of the New Testament was written to local churches. In the New Testament we find letters to churches at Rome, Corinth, Galatia, Ephesus, Philippi, Colosse, Smyrna, Pergamos, Thyatira, Sardis, Philadelphia, and Laodicea. As the local churches go, so goes the Church of God. So, as we pray, "Jesus, take charge!" we are praying that He will take charge of our local churches.

We have some thriving local churches where sinners are continually being saved, churches where both numerical and spiritual growth is evident. In these churches members are excited about what God is doing and they are dedicating themselves to even greater efforts of outreach as they experience a growing relationship with their Saviour. In too many places this is not the case, however, and without an infusion of new life some of these churches will soon cease to exist.

We must give more attention to the development of strong local churches. This demands strong, able leadership. Thank God for those pastors who are dedicating themselves to the greatest challenge in the Church of God, that of providing leadership to build strong local churches. There is no higher ministry in the Church.

In the past there seems to have been a pervasive feeling that if a pastor did well he might get elevated to a higher office. In my opinion there is no higher office, and I hope we can squash that kind of thinking. The Assembly last year recommended a rotation of those under General Appointment periodically into other types of ministry. Because of the mentality which has developed over the years, it is difficult for some to feel they are not receiving a demotion when this occurs.

To me, some of the finest ministers we have in the Church are in pastoral ministry, and to join their ranks is not a demotion.

The ministries we have at our General Headquarters and in our National/State offices are supportive ministries to support our local churches. The pastors and local churches are not there to serve us; we exist to aid them. Some work seems more effective through the combined efforts of our local churches coordinated through our administrative offices, such as world missions, literature preparation, etc., and in these efforts we here at headquarters are seen as laborers together with you. Otherwise, however, the National/State and the General level must be viewed as supporting ministries of our local churches. That is where growth occurs, that is where souls are saved, and that is where members are added to the Body of Christ.

I believe our efforts to plant new churches would be more effective if they were directed through local churches. Each church should view itself as a mission station, reaching out to its area in an ongoing mission of evangelization, with a burden to reach people with the gospel which will change their lives. I believe this burden can produce growth, and a growing church having this burden will soon be extending itself into neighboring communities, establishing branches of itself which can be "mothered" to become other strong local congregations.

I am not speaking of simply splitting an existing church just to create two weaker congregations. Rather, we must pray for the burden to evangelize to take such possession of us that we will be continually growing. A strong local church can develop to where it soon will have grown outside its own community. At first it may be the development of a satellite mission, but this can be nurtured or "mothered" to become a local congregation, which before long could repeat the process and become the mother of yet another local church.

We may have left church planting too much to the National/State offices. While they can be supportive, and there may be a mission field which develops that is not near any existing local church, in which the National/State office must be heavily involved, yet the idea of new churches being "mothered" by strong local churches seems most practical.

I believe we need a new vision of the need for, and the potential of, these strong local churches. Whatever is hindering their development must be discovered and eliminated. This world must be evangelized and the New Testament shows the heavy involvement in this mission by the local church. The church at Antioch as a case study can be enlightening.

The church at Antioch evidently was a strong church with strong leadership. "Now there were in the church that was at Antioch certain prophets and teachers; as Barnabas, and Simeon . . . and Lucius . . . and Manaen . . . and Saul. As they ministered to the Lord, and fasted, the Holy Ghost said, Separate me Barnabas and Saul for the work whereunto I have called them. And when they had fasted and prayed, and laid their hands on them, they sent them away. So they, being sent forth by the Holy Ghost, departed unto Seleucia; and from thence they sailed to Cyprus" (Acts 13:1-4).

As Luke recounts this missionary journey of Paul and Barnabas, he concludes it by saying, "And after they had passed throughout Pisidia, they came to Pamphylia. And when they had preached the word in Perga, they went down into Attalia: And thence sailed to Antioch, from whence they had been recommended to the grace of God for the work which they fulfilled. And when they were come, and had gathered the church together, they rehearsed all that God had done with them" (Acts 14:24-27).

We see here a local church with which the Holy Ghost was much involved as He directed them in sending out two great missionaries. It was a fasting church, it was a praying church, a church sensitive to the Spirit. It was in this local church that hands were laid upon these two men, separating them unto this special assignment by God. This was a matter taken care of by these brethren's local church.

It seems proper that our local churches bear responsibility in setting apart members of their congregation for ministry according to the will of God. Of course, this has been practiced for many years as members have been set forth in the business meetings to be examined by the presbytery for licensure in different ministries.

If our churches are to be strengthened there must be a proper function of spiritually gifted members. Deacons, for example, can relieve a pastor from becoming cumbered with duties which distract him from his primary task of prayer and the ministry of the Word. As deacons assume their supportive roles as servants of the local church they are to be appreciated.

The question has arisen as to whether the deacon is a purely local church servant, or whether he is a minister to be recognized by the General Church. Our practice has been to license him as a General Church minister and to ordain him by the laying on of hands by the presbytery. By this he has been honored, in many cases beyond the one who serves as his pastor, many of whom have never been ordained.

While pastors have been called upon to be willing to leave their homes and to go anywhere in order to fulfill their ministry, deacons have not been asked to make such sacrifices. Is it proper to make such a distinction, then, by ordination by the presbytery for deacons, or should this be a ministry for recognition by the local churches?

This is not to downplay the importance of deacons, because it is a biblical function. However, it may be more proper that these be chosen and ordained within the local church, rather than to become licensed ministers whose credentials are signed by the General and State/National Overseers.

We have some who are referred to as preaching deacons. It might be better for these to be relicensed in the preaching ministry.

I have asked the Questions and Subjects Committee to study this matter for presentation to the Assembly if they should feel it proper. Whatever we do, we want it to be a means of building strong local churches.

Reaching Forth

16

Annual Address to the 87th General Assembly, 1992

"Not as though I had already attained, either were already perfect: but I follow after, if that I may apprehend that for which also I am apprehended of Christ Jesus. Brethren, I count not myself to have apprehended: but this one thing I do, forgetting those things which are behind, and reaching forth unto those things which are before, I press toward the mark for the prize of the high calling of God in Christ Jesus" (Philippians 3:12-14).

There was no greater apostle than Paul. He had experiences none of the others had known. His conversion experience was powerful. Being caught up into the third heaven to hear words unlawful to utter was something experienced uniquely by this apostle to the Gentiles. We are thrilled by the account of his deliverance from a Philippian jail, of the story of his shipwreck and of his shaking a venomous serpent into the fire, suffering no harm from its poisonous bite. Our imaginations soar as to what it was like when an angel stood beside him on a ship, assuring him that he would arrive safely at Rome with all those who were traveling with him. We read the account of his plans being changed when the Spirit forbade his going to Bithynia and a man appeared in a vision praying him to come to Macedonia. All of us have longed at times for such direct guidance by God.

Now this man writing from prison in Rome, with such a remarkable history of powerful ministry, who might have rested in the reminiscences of a full and eventful life, had no disposition for spending his time in such reflections. We see him, rather, saying, ". . . forgetting those things which are behind, and reaching forth unto those things which are before." Paul was not content with the present measures of God's grace. He was not content to dwell in a familiar spiritual place; he felt in his spirit that there was more for him to know, more for him to experience.

The term "reaching forth" indicates a "stretching forward." It is expressive of a vehement desire. His spirit was akin to David's as he wrote, "As the hart panteth after the water brooks, so panteth my soul after thee, O God. My soul thirsteth for God, for the living God" (Psalms 42:1, 2). To rest on any plateau of spiritual attainment is to insure the setting in of Laodicean lukewarmness, a state which God despises. It is His desire to reveal Himself to His creatures, and the provision for this revelation has been so wondrously wrought in Jesus. And now the Holy Ghost is active in giving illumination to this glorious revelation to all who will respond to Him as He visits them.

Paul knew and appreciated the ministry of the Holy Ghost. He knew what it was to pray with the spirit, and to pray with the understanding also. He knew from experience the Spirit's praying for him with groanings that could not be uttered (cf. Romans 8:26). In short, Paul knew the meaning of life in the Spirit. It was this vibrant relationship with the Holy Ghost that caused him to be continually reaching forth for a yet fuller knowledge of his Lord. He was totally captivated by God's revelation of Himself in Jesus Christ, and his vehement desire to know this incomprehensible God forbade his resting at any plateau of spiritual growth. He, rather, was always "reaching forth."

For Paul, this was a personal matter. Notice his use of the personal pronoun "I." "I count all things but loss . . . that I may win Christ . . . That I may know him . . . I follow after . . . that I may apprehend that for which also I am apprehended. . . . reaching forth unto those things which are before, I press toward the mark" (Philippians 3:8-14). He did not hide himself within a local church, waiting for the church's response to the Spirit to somehow pull him along with it.

His initial encounter with Jesus on the road to Damascus was a very personal one which he recounted many times: ". . . suddenly there shone from heaven a great light round about me. And I fell unto the ground, and heard a voice saying unto me, Saul, Saul, why persecutest thou me? . . . . And they that were with me saw indeed the light, and were afraid; but they heard not the voice of him that spake to me. And I said, What shall I do, Lord? And the Lord said unto me, Arise, and go into Damascus" (Acts 22:6-10).

His call into the ministry was personal: "And I thank Christ Jesus our Lord . . . for that he counted me faithful, putting me into the ministry" (1 Timothy 1:12). His recounting of this experience to the Galatians was like this: "But when it pleased God, who separated me from my mother's womb, and called me by his grace, to reveal his Son in me, that I might preach him among the heathen [Gentiles]; immediately I conferred not with flesh and blood: Neither went I up to Jerusalem to them which were apostles before me; but I went into Arabia . . ." (Galatians 1:15-17).

Yes, Paul's conversion was very personal; his call to preach was very personal; and now, as he nears the end of his life in prison at Rome, his commitment of reaching forth, of pressing toward a mark that was yet higher, was a personal one. Even so it must be a personal matter with each of us. No one can do your spiritual growing for you.

Then he suddenly turns his attention toward the Church, as he writes, "Let us therefore, as many as he perfect, be thus minded. . . . Nevertheless, whereto we have already attained, let us walk . . ." (Philippians 3:15, 16). The local church at Philippi needed to catch that same spirit which Paul had personally, the spirit of reaching forth. This apostle was captivated by a heavenly vision of what was possible for him to apprehend, of what he, by God's grace, could attain, and this local church needed to be "thus minded."

Our local churches today need to be captivated by a vision, a vision as to just what God's purposes for them are, and then to be reaching forth to become what God has designed that they be. The success of the universal Church depends upon the success of our local churches. It is of God's design to place within the local church divinely gifted ministries to create the functioning Body of Christ in that church's locality. Why should not all the gifts of the Spirit be manifested in each local church? This would include not only the manifestations listed in 1 Corinthians 12, but the grace gifts of Romans 12, as well as the gifted ministries of Ephesians 4. Each local church needs to be a microcosm of the whole Church, functioning to show forth God's glory, bringing men and women, boys and girls to the only Saviour they can ever know.

Our local churches must come alive in the Spirit! They must be ministering bodies which offer help to hurting people, people whose lives have been devastated by Satan. If people cannot find help in our local churches, where will they find it? Oh, for pastors with vision, teachers with vision, leaders with vision, members with vision! We must have a local church leadership which sees that which is now invisible, a leadership that is reaching forth to bring that vision to reality through strong local churches. We cannot be satisfied with things as they are.

Then these local churches are not to be totally autonomous, independent of one another. They are a part of the whole which we call the Body of Christ. This is the Church which Jesus began in Galilee and which John described in Revelation 19 as the Lamb's wife which had made herself ready for the marriage. This Assembly is representative of that larger Body of Christ of which each of our local churches is a part. Here in this Assembly there must prevail the spirit of reaching forth. We are firmly committed to being the Church of God of the Bible, that Church which we see functioning embryonically in the gospels, then with great power in the Book of Acts, the Church whose doctrine is further set forth in the epistles.

Other groups may feel free to embrace only those things which would be acceptable or palatable to their constituency, but God's Church cannot do so. It must be faithful to Him. Christ is its Head and we must make certain that we submit to the exercise of His headship among us at all times. We must not limit ourselves to a certain list of prominent teachings, we must be reaching forth as a body to understand and observe every principle contained in this New Testament which comes to us through His blood.

Not only must we stand firm against the divorce and remarriage evil, we must know that to look on another person with lustful desire is to commit adultery in the heart. The principles of the New Testament are fully observable only by sanctified hearts. Let us know that Church doctrine is more than a list of what could be construed as creedal statements. Christ's Church must take the New Testament as its rule of faith [doctrine], and within this blessed gospel of grace, we must search to understand all its principles.

Not even Paul seemed able to spell out everything in detail. In his letter to the Galatians, when he was enumerating the works of the flesh, after naming adultery, fornication, uncleanness, lasciviousness, idolatry, witchcraft, hatred, variance, emulations, wrath, strife, seditions, heresies, envyings, murders, drunkenness and revellings, he concluded the list by saying "and such like" (Galatians 5:21). The "such like" will be recognizable by people who are sanctified.

Grace never seeks to justify any wrongdoing simply because a certain word to describe that wrongdoing may not be found in the Bible. Grace has its strength in relationship with Jesus, and the principles which meet His approval are clearly set forth in the Scriptures. Let us not get caught up in creedal living. Some seem to feel they must give their support only to what may be included in a list of teachings or advice. This could cause a person to be lost.

Is not the commandment to love one another, for example, Church of God doctrine? I believe it is. A commandment of Jesus is a teaching of Jesus, and the teachings of Jesus are the doctrines of Jesus, and His doctrine and Church doctrine should be one and the same. There is no greater doctrine than to love God and to love one another. In John 13:34, Jesus said, "A new commandment I give unto you, That ye love one another; as I have loved you, that ye also love one another."

There are members of the Church who would not dare use tobacco, drink alcoholic beverages, join a lodge, or swear in court, because these things are all included in a list of prohibitions. These same people have little reticence to join in a smear campaign of gossip or rumor-mongering against a brother or sister. Such actions must surely be deplorable to the God of all grace. These people obviously know little about the grace of God which teaches us to live godly in this present world.

Those people who are possessed by a spirit of reaching forth to know Jesus are not going to get caught up in critical attitudes where they will try to destroy a fellow Christian's credibility through rumor-mongering and gossip. That spirit belongs to the "accuser of the brethren," as John described Satan (cf. Revelation 12:10).

The people who are reaching forth to know Jesus—stretching forward with vehement desire—are the people who will one day arrive at the knowledge of the Son of God. They will have come into the unity of the faith, they will have become a glorious Church, holy and without blemish.

A complacent, legalistic Church will never qualify for the Rapture—it will be the people who do know their God. This glorious knowledge is the product of a fervent spirit of reaching forth to what is yet ahead.

Headquarters and the Local Churches

Within the past few months, we have been forced to review the role and function of our General Headquarters.

Through the years we have advocated a strong central government with a view to maintaining unity of faith and purpose. The mandate for unity within Christ's Church is clearly set forth in the Scriptures, and we do not want to do anything to prevent its realization. In fact, we want to do all we can through the power of God's grace to expedite the true biblical unity of our churches and among all the family of God. At the same time, we must recognize and acknowledge that this is truly a work of the Spirit, a work which human strategies can never accomplish. Some of our plans and projections of the past, we are now able to see, were evidently of our own thinking, rather than being the product of Holy Ghost direction—not all, but some. Misguided zeal without knowledge can take us away from the course that God's will dictates.

Now we are having to determine where we have followed God and where human wisdom may have been accepted as being divine. Theocratic government is a "must" for God's Church. Of that fact, there is no room for argument. That does not mean, however, that all direction must proceed from a General Headquarters. Theocracy literally means, "God rule." God can speak to sincere and searching hearts everywhere and exercise His rule in their lives. We do know that He never contradicts Himself, because in His wisdom and knowledge He is absolutely perfect; so, there is the need for spiritual organization to resolve the differences between what actually proceeded from God and what was incorrectly presumed to have proceeded from God. The New Testament is very plain in its teaching of order and government for Christ's Church and of submitting one to another.

In our emphasis upon a strong central government, we may not have placed enough emphasis upon the development of strong local churches. We must acknowledge that this is the emphasis of the New Testament. It was local churches to which Paul's letters were written. In the Book of Revelation, it was seven local churches to which Christ addressed His concerns through John. When God would send Paul and Barnabas on their missionary journey, He visited their local church to initiate this action.

Within that local church at Antioch, there was strong leadership referred to as prophets and teachers. Luke records it like this: "Now there were in the church . . . at Antioch certain prophets and teachers. . . . As they ministered to the Lord, and fasted, the Holy Ghost said, Separate me Barnabas and Saul for the work whereunto I have called them. And when they had fasted and prayed, and laid their hands on them, they sent them away. So they, being sent forth by the Holy Ghost, departed unto Seleucia; and from thence they sailed to Cyprus" (Acts 13:1-4). Thus, we see the Holy Ghost at work in a local church to initiate a missionary ministry that has been without parallel.

Today, I believe there is a need for a central headquarters. There are some things we can do better collectively than we can do individually, such as translating and publishing literature, initiating and supervising global missions, involving ourselves in mass communications and in ministerial leadership development. Even in some of these things, I see the function of our General Headquarters as being to serve the local churches. Then, for sure, such Headquarters' ministries as Sunday School, Pastoral Care, Children's Ministries, etc., definitely are to support the local churches' ministries.

It is my feeling that the General Headquarters should be a resource center for many of the ministries in which our churches are engaged, but with growth and enlargement, more of these eventually can be shifted to the national and regional levels. It is there that the specific needs of the various areas will be better understood, and from there they can be serviced more effectively.

Pastors must assume a more aggressive leadership role in pursuing ministries for reaching and discipling people in their communities. The local community is where growth will occur. It cannot be taken for granted any longer that just to have regular services faithfully will assure that new people will be reached. We must have in place inspirational ministries. The dynamics of small group ministries, for example, has not yet taken hold in most of our churches, although this has been promoted from General Headquarters since 1916. It was first called Watchers Over Tens, then Assembly Band Movement and now Pastoral Care.

Maintaining a department for the promotion of this concept from General Headquarters, through the years, has cost the Church millions of dollars, yet for the most part, it still has not taken hold where it counts—that is, in our local churches. And until our pastors catch the vision, until they sense the benefit of this ministry, our churches will continue to suffer from the lack of its implementation. I see this ministry as necessary for developing strong local churches. Pastoral vision is essential for this ministry to flourish. They must see it as more than just an auxiliary promotion from General Headquarters, but as a means for true fellowship in reaching out through body ministry to penetrate our communities.

So long as pastors feel their activities are being planned for them from the General, National or State offices, they will not take the initiative of true inspirational leadership which God intended. The time has come for these offices to become resource centers for pastors and local churches, with the initiative for accessing these resources coming from aggressive pastors who have a vision of what their churches can become. Perhaps it is time for us to listen to our pastors and churches tell us what services they need that we can provide. It has been over twenty-five years since I pastored a local church, and I know that times have changed. As for me, I'm willing to listen and then to respond to what can be done from my office to help build strong local churches. When we see ourselves as being support ministries, we will no longer hold a view that we are directing the work. This direction will come from God to our local churches, and we will make ourselves available and accessible to provide certain valuable services of assistance.

Discipleship ministering is necessary—which I take to mean assisting people toward their Christian development and maturity. We need sound spiritual teaching ministries in all our churches. It is of God's design that every member be a worker. In respect to the ministering that every church is to be involved in, we may have made too great a separation between the responsibilities of clergy and laity. I believe it is God's will that each local church be a ministering body, with every member functioning according to his particular giftedness which he has received from God. We must ask whether pastoral leadership has been sensitive enough to the Spirit in equipping all the members to be able to fulfill their personal ministries for which God has uniquely set each of them in the body.

Pastors must take a new look at what is being done toward this end. It is time for a new emphasis on teaching, nurturing and equipping members to minister. Sunday school can be a wasted hour or it can be a productive ministry. Real progress for nurturing and equipping through this arm of the church will not just happen. It will come about through teachers who have a vision of discipling, who are willing to pour their lives into the lives of others. Sunday morning can be one of the times for this to occur, but it must not be the only time.

In some places, we are seeing a decreasing interest in Sunday school, with the morning worship hour drawing more people than are in attendance for Sunday school. This has caused some churches to consider abandoning Sunday school in lieu of Wednesday evening Bible studies, thus having an extended worship time on Sunday morning. Worship is very important, but we must make certain that teaching and discipling is being pursued. We do know that Sunday school offers a means of use for the gifted ministries of many individuals. Let me reiterate, however, that these ministries must not be limited to one hour on Sunday morning. Instead of abandoning that time on Sunday morning, perhaps we should consider extending this teaching and discipling ministry through some midweek sessions. Aggressive pastors with vision will be able to see what possibilities exist. May we all be directed by God's grace!

The Ladies Retreats that have been supervised from General Headquarters have blessed many people. I foresee the time when these functions will be directed more from the national, regional or state offices. In fact, with the development of large, strong churches such activities can be carried out by local churches, as could be Men's Retreats, Couples or Family Retreats. There are resources currently available for local churches to become involved in family ministries from some excellent para-church organizations. With the family institution under such strong attack by Satanic forces, there is a pressing need for our churches to pursue more aggressive ministries to their families.

I had considered appointing someone to head a department of family ministries in this Assembly, but this might be simply perpetuating a system of our trying to provide from here what could be done at the local church level. We must ask why at General Headquarters we should try to produce and duplicate materials that are accessible from other sources and are based on sound biblical principles. Our national, regional and state offices can be resourceful in directing pastors to the availability of helpful video, audio and printed materials. We must minister to the family, God's primary institution.

National, Regional and State Overseers should take stock of the local churches under their supervision, and where there are churches having successful ministries, they can encourage the sharing by these pastors with other pastors who are needing some help. Things may not work exactly the same way in every church, and pastors should be given liberty to be resourceful in making adaptations for what is most suitable in their respective churches. Everything cannot be dictated or administrated from the general, national, regional or state offices. God's design is to communicate personally to individuals and to local churches. It was so in the days of the Apostles, and it is still so today. The ministries of our administrative offices are limited. It is in local churches that people come to the Lord. There they are baptized and nurtured as fellow members in a local body.

Your General Headquarters, as I view it, must become more of a resource facility, providing video, audio and printed materials for helping to develop leadership for strong, growing churches—for youth and children's ministries, women's ministries, small group ministries, for Sunday school and Bible studies, and other needs our churches may require. As we redirect our Headquarters operations, we must admit that in the past we have tried to do too much from here. Local churches have been made to feel that their direction should be received from the administrative offices. This is neither proper nor biblical. The New Testament does not support this principle.

True, there was a council at Jerusalem to deal with the questions of Jewish law and traditions being imposed upon the Gentiles, but the decrees handed down were for assuring freedom for a Spirit-led Church. And now we must emphasize a greater responsibility of the pastors and the local church to look to God for guidance and direction. Pastors need to provide inspirational leadership as they feed with knowledge and understanding, and gifted members must function with divine anointing. Local churches must make their presence felt in their communities. It is of God's design that they be salt and light. People are lost and hurting and we must recognize that we have been commissioned and sent by God to minister to them.

It was never intended that a state, national or General Headquarters should dictate the ministering to your communities. The Holy Ghost can still break in upon a local congregation to give direction and guidance as He did to the church at Antioch. It is most likely to occur as that church assumes the posture held by the Antioch church, which was "as they ministered to the Lord and fasted."

Nothing can take the place of spiritual life and power. Each member's personal relationship with Jesus Christ must be given top priority. We cannot share what we do not have. God waits to work through yielded instruments, and He will do it in your city, your town, your community. May His grace abound in every life to give richness to the testimony of our local churches.

The Battle Is the Lord's

"Then said David to the Philistine, Thou comest to me with a sword, and with a spear, and with a shield: but I come to thee in the name of the Lord of hosts, the God of the armies of Israel, whom thou hast defied. This day will the Lord deliver thee into mine hand . . . that all the earth may know that there is a God in Israel. And all this assembly shall know that the Lord saveth not with sword and spear: for the battle is the Lord's" (1 Samuel 17:45-47).

All of us, including our children, know the outcome of this battle. With his sling, David released a stone, but it was God who directed the stone to its mark and caused it to sink deep into the forehead of this Philistine giant. David's assertion was correct for that particular day which is imprinted in Israel's history, and it is also correct for the Church of God in 1992, as we stand upon the battlefield where a far more important battle is being decided, that assertion being, "for the battle is the Lord's."

Our enemy is Satan. He is not a mythological character. He is real, and he opposes everything that is good, pure and wholesome—everything that is decent, everything that is of God. Except for this Deceiver, we would not know sin, trouble, sorrow or grief. We would all be at peace with God and with one another. There would be no divisions and no strife. We can be comforted by the fact that one day he will be banished forever into the darkness of eternity.

At the present moment, he is alive on this earth to enslave and to destroy all God's creatures, as much as it is in his power to do so. Our victories over this vile enemy are assured not by any human strategies, but by the victory that was won over him by Jesus Christ when He triumphed over him through His death and resurrection. Jesus descended from heaven into Satan's domain and on his own territory won the victory over him for every one of us.

What Satan must have thought was a sure victory over the Son of God, as he beheld Him being nailed to the cross, was God's means of providing for every man the way of release from this Deceiver's power. Then when within three days Jesus arose from Joseph's tomb, our victory over the devil was guaranteed. Jesus assures to everyone who trusts Him complete deliverance, glorious liberty forevermore from all the power of this enemy. What a perfect victory, indeed, that Jesus won for us. There is no victory over Satan's power for anyone apart from Jesus Christ. We literally enter into this victory by entering into Christ's death and resurrection. It was Paul who wrote, "I am crucified with Christ: nevertheless I live; yet not I, but Christ liveth in me" (Galatians 2:20). Paul realized he had virtually entered into Christ's death at Calvary, but he also knew that he was alive from the dead because Christ arose. It is this life in Jesus that brings such great rejoicing for a child of God.

It is this vital relationship with Jesus that Satan is continually attempting to sever. He seeks to pull us away from true life in the Spirit by offering substitutes. His kingdoms are not threatened by forms of godliness which are void of power and life. This spiritual warfare will not be waged successfully by employing fleshly weapons or techniques. The weapons of our warfare are not carnal (fleshly).

Yet, on this great battlefield, the constant struggle is between the flesh and the Spirit. The only means of doing battle with which some seem comfortable is through the strength of the flesh. They plot, they scheme, they strategize—all the while working against what the Spirit is wanting to do. "For the flesh lusteth against the Spirit, and the Spirit against the flesh: and these are contrary the one to the other" (Galatians 5:17).

The Church is engaged in a war of liberation. Millions are still being held captive, and we have been sent to rescue them. We sometimes view this world as a harvest field, but the harvest field is in reality a battlefield. This is a battle that will not be won by fleshly ingenuity. The battle is the Lord's.

Satan's strategy is to divert our attention from the purpose of this war, which is to liberate millions of captives; he would distract us by causing us to focus upon ourselves. He would have us fighting among ourselves, "biting and devouring one another" while millions remain enslaved with no hope. May God help us to recognize our enemies! May we be able to recognize his tactics of diversion, diverting our attention from what is primary, which is rescuing souls from Satan's grasp by the power of the gospel.

This gospel, which has been committed to us, is described in the Bible as the glorious gospel, the gospel of peace, the gospel of your salvation, the gospel of the grace of God. What a blessed gospel it is! It is a gospel to be delivered not in word only but in power. It was never intended to be a source of debating and strife—it is God's good news for fallen man, that there is hope for him, that in Jesus he has a Saviour. Each of us at one time received that good news. Each of us was begotten by the power of the gospel and each of us who maintains a growing relationship with Jesus will do so through the nurture of the gospel's power.

Paul's letter to the Galatians was written to correct an attempt by some false teachers to pervert this glorious gospel of grace. He wrote, "I marvel that ye are so soon removed from him that called you into the grace of Christ unto another gospel: Which is not another; but there be some that trouble you, and would pervert the gospel of Christ" (Galatians 1:6, 7).

The good news of all time is that Jesus came into the world to save sinners, to save us from ourselves, to save us from the lusts of the flesh and to one day present us blameless to His Father. Any other gospel is not *the* gospel. Paul realized the enemy had been at work among the Galatians, and he longed for their restoration to life in the Spirit. He was willing to "travail in birth again" for their reformation in Christ. Paul knew the folly of trusting in the flesh, of relying upon anything less than the amazing grace of God, and he stood for this gospel of grace.

This apostle to the Gentiles felt so strongly about this that he wrote, "But though we, or an angel from heaven, preach any other gospel unto you than that we have preached unto you, let him be accursed"(Galatians 1:8). Then, as if to bring emphasis to his statement he went on to say, "As we said before, so say I now again, If any man preach any other gospel unto you than that ye have received, let him be accursed" (v. 9).

This is the gospel the Church has been commissioned to carry, the gospel which offers freedom, life and power. This gospel is that of which Jesus spoke when He said, "And this gospel of the kingdom shall be preached in all the world for a witness unto all nations; and then shall the end come" (Matthew 24:14).

It is for us now to question the effectiveness with which we are communicating this blessed gospel. I believe most of us would confess our disappointment with the degree of our effectiveness. It is proper that we seek to understand what the reason for this is. What made the ministry of Jesus so powerful? I believe this may be discovered by listening to Him in the synagogue at Nazareth after He had just returned from His wilderness temptation, where for forty days He had eaten nothing. There in that Jewish synagogue where lifeless religion prevailed, Jesus read, "The Spirit of the Lord is upon me, because he hath anointed me to preach the gospel to the poor . . ." (Luke 4:18), and He declared, "This day is this scripture fulfilled in your ears" (v. 21). Was this not the key to Jesus' effectiveness—His anointing?

At Cornelius' house, Peter preached, "How God anointed Jesus of Nazareth with the Holy Ghost and with power: who went about doing good, and healing all that were oppressed by the devil; for God was with him" (Acts 10:38). It was in Jerusalem at the pool of Bethesda, where He had just healed a man who had been sick for thirty-eight years, that Jesus said, "My Father worketh hitherto, and I work. . . . I can of mine own self do nothing" (John 5:17, 30). If Jesus could of Himself do nothing apart from divine anointing, how much more should we recognize our insufficiency apart from this supernatural power?

Attempts to minister without heavenly anointing are going on in far too many of our churches. If Jesus couldn't do it, neither can we. Only God knows the sermons that have been preached which received men's applause, sermons which appealed to their minds but which, being void of divine anointing, failed to effect any changes in these people's lives. Emotions can be stirred while hearts remain unaffected to any degree of changing the lives of listeners. Entertainment can stir emotions, some of which is done in the name of worship. There are singing groups who can bring an audience to their feet in thunderous applause, where no one can deny that emotions have been raised to a high pitch. At the same time, it may not mean any change in lives. We need anointed preaching and anointed singing, through which God's Spirit speaks to the human spirit in such a way that people will know they have been in the presence of God.

Jesus possessed such anointing and those He commissioned, about whom we read in the New Testament, had this empowering. When Peter preached on the Day of Pentecost, was it his eloquence, or was it the divine empowering flowing through him that pricked the hearts of the multitude? The answer is obvious. What made Paul's ministry so effective? An explanation may be found in his letter to the Thessalonians: "For our gospel came not unto you in word only, but also in power, and in the Holy Ghost, and in much assurance" (1 Thessalonians 1:5).

If we should listen to Paul's explanation of the gospel's power through his ministry to the church at Corinth we would hear him say, "And I, brethren, when I came to you, came not with excellency of speech or of wisdom, declaring unto you the testimony of God. . . . I was with you in weakness, and in fear, and in much trembling. And my speech and my preaching was not with enticing words of man's wisdom, but in demonstration of the Spirit and of power: that your faith should not stand in the wisdom of men, but in the power of God" (1 Corinthians 2:1, 3-5). "For the kingdom of God is not in word, but in power" (4:20).

Paul's confidence was not in his training at the feet of Gamaliel. He wrote, ". . . I have no confidence in the flesh. . . . If any other man thinketh he hath reason whereof he might trust in the flesh, I more" (cf. Philippians 3:3, 4). He had a list of credentials of which he could have boasted, but he knew these were not to be depended upon. Paul knew the effectiveness of his ministry depended upon one thing—divine anointing, to which he referred as "his working, which worketh in me mightily" (Colossians 1:29).

Paul did not get to spend time with Jesus while He walked on earth in Galilee, Judaea or Samaria, but he had the privilege of being gloriously transported into His presence for a special time of communion with his Saviour whom he had met earlier on the road to Damascus. We do not know everything Jesus shared with Paul while he was there with Him in the "third heaven." If Paul had asked Jesus on this occasion what the key was to His ministry's success while He walked on earth, Jesus might have said, "It was the anointing I received from my Father."

Anointed ministries—that is the key! Anointed with Holy Ghost power! Anointed with Holy Ghost fire! The Church must have men and women who have heard from Heaven, men and women who have spent time with Jesus. Our experiences may not exactly match that of Paul's when he was "caught up into the third heaven," but somehow we will be provided the means of being with Jesus, of communicating with Him. Only then will our ministries have freshness and power.

Our local churches need to hear the prophet's voice among them and not just that of the scribe. The prophet tells what he has seen and heard from Heaven; the scribe tells what he has read. Scribes most often become parrots of other men's revelation and anointing. Their words are without power and effect. Not so with the prophet! The effect of the prophet's message will be attested to in much the same way as was that of Jesus' words by the two men on the road to Emmaus who said, "Did not our heart burn with in us, while he talked with us by the way, and while he opened to us the scriptures?" (Luke 24:32).

Our churches need to hear "burning words" from our pulpits. Sunday school classes need to hear "burning words" from their teachers. We need to hear "burning songs" from our choirs and from others who are truly anointed to sing. Nothing less will start the fire that is needed in our churches right now, and keep it burning.

Matthew wrote of Jesus, "For he taught them as one having authority, and not as the scribes" (Matthew 7:29). There was such a contrast! Why? Jesus would say, "the Spirit of the Lord is upon me, because he hath anointed me...." The scribes were correct with their words; they could hand down faithfully what had been written, but they lacked anointing and power. They could not say, "The Spirit of the Lord is upon me." The scribes were said by Jesus to have shut up the kingdom of heaven against men. "For ye neither go in yourselves," He said, "neither suffer ye them that are entering to go in" (Matthew 23:13).

Within Christ's kingdom there is freshness, there is joy—unlike the staleness offered by the scribes. It is sad that so many ministers, who were called by God to lead people into kingdom righteousness, peace and joy in the Holy Ghost, have apathetically become little more than scribes who themselves will not go on into kingdom power and blessings, and who literally block the way for those who would go forward.

In a meeting I attended recently with nine other leaders of the largest Pentecostal groups in the United States, I listened to one of these brothers describe the condition of his group. He said, "If I could compare our local churches with patients in a hospital, most of them right now would be in intensive care. And while they lie there dying, our leadership is walking around like men with their white coats on, talking about how they might redecorate the rooms." I could not help but make some comparison to many of our local churches.

This must change! And it will change! I believe God is raising up a generation who will not settle for anything less than a heavenly anointing! There is a price to be paid, but they are willing to pay it. For Jesus, it included forty days of fasting during His wilderness temptation. For Paul, it was the Arabian desert. For all of us, it is crucifixion of the flesh.

Jesus said, "Whosoever will come after me, let him deny himself, and take up his cross, and follow me" (Mark 8:34). Sometimes people refer to some particular burden they must bear as their cross, but these people to whom Jesus was speaking knew full well what taking up a cross meant.

The Romans had introduced it as an instrument of death. And that is precisely what it meant for those Christians. To take up the cross meant to take it up and go with Him to Calvary, and to there be crucified with Him.

Paul said, "I am crucified with Christ: nevertheless I live; yet not I, but Christ liveth in me" (Galatians 2:20). The flesh must die, and crucifixion with Christ is the only way. "For the flesh lusteth against the Spirit, and the Spirit against the flesh: and these are contrary the one to the other: so that ye cannot do the things that ye would" (Galatians 5:17). "So then they that are in the flesh cannot please God" (Romans 8:8).

The power of Christ's crucifixion must precede the power of His resurrection. To experience resurrection power, we first must be crucified with Him. I am convinced that too much of the flesh is still alive among us. This must die! Only then can we go forth to minister in the power of His resurrection. Only those who are crucified with Him can experience this power. Only these can say, "The Spirit of the Lord is upon me, because He has anointed me."

Only by divine power will this great battle be won. The battle is the Lord's, and He is not a loser. He will have a people who are crucified with Him and who are walking in the power of His resurrection, assaulting the strongholds of Satan. Holy Ghost power, Holy Ghost fire, Holy Ghost anointing—this is the key to victory!

Leadership Development

Inspired, spiritual leadership is in great demand for God's Church in these challenging days. The Church is not likely to rise above its leadership—"able men, such as fear God, men of truth, hating covetousness"—these are basic qualities that spiritual leaders must possess. Whatever other virtues may be developed or enhanced, they must be in addition to these basics for those men and women who are to lead God's people.

At this time we are in the process of restructuring our educational ministries with a view toward ministerial leadership development. Such development will include both spiritual and academic growth. As Jesus increased in wisdom, and in stature, and in favor with God and man, so must the Church's leadership. It is important that we be equipped to minister effectively to a society of diverse cultures and intellectual backgrounds. We are involved in the greatest work on earth, laboring together with the God of all creation who deserves the best we can become for His glory and honor.

He deserves better than what is now being offered Him in many places of leadership. Consecrated ignorance is not enough to offer our God if we are capable of improvement through learning, and most of us are. Leadership preparation requires time, marked by an earnest desire to please the One by whom you have been chosen. For Moses it required forty years of desert refining. For Paul, years of desert solitude with his Saviour enabled him to put his years of learning at the feet of Gamaliel in proper perspective. Being chosen by God for leadership does not automatically qualify a person to lead, but there is help for the man or woman who truly wants help.

The suspension of Tomlinson College classes and of Bible Training Institute was not to signal a lessening of the Church's emphasis upon the importance of teaching and learning. It is my hope that the financial crisis through which we have been passing at our General Headquarters will be the means not for a diminishing of, but for a new emphasis upon leadership preparedness. For this to materialize will require the support of the entire Church. These times demand a more able ministry, and I feel that we must be willing to devote resources as may be required for an intensive approach toward upgrading our ministerial leadership all around the world.

In addition to our campus in Cleveland, it will be necessary to establish centers of learning on the field, in many nations. There will be some who are not ready to pursue a degree program, and courses of study must be prepared and made available to them. For others, a degree program will be the appropriate course to follow, and we want to offer them an environment of academic excellence whereby they will be able to mark their academic progress. But I want to emphasize the importance of affecting more than the minds of those who will be studying. We must have learning centers where genuine spiritual fervor is nurtured.

I have repeated many times that on the campus in Cleveland I would like to see "prayer paths" going into the woods on the backside of the campus. We must develop a leadership who knows how to pray, who has a vibrant relationship with the Holy Ghost. We have no desire to glorify ignorance, but neither do we want to glorify academic knowledge that is void of spiritual life and power.

I envision a campus and centers of learning where evangelistic fervor is hot, blazing with Holy Ghost fire. A vision of the great Commission must be kept before the students at all times. A vision of the lost for whom Jesus died must live within them, creating a burden which they cannot dismiss. I see no reason why intellectual excellence cannot coexist with spiritual excellence. We can have refined intellects that are also sanctified intellects, intellects which do not interfere with the Spirit's speaking through these vessels of clay.

I am calling upon our churches to get behind this endeavor of ministerial leadership development. We need you to stand behind it with your moral and financial support. It must have a degree of support which Tomlinson College never received. It will not be possible at the present time for those availing themselves of these educational opportunities to receive financial aid from government-funded programs. This means a greater financial involvement by the entire Church. National and state offices must rally with their support. I am calling upon the Ways and Means Committee to give this their attention.

Then, it will also be necessary for our churches to encourage their pastor's desire, plus that of other young ministers in their number, to take advantage of the opportunity to enrich their ministerial preparedness. This must be a concentrated endeavor. We are facing the greatest opportunities the Church has ever known. Our churches must become set on fire with evangelistic zeal, reaching the lost, ministering to people in their needs. It is time for a new thrust of getting this gospel to the world, starting in our communities. Our churches are needing leaders who can lead. If we all are willing to pay the price, I believe God is ready to help us.

Proper leadership development will require teachers who are prepared to teach, prepared not only intellectually but who are full of the Holy Ghost. What they impart must not be mere theory, but a sharing of what is real and vital, what they themselves have experienced. Spiritual teaching is pouring one's life, a life that is under the Spirit's control, into another. In the truest sense we do not share Jesus with others; we share with them our relationship with Jesus, allowing Him to express Himself, His power, His love through us. Experiential knowledge is the kind that can be shared from the heart and not just from the head.

The new school of ministry must be a joint venture between the local church, national, regional or state headquarters and General Headquarters. We must see it as our school, belonging to all the churches. Otherwise, I see no chance for its success. But it must succeed! The need for qualified leadership is urgent, a leadership which can lead members in the exercise of their spiritual giftedness. Churches must be awakened to a vibrant, effective Body ministry. They must understand what that means. It is time for total mobilization of all the resources Christ has placed in His Church. God has the power to communicate without our help, but He has chosen to speak to the world through His Church.

We must be more effective in reaching people. People are the only thing going up in the rapture—not beautiful buildings, not attractive landscaping, but people. Let's concentrate upon what is primary! Let's keep the main thing the main thing! O God, give us leaders who can lead! O God, help us to understand our responsibility in leadership development! We must understand our limits in this matter. We dare not intrude into areas which God reserves for Himself in dealing with a man or woman's heart. At the same time, we want to foster a climate which encourages ministers to seek God and to listen to God, to cultivate a vital relationship with Him.

I want to express my sincere appreciation for all of those who have worked in Bible Training Institute and in Tomlinson College. Years of dedicated service by devoted men and women have gone into each of these departments, and many can testify along with me of the blessings received through their labors.

With the merging of these two departments into one new entity, we want to identify the weaknesses of each and seek to eliminate these. At the same time, we desire to identify the strengths of each and build upon these strengths.

When I announced the suspension of the operations of these two departments this past May, while effecting a merger of the two into one, some questioned the reason for including Bible Training Institute in this suspension. The idea seemed to exist that BTI was more or less financially self-sufficient. Perhaps this was because they saw in the Assembly Minutes the listing of a substantial reserve in Bible Training Institute funds. Actually, this fund reserve consists of monies that have been raised for conducting Bible Training Institute in countries outside the United States. This includes the convention offerings raised by our churches. These funds have been set aside to bring students together in these countries, principally what we term "third-world countries," providing food, lodging, books, etc., for those who otherwise could not have afforded this training.

These funds have not been used to finance the operation of the department such as staffing the offices, paying the travel expenses of the BTI Superintendent and Representatives, etc. These expenses are borne by the General Tithe Fund. For the past year, this amounted to some $266,000.

So, when we became aware of the financial crisis back in May, we had to look at what was being required from our

Tithe Fund to support both Tomlinson College and Bible Training Institute, and the decision was made to bring them together in one new school. It is our hope that this will be a more effective means of equipping ministerial leadership.

Financial limitations will forbid our staffing enough teachers in this department to have schools going on in every state and nation around the world. Yet, we believe this to be the necessary approach. Many will not be able to leave their homes for extended periods of time to live on a campus. So, we must establish centers of learning in a close enough proximity to their homes to where they can avail themselves of learning opportunities.

Inasmuch as our staff working out of Headquarters in this new school of ministry will be limited in number, we will have to rely upon overseers and other capable teachers in the states and nations to join us in a cooperative effort. It may be necessary for overseers to alter some of the routines they have traditionally followed in their "calendar of events," in order to give their time specifically to this ministerial leadership development. We must have leadership, spiritual leadership—able men such as fear God. Whatever is required for this, we must establish as a priority. Initially, the principal emphasis will be on the field. We hope to have something to offer our ministers which they can see to be of immediate benefit to them. In some cases, it is going to be necessary to overcome the apprehensions that exist about their abilities to achieve in a study program. No one should have fears of learning. Each one of us is ignorant in varying degrees, and all of us need a greater personal knowledge of Jesus Christ and of the blessed Book which God has given to us.

As was the case with Bible Training Institute, the General Overseer will be president of this school of ministry. I do not propose to be a mere figurehead. It is my intention to be personally involved, to demonstrate how strongly I feel about the development of truly spiritual leadership. I am inviting the state overseers, as well as other national overseers who are nearby, to Cleveland in January where they will be staying in a dorm on campus for a week of intensive study and preparation for schools in their states and nations. We also have plans to take this to other areas of the world. We want all our overseers to catch the vision and to get under the burden of spiritual, ministerial leadership development. We must accelerate our efforts to reach and impact this world with the greatest message they will ever hear.

The Arise of the Day Star

"For God, who commanded the light to shine out of darkness, hath shined in our hearts, to give the light of the knowledge of the glory of God in the face of Jesus Christ" (2 Corinthians 4:6).

In this verse of Scripture, Paul likens the illumination which comes to human hearts through the revelation of Jesus Christ, to the Creation which is recorded in Genesis, chapter one. In the second verse of this chapter, we read, "And the earth was without form, and void; and darkness was upon the face of the deep." It was God's creation, yet it lay in darkness. Where there is no light there is no discernible form. Light is required to give visible form to that which exists. So, God said, "Let there be light: and there was light" (v. 3).

This light is mysterious to us, in that it was manifest on the first day, while the sun was not created until the fourth day of that first week. But when God said, "Let there be light," there had to be light. May it not be said that this light was of His own immanence? John wrote, "God is light, and in him there is no darkness at all" (1 John 1:5). Of Him Paul wrote, ". . . dwelling in the light which no man can approach unto; whom no man hath seen, nor can see: to whom be honour and power everlasting. Amen" (l Timothy 6:16).

David wrote, "The heavens declare the glory of God; and the firmament sheweth his handiwork" (Psalms 19:1). To me, it is wondrous to sense that God was declaring His glory in the creation of the heavens. First, there was this light of Genesis one, verse two, light which gave form to His creation. Perhaps this light of His immanence, of His eternal being, the light of His presence, would have been far too brilliant for the mortals whom He would create on the sixth day. So, on the fourth day, God made the sun and the stars, all of which have light in themselves, and they are sources of light. This is not true of the moon or the planets in this solar system, each of which from a distance appears to be a light, but which shines with a reflected light from the sun.

While we make distinction between the sun and the stars, and the Bible makes this distinction, we are told by those who study the heavens that the sun is a star also. This presents no problem for me, since I can refer to it as the "day star." I admire all the stars of the night, but I know it is this "day star" which is the source of light and life for this planet. Peter referred to Jesus as the "day star" as he wrote, ". . . until the day dawn, and the day star arise in your hearts" (2 Peter 1:19). In Luke, chapter one, we hear Zacharias prophesying of Him as the "dayspring from on high." He said, "Through the tender mercy of our God; whereby the dayspring from on high hath visited us, To give light to them that sit in darkness and in the shadow of death, to guide our feet into the way of peace" (vv. 78, 79).

As I meditate upon the heavens declaring the glory of God, I like to think upon this great, pervasive light of Genesis one, verse two, which might have been far too brilliant for mortals. Then, I think of God setting the sun in place to give us precisely the light we needed. And now the God who dwells in a light that no man can approach unto has "shined in our hearts, to give the light of the knowledge of the glory of God in the face of Jesus Christ," the One whom Malachi called the "Sun of righteousness [risen] with healing in his wings" (Malachi 4:2). That measure of himself which God would allow us to understand, He has revealed to us in Jesus. Though dwelling in a light no man can approach unto, He chose to give us light, glorious illumination through Jesus.

Jesus Christ—the day star from on high—is for us the Source of all spiritual light and life. John wrote, "In him was life; and the life was the light of men. . . . the true Light, which lighteth every man that cometh into the world" (John 1:4, 9). Isaiah prophesied of Jesus like this, "The people that walked in darkness have seen a great light: they that dwell in the land of the shadow of death, upon them hath the light shined" (Isaiah 9:2). Jesus referred to Himself as "the bright and morning star" (Revelation 22:16).

The powers of darkness had prevailed for such a long time, but suddenly there was a dawning. As the Sun of righteousness appeared on the horizon, darkness had to flee. The angels sang, "Glory to God in the highest," as the "dayspring from on high" sprang forth. Darkness has no power over light. Light dispels darkness always. It is only when light is withdrawn that darkness can exist. Oh, what great hope this glorious dawning held for all mankind. Such light for the whole earth had never been known.

Thousands bound by darkness rejoiced in the freedom brought to them by Heaven's light. The fear in which they were held as they stumbled in the darkness was dispelled as they began walking in the light of life. Light—what a blessed thing! And it came by this "day star" who called himself "the light of the world."

Thank God that our darkness has passed! It is true that the Church Jesus established eventually rejected His headship, His authority over her, and that He withdrew Himself from her to let her learn a hard lesson of being "on her own," having scorned His love. For awhile He hid Himself from her. The ensuing period of darkness was terrible. The constancy of His love did not fail, however, and Jesus returned to make His presence known to her once more.

Being drawn by His love, she came forth out of this awful darkness to be joined to Him again, to walk with Him in the glorious light of His presence. In Solomon's Song we hear the question, "Who is she that looketh forth as the morning, fair as the moon, clear as the sun, and terrible as an army with banners?" (6:10). As the morning emerges out of the night's darkness, so the Church, being drawn by her Redeemer's love, emerged from the prevailing darkness, looking forth as the morning.

She that looketh forth as the morning—this is a significant phrase. From the haziness of the morning's dawning to its zenith at noonday, there is growing brightness and clarity. For the Church to remain in the haziness of the morning's dawning is to fail to walk with the Day Star from on high. In the Book of Proverbs we read, "But the path of the just is as the shining light, that shineth more and more unto the perfect day" (4:18). Perfect day, perfect brightness—the noonday zenith—are not these expressions synonymous? And would not this zenith of brightness be marked by the rapture, when Jesus could say of His bride, "Thou art all fair, my love; there is no spot in thee" (Song of Solomon 4:7). I believe so!

In Peter's second epistle he wrote, "We have also a more sure word of prophecy; whereunto ye do well that ye take heed, as unto a light that shineth in a dark place, until the day dawn, and the day star arise in your hearts" (2 Peter 1:19). Here Peter speaks of the certainty of God's Word, compared to the experience he had undergone on the Mount of Transfiguration when a voice from heaven had identified Jesus as the Son of God. Then he says of God's Word, "... whereunto ye do well that ye take heed . . . until the day dawn, and the day star arise in your hearts."

Obviously, he is not saying there comes a time when one no longer is to take heed to God's Word. Instead, he points to the moment when there is a blessed illumination in the heart, and not just an academic knowing of what is written. Peter says, ". . . until the day dawn," or until the Sun arises, until "the day star arise in your hearts."

This is the key to walking with Jesus in a growing illumination that will peak at the Rapture. It is in a relationship with Him that has its roots in the heart. It is a love relationship, and love is not merely academic or intellectual. It is felt when the Day Star arises in your heart. We speak often of our responsibility to people who are lost. We speak of compassion, of needing a greater burden for the lost, and this is indeed a great need among us. We can recognize this need, and talk about it from now on, which means it is in our minds, in our heads. This burden will become real, however, only as the Day Star arises in our hearts. That is where the burden will be felt.

We have a sure word of prophecy, all right—the written Word. This is something to be treasured. We have been blessed to hear it preached and taught. At the same time, we must question the degree to which it is working in our hearts. In other words, to what degree has the Day Star arisen in our hearts? This is a vital question.

Some among us have been preaching and teaching for 30 or 40 years or more. The "sure word of prophecy" is in their heads, but it is obvious that the Day Star has not yet risen in their hearts. This seems so sad. These people do not hesitate to gossip, slander, criticize, attack, accuse, all the while knowing the Bible forbids the kind of behavior they are exercising. Something is sadly missing in their hearts. They proclaim loudly their loyalty to the Church, boasting of how they will never compromise, but something is missing in their hearts. Sure, we need to be loyal, and certainly we have no right to compromise God's Word, but where is the respect, the kindness, the love, the care for fellow Christians? Where is the burden for reaching the lost? Knowledge is not enough. Paul wrote, "Knowledge puffeth up, but charity edifieth. And if any man think that he knoweth any thing, he knoweth nothing yet as he ought to know. But if any man love God, the same is known of him" (1 Corinthians 8:1-3). This love comes as the Day Star arises in your heart. You can then love with His love.

The judgment of Jesus Christ is not a harsh, uncaring judgment. The judgment of Moses' law was unto condemnation, but of Jesus it is written, ". . . till he send forth judgment unto victory" (Matthew 12:20). When the Day Star has arisen in one's heart, he will not take delight in condemning, and hoping for a vindication of his "judgment" message. He will be more concerned with a judgment that leads to victory. When Jonah preached a message of judgment against Nineveh, he was disappointed by their repentance which caused them to be spared. His reaction was one of wishing he could die. He said, "It is better for me to die than to live" (Jonah 4:8).

Jonah evidently did not love people. He desired to see his message vindicated. That would have made him look better, but God loves people, and He spared Nineveh. When the Day Star arises in your heart, you, too, will love people. Jesus came not to condemn the world, "but that the world through him might be saved" (John 3:17).

As this Day Star arises in our hearts, we will proceed with a heart-burden to carry out the Great Commission. Generally speaking, the Church knows what Jesus said. We know He said, "Go ye into all the world and preach the gospel to every creature" (Mark 16:15). But why are we so slow about going? How is it that God's people can be so apathetic when they know souls are dropping into hell every day? Do we not know this? Do we not have as one of our teachings made prominent, "Eternal Punishment for the Wicked"—with no liberation or annihilation?

Yes, we know this important Bible truth—we know it in our heads. And we are willing to fight to defend our teachings, even to the point of destroying one another with our debating, while souls continue every hour to depart this life unprepared to meet God—lost forever.

As the Day Star, this Sun of righteousness, arises within us, we will have a brighter and brighter illumination of spiritual truth. We will see more clearly, we will know better, the eyes of our understanding being enlightened. And it will be the kind of knowing that surpasses intellectual knowledge. It simply brings us into a greater unity with Jesus, and the more perfect our unity becomes with Him, the more perfect it will be with one another.

A. W. Tozer pointed out in his book, *The Pursuit of God*, that one hundred pianos all tuned to the same tuning fork are automatically tuned to each other. He emphasized that they are of one accord by being tuned, not to each other, but to another standard to which each one must individually bow. What a wonderful thing will be wrought among us as the Day Star arises in our hearts to bring us to the perfect knowledge of, and in perfect unity with the Son of God!

Thank God for the "more sure word of prophecy"—God's eternal Word, settled forever in heaven. We must hold fast to it—as Peter wrote, "whereunto ye do well that ye take heed, as unto a light that shineth in a dark place, until the day dawn, and the day star arise in your hearts." Oh, for a deep compassion to arise in our hearts! But this will not happen as long as we major in knowing and defending doctrine just from our heads, knowing with a knowledge that "puffeth up."

We must pray for something to happen in our hearts, indeed, for the Day Star to arise in our hearts. This will move us from simply knowing to doing. We will then truly become one with Him. His burden will become our burden. Jesus could have spent all His time debating with the Pharisees, and He would have won the debates every time. Whenever He did take the time to reply to their attempts to engage Him in argument, they always lost. He knew what He was talking about.

Jesus had more important things to do. He loved people, and as He looked at the multitudes, He saw them as people who had been victimized by Satan, people who were hurting, suffering, lost, and His heart was moved with compassion toward them.

I pray that as we leave this Assembly we will go with this blessed gospel not just in our heads but burning in our hearts. Every local church is surrounded by people who need the good news of their Saviour's redeeming love. They are lost. Jesus cares that they are lost. He suffered, He died that they might be saved. His heart toward them is still one of compassion.

Will we allow Him, with His love, to arise in our hearts? I pray that we will!

88th General Assembly Sermons

Sermons preached to the 88th General Assembly, 1994

Turning to the Harvest With Grace and Truth

"And the angel said unto them, Fear not: for, behold, I bring you good tidings of great joy, which shall be to all people. For unto you is born this day in the city of David a Saviour, which is Christ the Lord" (Luke 2:10, 11).

It was the announcement of the ages, reserved from the foundation of the world. It was made to a small group of shepherds in a Judean field. Little could they have known that it would be recorded later in a Book to be published by the millions throughout the world, and that 2,000 years later this announcement would be translated into 2,564 languages.

It was direct and it was stated simply: "good tidings of great joy, which shall be to all people;" good news that was going to bring great joy, not just for these Jewish people there in Palestine, but it was good news that would go to all people—a Savior, Christ the Lord, a Savior for everyone. Both Jesus and Paul called it the gospel!

All people everywhere—past, present and future—were victims of sin, separated from God, a separation which, without divine intervention, would be for eternity. But, thank God, there came a Savior. His name is Jesus! He was not an ordinary man. No ordinary man's death would have sufficed as an atonement for the sins of the whole world. But when there was no other way, God became man, became one of us to offer Himself for our sins, to redeem us from our sins and reconcile us to Himself.

John called Jesus "the Word," declaring that **the Word** was God. "And the Word was made flesh, and dwelt among us, (and we beheld his glory, the glory as of the only begotten of the Father,) full of grace and truth" (John 1:14).

His very title, *the Word*, is expressive of communication, of revelation, and God chose to communicate with us powerfully through this One whom John called "the Word made flesh." Of course, this same Word, being Creator of this universe and everything in it, had communicated already much of His power and of His wisdom through His creation: "The heavens declare the glory of God; and the firmament sheweth his handiwork (Psalms 19:1). While we stand in awe at His great power by which all His creation is now being upheld, something greater than this is **His great love**! Apart from this love, what would His great power and great wisdom mean to us? Our relationship with Him, our love for Him, stems not from the greatness of His power, but from the greatness of His love. John said it well, "We love him, because he first loved us" (1 John 4:19).

He loved us in our sins, and He loves each of those who still live in sinfulness just as much as He loves any one of us. Jesus came as a Savior for them all. It remains His will that none of them be lost. He would have all men to be saved. He came to earth as a Savior to express this desire, and He expressed it strongly at Calvary. Oh, that our hearts might be knit with His heart in His love for every lost person!

It seems easy for us to sit in judgment upon a decadent society, decrying the sinfulness that abounds. Jesus came to this earth for judgment all right, but His was not a judgment to condemnation. The people were condemned already. Matthew wrote, in reference to Isaiah's prophecy, that Jesus would "send forth judgment unto victory" (Matthew 12:20).

His judgment differed from the judgment of Moses' law by which they stood condemned. In Him was the power for deliverance from condemning sins, the power for restoration to a loving relationship with their Creator.

Jesus was able to say to the woman brought to Him by the "law-keepers," the woman they were condemning to be stoned, "Go, and sin no more" (John 8:11). He had not come to condemn the world, "but that the world through him might be saved" (3:17). He had not come to condemn this poor woman further. He came *to set the captive free.*

John reminds us that the law was given by Moses, "but **grace** and truth came by Jesus Christ" (1:17). The law was truth—it was God's Word, but in Jesus truth was accompanied by grace. The law was weak in that while condemning sin, it did not offer grace for deliverance. In the light of God's holiness sin is always condemned. Both the judgment of the law and the judgment of Jesus condemns all sin, but Jesus comes with *judgment unto victory,* with truth **and grace**, the grace to set free.

It is possible for us to develop an unholy pride in being able to interpret the Scriptures correctly, to where we can identify what is sin, and thus condemn as sinners those who are transgressors of scriptural teachings. Too often, however, there is not an accompanying compassion to set the captives free, and our judgment becomes not a *judgment unto victory,* but a judgment unto condemnation. If our hearts are attuned to the heart of Jesus, if indeed we have become one with Him, we will never condone or approve of sin. Sin is still an affront to the holiness of God, and its penalty is death—eternal death. This is a message we must declare with a holy fervor! This world regards sin so lightly, but God does not. Sin is what made necessary Jesus' awful death at Calvary. But if we have union with Christ, we will also share His compassion for the lost, a compassion that calls us to sacrificial living and service in an effort to rescue souls from Satan's power.

It is important that we know the truth. How blessed we are to know God's Word to the degree we do know it. It is possible, however, for us to know the Word, yet to be out of touch with its Author. More important than an academic knowledge of the truth is our relationship with the One who declared "I am the Truth." We must become one with Him.

Through the years we have felt the need for indoctrination, for establishing our people in the doctrine. And we do not want to minimize the importance of sound theology, of sound doctrine. Paul's instruction to Timothy was, "Take heed unto thyself, and unto the doctrine; continue in them: for in doing this thou shalt both save thyself, and them that hear thee" (1 Timothy 4:16). Yes, doctrine is important. The problem arises, however, when our knowledge of the doctrine becomes more academic than experiential. Jesus came to bring not just truth but *the grace that restores*, the grace that brings us into a blessed relationship with our Lord.

It does not disturb Satan greatly for us to be able to defend scripturally the doctrine of sanctification and holiness, for example, so long as the fruit of holiness is not being reflected in our lives. It has been borne out in our history, regrettably, that ministers can preach and defend these doctrines while in secret they are living shameful, sinful lives.

How profitable is it to be able to recite 29 prominent teachings of the Church and to support each one with verses of Scripture, when it is only academic and not experiential. The power of our witness is not in being able to preach "Full Restoration of the Gifts of the Spirit," but in being filled with the Spirit to where these gifts of the Spirit are being manifested through us as a witness to people who need to know Jesus Christ.

The power of the Early Church's ministry was not demonstrated in quoting what Jesus had said about *signs following believers*, or in their ability to defend this as a doctrine. Their ministry was powerful, rather, as "they went forth, and preached every where, the Lord working with them, and confirming the word with signs following" (Mark 16:20). A skeptical world is going to be little affected by rhetoric. To *turn to the harvest* with effect, it will be necessary to identify with Paul, who said, "For our gospel came not unto you in word only, but also in power. . . ." (1 Thessalonians 1:5).

We have been strong in our teaching against the divorce and remarriage evil. It is an **evil** which plagues our society and is having a devastating effect upon this generation. At the same time, we must ask what we are doing by the examples we set forth before others in our own marriages to make marriage the beautiful, loving relationship which is prefigured by the love relationship of Christ and His Church.

In marriage, the husband and wife are involved in the most intimate relationship that humans can know, apart from the relationship an individual can have with God. It is a mysterious "one flesh" union, which the world needs to see being lived out among those who are the light of the world. It seems easier oftentimes for a preacher to preach against the divorce and remarriage evil, condemning those who have become victims of this evil, than for him to be a loving husband and father, living out within his family the example of what God has ordered for marriage.

In the Creation account we read, "And the rib, which the LORD God had taken from man, made he a woman, and brought her unto the man. And Adam said, This is now bone of my bones, and flesh of my flesh: she shall be called Woman, because she was taken out of Man. Therefore shall a man leave his father and his mother, and shall cleave unto his wife: and they shall be one flesh" (Genesis 2:22-24).

Referring to this Genesis account, Jesus said, "Have ye not read, that he which made them at the beginning made them male and female, And said, For this cause shall a man leave father and mother, and shall cleave to his wife: and they twain shall be one flesh? Wherefore they are no more twain, but one flesh. What therefore God hath joined together, let not man put asunder" (Matthew 19:4-6).

Human history literally began with marriage, and the family thus became God's primary institution. At times we have placed the Church above the family, sacrificing the family to the Church, but I believe the Church exists to serve the family. The family is God's primary institution, not the Church. God did not begin this creation of the family with two bodies. He began with one, and from this one He made the second. One body became two. Moses described it like this: "So God created man in his own image, in the image of God created he him; male and female created he them" (Genesis 1:27).

When God brought Eve to Adam, in order to make the man He had created complete, Adam recognized her as "bone of my bones, and flesh of my flesh." Jesus' reminder was, "For this cause shall a man leave his father and his mother, and shall cleave unto his wife: and they shall be one flesh." In the **Creation**, one became two, but in **marriage**, two become one.

To the questioning Jews Jesus admitted that Moses had allowed divorce, but He emphasized that "from the beginning it was not so" (Matthew 19:8).

Thus was man created in *the image of God*, being made **in His likeness**—like Him in a union of oneness, like Him in sharing love within this union, like Him in this union in the power to produce life. For the purpose of producing life, notice that God made them **male** and **female**. Two males cannot reproduce—there is no divine image in homosexuality. Two females cannot reproduce—there is no divine image in lesbianism. Such unions are abominable to God!

Whatever Satan can do to weaken the union of marriage mars the image of God in His creation. This enemy of God is using a diversity of tactics to belittle what God has purposed for this sacred union from the beginning. He has promoted homosexuality, lesbianism, divorce and remarriage, premarital sex, extra-marital sex, male chauvinism for man's assertive dominance of his family, instead of demonstrating a loving servanthood, loving his wife as Christ loved the Church. Then again Satan has foisted upon woman ideas of irrational feminism which have adversely affected her role of a loving and supportive wife and mother. With a faulty ideal of liberation, abortion is offered her as a means of freedom by this enemy of God.

An unprecedented increase of divorcing and remarrying is having a devastating effect upon families. Only time will reveal this evil's impact upon children, where marriage is being looked upon as a merely human contractual arrangement that can be ended by mutual agreement. This ploy of Satan in no way alters God's design of "one man for one woman for life" in a union whereby they are no more twain but one flesh, having no such option for the dissolution of marriage.

To be salt in a decaying society, we must continue to emphasize the sanctity of marriage, and the divine lawfulness of sex only within the marriage bond. (I applaud those Baptist young people in this nation who pledged themselves recently to retain their virginity until marriage.) So-called experts would have us believe the traditional family as we have known it is merely changing. The truth is that the family institution is decaying, and will continue to do so until the sanctity of marriage and family is restored.

To judge an action properly, one must know the motivation behind that action, or in this case, the Motivator. Who is the Author of marriage? Who is the author of all those things being employed to weaken and destroy marriage and the family as he encourages premarital sex, extra-marital sex, divorce, homosexuality, lesbianism, male chauvinism, irrational feminism and abortion? The answers are evident. Satan opposes everything that is holy, everything that is wholesome, decent and virtuous. When God's laws are in opposition to their fleshly desires, carnal people will listen to Satan.

Young people, I wish I could stamp upon your minds and hearts tonight the sacredness of the marriage bond. This is something which many of you within the next few years will be considering. The worldly system in which you live will minimize its permanence—the fact that true marriage is something which only death can sever. You will be influenced to look upon it as a contract between two persons with certain terms to be met, and if your partner should break these terms then the contract is no longer binding.

Marriage is much more than a contract. It is a divinely purposed union wherein two persons, male and female, are joined together to become one flesh for life. When this occurs they are no longer two but one. Love and trust can make it a beautiful union which honors its Author. There is a completeness for both partners which cannot be found outside this union.

The commitment to marriage is a sobering one, and many in this generation are unwilling to make it. This accounts for those who just decide to live together in an adulterous arrangement without becoming married. This surely dishonors God who created man in His image, and designed marriage to portray this divine image.

We can decry and denounce all those things Satan employs to corrupt the sacredness and beauty of marriage. We can heap condemnation upon all his victims, and we can call this, "standing for the truth," and this we have done. We may also observe, however, that all this was done under the law. How much is God honored by the preacher who, with a sound interpretation of the Scriptures, *lays down the law* in the pulpit, but who demonstrates harshness by unkind words toward his own wife and children on his way to or from the service where he *stands for the doctrine*?

Remember, Jesus came to bring **grace** and **truth**. Grace enables truth to become relational. It removes it beyond being purely doctrinal, and causes it to be a matter of experience, written and known in our hearts. It can then be *lived out* in practical expression before those among whom we shine as lights in a world of darkness—*turning to the harvest*.

There is a place for expository preaching where scriptural truth is set forth with correctness. We can do this, however, while our own relationship with Jesus is deteriorating. Expository truth must become relational truth. Our children need to see in their own homes what a Christian marriage and family is really like. It is very difficult for them to establish a marriage and home which they have only been told about and not shown. We may well ask ourselves whether it is *law* or *grace* that is the predominant force in our homes. We do not want to just preach against the divorce and remarriage evil. We want to foster loving relationships which will be a light to the world, showing them the beauty of marriage which God intends.

This world is in darkness. People have lost their direction. What is their hope? Not in just hearing God's law, but in being introduced to a **Person**, and, by God's amazing grace, finding a relationship with Him. His name is Jesus! He is their Savior! Apart from Him they are forever lost.

As a whole, we have been fairly proficient in proclaiming and defending doctrine, but while doing this we have often been deficient in fervent love, a caring love for a world that has lost its direction, a deep concern for people who are lost. Do we condemn more than we weep for the thousands who have been victimized by Satan, for all those who drop into hell daily, entering into that horrible pit from which there is no escape ever?

It is now time for God's Church to truly *turn to the harvest*, to turn to the harvesting of these souls who are going to be lost forever unless someone reaches them. There is hope to be offered them—it is a glorious hope. Oh, what a glorious salvation we ourselves have received! Gathered here in this place we will rejoice together, and rightfully so. We have been introduced to Jesus! But in the midst of our rejoicing, I pray we shall be seized with a passion for reaching lost people, a passion such as we have never experienced prior to this week.

"Turning to the Harvest" must not be viewed as just a promotional theme for this Assembly. It is not a promotion! It is not a program! It must become a passion, extending not just for this coming year, but continuing until the Rapture. This will happen only when a fire is ignited within our hearts—a fire in our hearts to save souls from the flames of hell!

Promotions and programs will not suffice; a compelling passion must be our driving force. Programs are designed by the mind, while passion is of the heart; it sets the spirit aflame. Passion is defined as "extreme, compelling emotion; intense emotional drive or excitement."

The passion being called for by God is not a "pumped up" emotion, one that rises and falls in proportion to someone's ability to excite or arouse feelings in a meeting like this. It is, rather, the passion which drove our Savior while He was "tabernacled" among us, and it will be felt in our hearts in proportion to our relationship with Him. Oh, to see with His eyes, to love with His love, to feel with His heart!

At this juncture in our history, here in this Assembly, we are being given by God a choice. We can continue with our routines, reassuring ourselves that we are on track, defending traditions, condemning, disputing with one another, or we can fall down before God, confessing a self-centeredness that is lacking in a deep compassion for the lost, and genuinely repent. This is what God is calling us to do. To repent is to confess and to forsake. It is to make a turn. Are we ready to turn? Can we do it? Will we do it? We will do it only as we become one with our Lord.

Then we will share His compassion for the lost; then we can weep with Him, as when He wept for Jerusalem, and as He still weeps with love, not willing that any should perish. As Jesus foresaw the impending destruction of Jerusalem, and how those He loved would be fleeing in vain from their torturers and murderers, He wept. And today, foreseeing the horrors awaiting all who are lost, I believe He still weeps.

Do we really carry a crushing burden for them? Some of them are our sons and daughters, our brothers and sisters, headed for hell while, too often, we carry on our routines. We should be, and we must be, instead, driven with a consuming passion. I further emphasize that it has been easier for us to focus upon the teachings of the Church, upon the doctrine of "Eternal Punishment for the Wicked," for another example, and to defend it with the Scripture, than to focus with compassion upon the reality that thousands are dropping into that horrible pit called hell every day.

Yes, we will memorize verses of Scripture to support and defend this teaching, arguing with those who may disagree with us, and we call it being *established*, but we can do that while having little real passion to *rescue the perishing*, to *care for the dying*, to *snatch them in pity from sin and the grave*.

Do you think it bothers Satan for us to spend our time disputing about Scripture instead of being driven by a burden for the lost? I rather think he delights in it. An academic knowledge of biblical doctrine does not assure relationship with Jesus. We can embrace and defend the doctrine of His second coming and still miss the Rapture. It is to those who are **looking for Him** that He will appear, not necessarily to those defending this teaching of His second coming.

To know Him—that is the key! To become one with Jesus, our hearts attuned to Heaven. Then the rejoicing of Heaven will be our rejoicing, also. There is rejoicing in heaven over one sinner that repents more than over ninety-nine "just persons" who are, dispassionately, *abiding in the faith*. When our hearts are united with Jesus' heart it will cause rejoicing among us also, **whenever** and **wherever** a sinner repents and finds Jesus as his Savior. Do we rejoice when we hear that someone got saved at a neighboring church, when that church is not one of our churches? Heaven does!

It is a sign of spiritual sickness when an altar invitation is given, and sinners respond to that invitation, and Christians walk out of the auditorium, showing little interest in what happens at that altar. This is where the attention of heaven is focused; this is what captivates the interest of the angels. How much are we attuned to the interests of heaven?

I have to ask whether we are ready for *turning to the harvest*? I know that Jesus is ready. Already He has enlisted thousands of harvesters to work with Him, and they are busily engaged. The greatest revival the world has ever experienced is underway right now. Credible estimates are that some 50,000 people are coming to Jesus every day, 20,000 of these daily converts being in China alone.

The Holy Ghost is doing His work. Hearts are being ignited by a divine fire, with a passion which only God can ignite. I believe that in this Assembly He is going to do a work among us. Make sure you are listening, that you are sensitive to Him. We must not allow distractions.

Everything done in this Assembly should be done with *the harvest* in mind. Souls who are lost must occupy our attention. The Assembly committees have worked hard to prepare their reports, but if these reports do not serve to help us focus on the harvest, they should not be given. Satan would like to use these business sessions to create strife among us in order to distract us from the primary goal of *turning to the harvest*. Preachers, singers, workshop leaders—our hearts must be attuned to Him who is saying, "Lift up your eyes, and look on the fields; for they are white already to harvest" (John 4:35).

Well-prepared committee reports do not produce passion. Entertaining songs and eloquent sermons do not produce passion. The passion needed right now is produced from heaven, from our union with that One who came from heaven, a union which is strengthened on our knees. Do you feel a oneness with Jesus? Do you believe His burden is your burden? Can you weep with Him over those who are lost, even for those who, here in this place tonight, are lost? Can you weep **with** them here in this altar tonight?

Oh, that those who are lost might feel the burden that Jesus has for them right now, that they might feel tonight the burden the Church has for them, as "the Spirit and the bride say, Come. And let him that heareth say, Come. And let him that is athirst come. And whosoever will, let him take the water of life freely" (Revelation 22:17).

Ministering From His Power

"If any man speak, let him speak as the oracles of God; if any man minister, let him do it as of the ability which God giveth: that God in all things may be glorified through Jesus Christ, to whom be praise and dominion for ever and ever. Amen" (1 Peter 4:11).

Abiding in Him, engulfed in His power—then we will not be ministering from our own limited abilities, but from His unlimited, infinite ability. His ability, infinite ability—we cannot fathom it with our human understanding; yet we know it is so. He is able to do immeasurably beyond what we can ask or think, and He does it, as Paul said, ". . . according to the power that worketh in us" (Ephesians 3:20). Paul further described this as a working that worked in him mightily (cf. Colossians 1:29).

If we are to *turn to the harvest* with real effect, as has been projected in this Assembly, it is an absolute necessity that we become engulfed in this power. Otherwise, what we have talked about will be viewed as just another Church promotion or program. That must not happen!

During a time of prayer during the week of fasting and prayer for this Assembly, on June 17, a new picture flashed into my mind from the verse in Hebrews 1:3, where the writer described Jesus as "upholding all things *by the word of his power.*" We are inclined to say that He is upholding all things by *the power of His Word,* and I'm sure it would not be altogether incorrect to say this, but the verse says, "by the word of his power."

As I knelt in prayer, I envisioned something of a fixed radiance which I viewed to be God, and projecting from this awesome radiance was an extension which was His Word. Then I saw it as *the word of His power,* the power being God Himself. But He desired to communicate with His creation, and the means was by the Word. So the Word proceeded from His eminence, from His very being, from the very Source of *all power.* I then envisioned us being engulfed in that same Power, with our ministering proceeding from this great Radiance which I perceived to be God.

When Jesus spoke, He spoke with power, with authority. It was an authority that had the backing of all power in heaven and in earth. And this is the power into which He invites us to come, by which we are to be engulfed. Jesus described it as *abiding* in Him. I have tried to fathom this relationship wherein He said, "If ye **abide in me**, and my words abide in you, ye shall ask what ye will, and it shall be done unto you" (John 15:7). *Abiding* **in Him**, *living* **in Him**—we know that **in Him** is all power, **in Him** is infinite love, **in Him** are hidden all the treasures of wisdom and knowledge; indeed, **in Him** dwells all the fulness of the Godhead. It is no wonder that Paul could write, "And ye are complete **in him**" (Colossians 2:10).

Outside Christ we are incomplete. To place our trust in anything, or anybody, apart from Jesus, is to have a misplaced trust. We must ask ourselves whether our trust has been completely in Him, and in Him alone. Paul wrote to the Philippians about how he had suffered the loss of all things in which he had trusted in order to *win Christ* and to be *found in Him*. He had trusted previously in his faithfulness to God's Word as it had been interpreted to him. Concerning keeping God's law, his testimony was that he was "blameless" (Philippians 3:6). To Paul this had assured him of his relationship with the Lord. However, he was mistaken. While he knew God's laws well, he did not know God.

Keeping divine rules does not insure divine relationship, but having this relationship wherein we are abiding **in Christ** will assure faithfulness to His Word. If following divine rules brought us into union with God, then salvation would be of works, and righteousness would be of the law. Then Christ would not have had to come and suffer as He suffered.

I recall being taught when younger that if I was faithful to the teachings of the Church and the Advice to Members, this would ultimately assure my perfection. I know it could be argued that I was taught correctly if, for example, I had understood the teaching of "holiness" correctly; this being that there could be no holiness apart from Him who is holy—thus, the necessity of abiding in Jesus in order to observe holiness. Regrettably, this was not the emphasis at that time so much as it was a matter of things I ought to do and things I ought not to do in order to have that holiness without which no man would see the Lord.

Paul wrote, "For ye are dead, and your life is hid with Christ in God." If we are living **in Christ** we are living in holiness, and the fruit of holiness will be manifested in our lives. Those who are dead to sin will no longer live in sin. If we are living **in Christ** we are living **in love**; then it is not difficult to have fervent love for one another. Self-centeredness will be gone. It is not possible to live **in Christ**, to live in love's Essence, and not to care deeply about others. We will care how our conduct and manner of living affects them. We will be troubled in our spirits when we know that what we are doing is offensive to a fellow-Christian for whom Jesus cared enough to die at Calvary. While we are attempting to make some corrections in judgments that seemed too harsh, some appear to be flaunting their liberties to thus become stumblingblocks to fellow-members of the Church. It is wrong to be inconsiderate of your brothers and sisters. I would urge each of you not to use your Christian liberty to satisfy fleshly vanities. Rather, make certain that you are crucified with Christ so that fleshly vanities no longer exist. Some seem to be saying "I don't care what so-and-so thinks," I'm going to express my liberties. "I don't care" should not be in the vocabulary of a Christian. Paul exhorted the Galatians not to use their liberties for an occasion to the flesh, but, by love, to serve one another (cf. Galatians 5:13). **Be one another's servants**!

To live in Christ is also to live in His power—to live in His authority over all the power of Satan. As we turn to the harvest we will be assaulting his kingdoms wherein millions remain enslaved. Without realizing it, many have been working for him who now, as they make this turn, are going to be assaulting his strongholds. They have served Satan's purposes by being faultfinders, slanderers (accusers of the brethren), continually agitating, stirring up strife within the Church. Some of this has been done under the guise of being "guardians of the faith." Since our last Assembly some of this has turned into open rebellion as they now go about openly trying to draw away disciples after them. I feel deep pity for these who have allowed themselves to be overcome, and who, by distorting the truth, indeed, by outright fabrications, have deceived some good people. Let us continue praying earnestly for all of these lest they be lost forever.

I suppose the soil was fertile for these things to take place. Whenever soldiers are not aggressively assaulting the enemy, they are likely to begin disputing among themselves, and are apt to start attacking one another. This is why we now must turn to the harvest with passion. And we must do so with a power we have by abiding **in Christ**. His authority over Satan is the only authority we can exercise. That is why we go in the name of Jesus, which is to say, "in the authority of Jesus."

In fact, the source of all our victories over Satan's power, over his domination of those needing to be set free, is in our being one with Christ—living in Him, abiding in Him. To the Galatians Paul called it being baptized into Christ. He said, "For as many of you as have been baptized into Christ have put on Christ" (Galatians 3:27). Now we believe that baptism is immersion; so, the apostle here is speaking of our being immersed into Christ. Have we been guilty of accepting "sprinkling" for baptism, of proceeding from a sprinkling of His power? For turning to the harvest with the power to assault the gates of hell and bring forth Satan's captives into the glorious liberty Jesus bought for them at Calvary, more will be required than a *sprinkling of power*. We must be immersed in Jesus, immersed in *All Power*, with our ministry proceeding out of that power.

"And they shall not teach every man his neighbour, and every man his brother, saying, Know the Lord: for all shall know me, from the least to the greatest" (Hebrews 8:11). When Moses ascended the mountain at Sinai the people could not go with him; they had to stay at the base of the mountain. He alone was to come into God's presence. Then he would deliver to the people what he had received from God.

When Moses descended from God's presence, his face shone so that the people were afraid to come to him, and it was necessary for him to put a vail upon his face in order for him to deliver to them what he had received from God. But now in Christ we can, as it were, all go up the mountain; we can all know Him, from the least to the greatest. All our faces can shine.

The unity now being needed for the Body of Christ cannot be attained apart from this kind of relationship with Jesus. He prayed, ". . . as thou, Father, art in me, and I in thee, that they also may be one **in us**: that the world may believe . . . " (John 17:21). More is involved in this relationship than merely verbalizing a covenant formula for church membership, although I hold this covenanting together which we have done to be important. I took that covenant fifty-two years ago this month, and it is more meaningful to me today than it was then. It is just that oneness with Jesus is not automatically attained by reciting certain words contained in a certain formula. Those people at the base of Mt. Sinai repeated a covenant formula, but they did not know the Lord.

The union we are needing now in Christ must be a work of the Holy Ghost. Paul's reminder to the church at Corinth was, "For by one Spirit are we all baptized into one body, whether we be Jews or Gentiles, whether we be bond or free; and have been all made to drink into one Spirit" (1 Corinthians 12:13). It was an emphasis upon the oneness in their relationship where Paul wrote to the Galatians, "For as many of you as have been baptized into Christ have put on Christ. There is neither Jew nor Greek, there is neither bond nor free, there is neither male nor female: for ye are all one in Christ Jesus" (Galatians 3:27, 28). Oh, the power of this immersion into Christ as we yield ourselves completely to the Holy Ghost!

I recall an illustration by Brother A. J. Tomlinson of the iron which is placed in the fire of a blacksmith's forge. As the heat is intensified, the iron begins to glow. Soon it assumes the color of the fire. At this point, the iron becomes very malleable. He described this as the iron in the fire and the fire in the iron. Is this not what is depicted when we speak of our being **in** Christ and of His being **in** us?

Jesus' baptism is with the Holy Ghost *and with fire*. Right now we should ask, "Where is the fire?" Where is the passion? Jesus could testify, "The Spirit of the Lord is upon me, because he hath anointed me . . ." (Luke 4:18). Peter testified, "How God anointed Jesus of Nazareth with the Holy Ghost and with power" (Acts 10:38).

In Mark's account of Jesus' wilderness experience, where our Savior defeated Satan's attempts to pull Him away from His mission, he writes as follows: "And immediately the Spirit **driveth** him into the wilderness" (Mark 1:12). We often refer to being directed by the Spirit or led by the Spirit, but Mark uses a more forceful term of being **driven** by the Spirit. Is this not the compelling urge we are feeling today? To be **driven** by the Spirit denotes a divine urgency.

Being Spirit-driven will create a willingness to make personal sacrifices in order to reach perishing people before it is too late. The harvest field is actually a battlefield, and on a battlefield there are casualties. Satan knows already what has been taking place in this Assembly, and he is scheming to stop this harvest-thrust by whatever means he can. As Paul felt driven by the Spirit to turn to the Gentile harvest, he encountered severe opposition and persecution, but he considered the offering of one's body as a living sacrifice to be his reasonable service.

For Paul, this reasonable service was to be beaten with stripes five times, to be beaten with rods three times, to be stoned, and to suffer shipwreck. He described some of his trials further as, "In weariness and painfulness . . . in hunger and thirst, in fastings often, in cold and nakedness" (2 Corinthians 11:27). Was it "reasonable" for Paul and thousands of others to suffer martyrdom as the result of being Spirit-driven? To the Philippians he wrote, "But I would ye should understand, brethren, that the things which happened unto me have fallen out rather unto the furtherance of the gospel" (Philippians 1:12). His testimony to the Ephesian elders who came to him at Miletus was, ". . . neither count I my life dear unto myself" (Acts 20:24).

Many today continue to offer themselves as *living sacrifices*. As I travel and see people who have left families and friends to go thousands of miles from home to labor in God's great harvest, some of them at great danger, my spirit is stirred, and I feel enriched to be in fellowship with them.

I have no desire to return to the day when success in the Church was viewed by one's appointment or by material achievement, often in competition with others to see who could have the finest cars, parsonages, or other buildings. A fascination with materialism has nothing in common with fasting, praying, weeping for the lost. Ten years ago, in 1984, we were called upon by God to repent.

Some may argue that this condition did not develop overnight, and that it will not be corrected suddenly. May I counter that argument with this thought? The Church is comprised of individual members, and the nature of the Church is reflected in the nature of an individual. An individual, we admit, does not backslide overnight. Failures begin to appear gradually in different areas of his relationship with the Lord, and his spiritual weakness becomes more apparent as time goes on, until finally it is acknowledged that he is backslidden.

That same person, however, when convicted by the Holy Ghost, can have an immediate turnaround. It does not require months wherein his relationship with the Lord is gradually restored. It is not a self-improvement plan that will do this. It is a work of the Spirit.

An individual is born again, not gradually over a period of months or years, but it is an instantaneous experience. I do not believe the Church will **turn to the harvest** until it experiences a *new birth*. This *new birth* will occur only through Holy Ghost conviction.

If this conviction has seized our hearts in this Assembly, we will be able to notice a real change. I believe where there is a core group that experiences real change, that group can travail before God until Holy Ghost conviction will seize others, and then for them also there can be immediate repentance and change. The process can spread throughout the Church.

There is hope for us! There can be change, not gradually, but suddenly! This change will cause us to **"turn to the harvest."** That's where Jesus' heart is, and that's where ours will be. Becoming one with Him, we will minister with His authority over all the power of the devil, with His love for those who now are unlovable; we will go with Heaven-born compassion, being **driven** by a sense of urgency. Are you ready to become a living sacrifice? God requires it! We must not fail Him!

Engaged In The Harvest

18

Annual Address to the 89th General Assembly, 1996

Tithing Joyfully

In addition to Abraham's obedience in leaving his homeland at God's command, and of his obedience in offering Isaac, we need to consider something else about this "father of faith." It concerns a manner of worship which he practiced. This is recorded in Genesis, chapter 14, as he was returning from the battle where he had rescued his nephew Lot, and had taken spoils from the battle. God's priest, Melchizedek, pronounced a blessing upon Abraham and the Scripture states that Abraham "gave him tithes of all."

This incident was significant enough that God inspired it to be recorded also in the New Testament. In Hebrews 7:1, 2 we read, ". . . Melchisedec, king of Salem, priest of the most high God . . . to whom also Abraham gave a tenth part of all."

We discover from the Scriptures that this expression of worship was practiced also among Abraham's descendants. When his grandson Jacob was enroute to Haran to seek a wife, he had a dream at Bethel. A ladder reached to heaven and the Lord stood above it. God's message to him, in part, was, "I am the Lord God of Abraham thy father, and the God of Isaac. . . . And, behold, I am with thee, and will keep thee in all places whither thou goest, and will bring thee again into this land; for I will not leave thee . . . " (Genesis 28:13, 15). The Bible says, "And Jacob vowed a vow, saying. . . . of all that thou shalt give me I will surely give the tenth unto thee" (vv. 20, 22).

For these men, tithing became very early an expression of their worship. They recognized that their blessings were from God, that they were dependent upon Him. This knowledge led them to adopt ways for expressing thanks and to make known their devotion. As they did so, God was pleased. Later, when He provided the nation of Israel with laws to govern their worship, He included tithing as a means of worship that would honor Him as their Provider.

As the Church has sought to understand those principles of worship in which God takes pleasure, the conclusion was reached many years ago that we should all practice tithing. Inasmuch as true worship cannot be forced, we have never sought to make tithing a compulsory practice. Yet, it is something that every Christian should take pleasure in doing. Certainly, it is not something to be done grudgingly. Tithing, like giving, should be done cheerfully, joyously. True worship can take tangible forms, such as the communion of the Lord's Supper, for example, in addition to tithing and giving. There is such a thing as superficial, shallow worship which makes little demand upon the participants. Some seem quite willing to lift their hands and sway to the beat of rhythmic music in so-called worship, but when it comes to being faithful in stewardship, especially in tithing and giving, they seem to regard this as being unimportant. It was not unimportant to Abraham, or to Jacob, and it is not unimportant to millions today who wouldn't consider **not** tithing.

Inasmuch as God has approved tithing as a form of worship which pleases Him, it seems a very small thing that His children bring a tenth of their increase into His "storehouse." This, in effect, is our way of saying, "Thank you, Lord, for the air we breathe, for health and strength You provide, and for all else of Your many provisions, and it is by means of our tithe that we worship You." Furthermore, God challenges His children to just prove Him by this act of worship, to give Him a chance to pour out a special blessing of abundance upon those who will bring **all** their tithes into His storehouse.

Tithing and giving should be joyful worship. Never should such become rituals carried out dutifully without feelings of thanksgiving and praise. In that vein, they could become burdensome to the participants, and God would be robbed of worship which He so richly deserves. Ritualistic worship is something of the past. We now worship in spirit and in truth.

When His people fail to tithe, the greatest tragedy is not the loss of finance to the Church. It is the loss of blessings suffered by people who fail to worship in the manner which God approves and prescribes. God, who owns the cattle on a thousand hills, who owns the world and everything in it, is not being robbed so much of material assets as He is being robbed of His people's love and devotion. Owning this world and all in it, our God places certain possessions in our hands to see how we handle them. We become stewards of His possessions. It is His choice that we put 10% of that with which He entrusts us into His storehouse as a form of worship. It is a mistake, then, for us to consider the remaining 90% to be ours. It remains His, and we remain stewards to manage it according to His will. Should not we have the same attitude as was manifested in the apostolic church where Luke wrote, ". . . neither said any of them that ought of the things which he possessed was his own" (Acts 4:32)?

It is true that tithing has provided needed funds for the Church's ministry. Thousands of ministers have thus been provided support so that they have been able to give their time to prayer and the ministry of the Word. This is always a blessing. The greatest blessing, however, comes to those who have offered genuine worship and praise to God by presenting to Him a tenth of their increase. This is a worship in which everyone can participate. No person is either too poor or too wealthy to tithe and give.

It seems sad for people who have been redeemed from their sins by the One who gave **all**, who sacrificed His very life, shedding His blood at Calvary for them, to approach tithing as though it is a form of taxation. People with this mindset will spend time looking for loopholes and deductions they may take to see how little they can "get by with." I have known even of ministers who would compute their so-called "expense in the ministry" to where the amount they submitted as their tithes was pitifully small. Some of these have pastored strong churches with good financial support; yet, after all their figuring and deducting in an attempt to reduce their tithe, the amount they would pay gave indication that they were living in absolute poverty. This is shameful! These people need to ask themselves whether they are tithing or "tipping."

It causes me to wonder whether such people consider tithing as worship, or whether they regard it as a form of taxation. When God's people worship Him "in spirit and in truth," it will not be indicated by how little of their hearts they can put into that worship. Wholehearted worship is marked by exuberance. Tithing and giving is worship which, when practiced exuberantly, brings pleasure to God and joy to the worshipper.

Under the law, it might have been practiced grudgingly at times, but the tithing in which God delights preceded the law, and is a form of grace worship. How delightful it will be when all those who are children of Abraham by faith bring all their tithes into the *storehouse* joyfully. Then God can pour out a blessing upon us that there shall not be room enough to receive. My prayer is that all of our people shall soon know and experience the joy of true worship through tithing and giving.

Vibrant local churches most likely will be churches where tithing and giving is done exuberantly!

Possessing the Enemy's Gates

"And the angel of the LORD called unto Abraham out of heaven the second time, And said, By myself have I sworn, saith the LORD, for because thou hast done this thing, and hast not withheld thy son, thine only son: That in blessing I will bless thee, and in multiplying I will multiply thy seed as the stars of the heaven, and as the sand which is upon the sea shore; and thy seed shall possess the gate of his enemies; And in thy seed shall all the nations of the earth be blessed; because thou hast obeyed my voice" (Genesis 22:15-18).

It was a severe test for Abraham, but his faith held fast. It was God who had promised to make of him a great nation. It was God who declared, ". . . in Isaac shall thy seed be called" (Genesis 21:12). It was the same God who then commanded Abraham to take the lad Isaac into the land of Moriah and there offer him for a burnt offering upon a certain mountain.

Abraham believed the promise that his seed for a great nation would come through Isaac, so he proceeded in preparation to take his son's life at God's command, "Accounting that God was able to raise him up, even from the dead" (Hebrews 11:19). In writing about this great patriarch, Paul said, "He staggered not at the promise of God through unbelief; but was strong in faith, giving glory to God" (Romans 4:20).

Recently, in reading again the account of this event at Mt. Moriah, I was intrigued by a portion of my text Scripture passage where God promised Abraham: **"and thy seed shall possess the gate of his enemies**." "Thy seed" could be a reference to Jesus, who came from Abraham's lineage. If so, we who are now *heirs with Christ* of God's promises would do no injustice to Scripture to make application of this promise as being to Christ's Church also, which is His Body, doing His work. In those days when a city's gate came into the possession of its attacker, or under the control of its attackers, its defeat was certain. This was God's promise to Abraham—**thy seed shall possess the gate of his enemies**.

Today, we who are *children of Abraham*, following in his footsteps of faith, are heirs of this promise. We were given reassurance by the promise of Jesus when He said: ". . .

upon this rock I will build my church; and the gates of hell shall not prevail against it" (Matthew 16:18) (shall not withstand its assaults). This is a promise of victory for the children of Abraham, the children of faith—victory in this battle in which we are now engaged. This battle is to attack Satan's dominion wherein souls are being held captive, to set those prisoners free. Millions are still being held in captivity, but does not this promise to Abraham pertain to us today? *"And thy seed shall possess the gate of his enemies."*

Zacharias, father of John the Baptist, referred to an oath God made to Abraham, that his seed would be delivered from the hand of their enemies and then serve God without fear in holiness and righteousness (cf. Luke 1:73-75). I believe these enemies referred to are **sin** and **Satan**.

Those who are set free, delivered from the grasp of their enemies, are to then turn back, joining in the assault to help liberate others from the power of sin and Satan. After we have been freed, it becomes our business to help rescue those still being held in captivity.

We must be certain that we are identified as the seed of Abraham, not just in our own assessments, but by God who searches hearts. We remember the occasion when Jesus addressed this issue with some Jews who asserted boldly that they were Abraham's seed. They were a part of the covenanted nation, not just generally, but they each, individually, had become a part through the covenant rite of circumcision as had been prescribed by God.

They were offended when Jesus told them that Abraham was not their father, but that they were of their father, the devil (cf. John 8:44). The criteria for such judgment by Jesus was their works: "If ye were Abraham's children," He said, "ye would do the works of Abraham" (v. 39). Now we do not become children of Abraham by any works we may do (this happens through faith), but if we are his children, according to Jesus' statement, we will do his works.

Abraham's *works* were acts of obedience to God. When he was told by God to leave his homeland and his kindred and go to a land to which God would lead him, "he went out, not knowing whither he went" (Hebrews 11:8). When told to offer Isaac as a burnt offering to God, he proceeded to obey God's command. Abraham simply **obeyed** God.

These Jews were trusting in their covenant relationship, in Israel's being God's "peculiar treasure . . . a kingdom of priests, and an holy nation" (Exodus 19:5, 6). Individually, they also bare in their own flesh the mark of circumcision which gave witness of their having become a member of this covenanted nation. In this membership they trusted, believing they were children of Abraham, children of God, but Jesus gave them the true picture.

Their mistake may well be repeated today. There can be a false sense of security in church membership. Rather than boast of our membership, or of its tenure, it is better for us to examine our obedience to the voice of the Lord. Jesus asked, "And why call ye me, Lord, Lord, and do not the things which I say?" (Luke 6:46).

In our last Assembly, He spoke powerfully to us, calling us to *turn to the harvest*. I believe many heard His voice, and the result is that thousands of souls have been set free. Where this has occurred, there has been much rejoicing, even as rejoicing has been taking place in heaven, where there is joy over one sinner that repents, "more than over ninety and nine just persons, which need no repentance" (Luke 15:7). We give thanks to God for each soul saved!

While thousands were saved these past two years, thousands of others departed this life, lost forever. Where they are, there is no hope. Then there are the millions still living whose lives are empty and meaningless. For each one of them, Jesus died, and it remains His will that not one of them perish. His words sound out to us today: "The harvest truly is plenteous, but the labourers are few; **Pray ye therefore** the Lord of the harvest, that he will send forth labourers into his harvest" (Matthew 9:37, 38). His command in the Great Commission seems to ring in my ears: "**Go ye therefore! Go ye therefore! Go ye therefore!**" *And thy seed shall possess the gate of his enemies.*

Are we being aggressive enough in attacking the enemy's strongholds? Is there such a thing as a *passive* assault upon the *gates of hell*? I think not! "Fervent in spirit" is the hallmark for those who will be effective in this war of liberation. We just must not lose this battle! There are millions of souls who are yet to be set free.

Also, fellow-soldiers cannot be bickering among themselves, attacking one another while assaulting the gates of their enemies. It is proper to ask, "But would Abraham's seed display such uncaring attitudes toward one another? Would Abraham's seed be attacking one another?" Abraham's attitude toward Lot was displayed as follows: "Let there be no strife, I pray thee, between me and thee, and between my herdsmen and thy herdsmen; for we be brethren" (Genesis 13:8). Remember Jesus' words: "If ye were Abraham's children, ye would do the works of Abraham."

We are not one another's enemies. *We be brethren!* How, then, can we be inconsiderate of one another? In an attempt to escape the spirit of legalism, for example, the Assembly has pointed out some of the freedoms, some of the liberties of living under grace. Some seem now to be pursuing such liberties with a reckless abandon, without due consideration for their brothers and sisters whose consciences do not allow them such liberties. We are all members one of another, and there is a need for caution lest we offend and bring disharmony in our ranks which hinders our ongoing battle against Satan.

Fervent love for one another will produce *moderation*. When Satan would tempt you to feel that you are being constrained too much, that an unnecessary burden is being imposed upon you by your having to respect the feelings of a fellow-Christian, just tell Satan, "He's not heavy; he's my brother." Such an attitude is appropriate for the *seed of Abraham*. Then, together we will continue our attack, not upon one another, but upon the *gates of hell*.

A New and Living Way

"Having therefore, brethren, boldness to enter into the holiest by the blood of Jesus, By a new and living way, which he hath consecrated for us, through the veil, that is to say, his flesh; And having an high priest over the house of God; Let us draw near with a true heart in full assurance of faith, having our hearts sprinkled from an evil conscience, and our bodies washed with pure water" (Hebrews 10:19-22).

The *old way* of having rules engraved in stone or written in a book had not worked. It had not brought about the relationship which God desired to have with His creation. Prophets had declared and priests had borne God's messages to the people, but without any lasting effect. There was a heart problem which preaching and teaching could not correct. Even the threats of impending judgment would deter unrighteous behavior only for brief periods. All the while, God did not desire cringing subjects who obeyed Him from the sheer fear of His power to crush them. He loved His people with a pure and perfect love, and He wanted His love for them to be reciprocated. However, He realized that in their fallen state, they were not capable of returning to Him such love.

The weakness of the law, which I am calling the *old way*, the old covenant, was thus evident. Its application was *external*, while mankind's problem was *internal*. Some 600 years before the solution came, Jeremiah prophesied of a new covenant God would make with His people. Through his prophecy, recorded in Jeremiah 31:32-34, God says, "Not according to the covenant that I made with their fathers in the day that I took them by the hand to bring them out of the land of Egypt; which my covenant they brake, although I was an husband unto them, saith the LORD.

"But this shall be the covenant that I will make with [them]; After those days, saith the LORD, I will put my law in their inward parts, and write it in their hearts; and will be their God, and they shall be my people. And they shall teach no more every man his neighbour, and every man his brother, saying; Know the LORD: for they shall all know me, from the least of them unto the greatest of them, saith the LORD."

The writer of Hebrews, in chapter 10, verse 9, wrote about this prophecy's fulfillment as follows: "Then said he, Lo, I come to do **thy will** [or, to perform what you have purposed], O God. He taketh away **the first**, that he may establish the second." Jesus came to replace the *first* covenant with a *new and better* covenant, one whose strength would reside in the human heart.

In speaking of the old covenant and the new covenant, or the Old Testament and the New Testament, we sometimes relate these terms to the two divisions of the Bible. The new testament of which I am speaking, however, is not confined to the pages of a book made of paper and ink. The new testament of which I am speaking, *this new and living way*, is in the blood of Jesus. It is the *new testament in His blood*.

It is possible for us to become legalistic, even with the new testament, if our mindset is that it is a book. It is, rather, a relationship that stems from an experience—an experience of the sanctifying power of Jesus' blood. This is the new covenant of which we are now made partakers. It is *a new and living way*!

Jesus came to bring forth life out of death. This life of the new testament was experienced by the apostles when no book existed called the New Testament. They were experiencing the new testament in His blood. Thousands of others experienced the same life-giving power. Through the work of the Holy Ghost, they were experiencing the power of their risen Lord. Like Paul, they had given up all else in which they trusted to know Jesus, to know the power of His resurrection. They had made an exchange of the *old* for the *new*, and how blessed they were in the *exchange*!

Oh, if only the Church had continued in that power which these early followers had found! They knew Jesus! They knew they were new creatures **in Him**! They knew they were abiding **in Him**! He had not come to show them **a way**; He was **the Way**! Abiding **in** Him provides a blessed assurance that *all is well*. Abiding in Him, trusting Him in this *new and living way*, provides an assurance which the old covenant could never give. He is the way! He is the truth! He is the life!

To illustrate, suppose you were wanting to go to a certain downtown hotel in Louisville but didn't know the way. I could give you detailed directions from here, telling you all the turns you would have to make, giving you the names of the streets you would need to observe. Or, I could say, "Just get in my car, and I will drive you there." Which would provide you the greatest degree of certainty in getting there that you would need? Jesus did not come just to show the way. He is the Way, and our certainty is assured by abiding in Him. He is the *new and living Way*!

As long as the Church maintained this living relationship, they moved forward with great power and success in their mission. When their relationship waned, they trusted less in the Person, who was and is the Way, and began to place their trust more in "roadmaps." This led eventually to the adoption of creeds and creedal living. This will always pull the Church toward a legalistic spirit of the old covenant, and this is unacceptable to our Lord, and it grieves Him.

Christian history shows where time after time the Spirit has visited and moved among God's people to lead them back from creedalism to a vital relationship with Him. The beginning of the Protestant Reformation was the result of such a visitation. History shows, however, the success Satan has enjoyed in pulling us away from life in the Spirit, to creedal disputings.

One might ask, "What is wrong with creeds? After all, a creed is simply a statement of faith." It is not that most creeds do not embody truth, for indeed they do. That their purpose is to fortify the Church against heresies has merit, but they tend to become static and rigid, discouraging further exploration into deeper spirituality. They tend to divert us from our trust in a personal relationship with Jesus, to where we set premiums upon certain doctrines while failing to give attention to others of equal importance.

Has any creed, for example, ever exalted the doctrine of forbearing and forgiving, of mutual respect for one another, of submitting to one another? Is it not the spirit of creedalism which has fostered denominationalism with its antagonisms toward other groups of Christian brothers and sisters?

In recent months, I have thought much upon the covenant of membership each of us took in becoming members of the Church. I have reflected upon what really took place in the early years of this century when our fathers formed the Holiness Church at Camp Creek in 1902, A. J. Tomlinson covenanting with them in 1903, and then in 1907, officially accepted the name, the Church of God.

Perhaps it would be good for us to review further a bit of Christian history. We are familiar with the account of the Church's drift from the *new and living way*, wherein they had experienced the vitality of the Spirit, and had ministered with apostolic authority, with Pentecostal power. More and more, they placed their trust in their statements of faith, in the creeds which were adopted. Having begun as a vibrant movement, depending on Jesus and the power of the Holy Ghost, their drift led them to become a religious institution.

What we know as the Reformation was a series of attempts to repudiate creedalism and to return to the kind of Christianity that was seen in the New Testament. Those who, being moved upon by God, led the way in these reformation attempts were noble men who subjected themselves to ridicule and persecution. Some gave their lives, being put to death as heretics.

All too often, however, the movements they were instrumental in bringing forth followed the ways of those who preceded them, drifting into becoming creedal religious bodies. Beginning as covenanted bodies of Christians, covenanting together to be faithful to the Scriptures, they would eventually become creedal organizations. For matters of protection and control, some of these organizations aligned themselves with civil governments, becoming state churches. This provided a kind of protectionism against "breakaway" groups who might actually be following the Spirit, but who would be discountenanced by the government.

When coming from Europe to the new world to escape governmental restrictions and persecution, there was a determination voiced strongly for the separation of Church and State. The freedom of religion this provided was good.

The result, however, was a proliferation of denominations, each outlining for themselves their various statements of faith, claiming for themselves a better doctrinal position than their rival groups. This great freedom allowed anyone who disagreed on a point of religious belief within a particular denomination to start a new one. Rivalries between some of these were intense.

Such was the scene as viewed by our fathers at the turn of this century. The hodgepodge of groups which fostered denominational divisiveness among Christians, they viewed as being contrary to the Church which they saw functioning in the New Testament Scriptures. The stirring within their hearts was calling for a return to pristine Christianity, a return to the power depicted in the Book of Acts. They felt that the spirit of creedalism had to be rejected, that the spirit of denominationalism had to be repudiated. It was their desire to see Christ's Church functioning once more as it functioned in the days of the apostles.

The so-called Christian church, divided as it was, was not offering a credible witness to a lost world. Jesus had prayed for the unity of all His believers, specifically, "that the world might believe." What the world was seeing was not an effective testimony.

So, the covenant they took with one another was actually a rejection of denominationalism, of sectarianism. It was a repudiation of creedalism as they pledged themselves to the New Testament as their rule of faith, practice, government and discipline. To be the Church of God, the Church Jesus is building and for which He will return, such a covenant seems very important. Some may argue that this kind of covenant is not apparent in the Book of Acts for the Church of that time, while others feel there is sufficient wording to support the concept. We must know that ours is more of a "reformation" covenant leading to a restoration, a kind of covenant that would not have been needed at the time of the apostles.

I believe the Church that soon is to be raptured and presented to Jesus as a glorious Church without spot or wrinkle must reject all substitutes that would interfere with, or prevent, a vital relationship with Jesus in this *new and living way*. Therefore, creedalism, legalism, sectarianism must be rejected. These things become barriers to the kind of unity for which Jesus prayed. It is a unity which He described as "I in them, and thou in me, that they may be made perfect in one" (John 17:23).

The covenant our fathers took as a repudiation of creedalism is the one I also took fifty-four years ago. I joined them in rejecting any creed that would limit an ongoing venture into the depths of spiritual experience which this *new and living way* offers. I literally said, "I will take this Bible as the Word of God. I will believe and practice its teachings, rightly divided. I will take the New Testament as my rule of faith, and practice, and government, and discipline." Furthermore, I said, "I will walk in the light to the best of my knowledge and ability."

Moreover, I became a member of a group who had covenanted likewise. Within this body there must be a spirit of mutual submission. Thousands gathered here today have joined together in this covenant. There should be no reluctance for us to persuade others to make the same commitment. It is a covenant that every Christian should be willing to make, and to keep. We have often used the term "perpetual covenant." This is a term used by Jeremiah (50:5). May we be reminded that its perpetuity is in our ongoing commitment to be faithful, our commitment to stay away from creedalism, to walk in the light of God's Word, to enjoy a daily relationship with Jesus in this *new and living way*.

I fear too many of our converts are not being received into the Church. This is a generation who is reluctant to make commitments. Many of them distrust what they view as institutions. Once they surrender to Jesus, however, they have already committed themselves to His lordship. May we then help them to know that the Church is not a static institution, but a living, growing, developing body. The covenant, then, is a commitment to reject everything that prevents

Christian growth, and we are placed within a fellowship where there is accountability, where there is protection.

God has designed that within the Body of Christ we will have those over us who watch for our souls as *they that must give account*. How important it is that we have a true picture of Christ's Church—not a rigid, static institution but a loving fellowship, caring for one another, exhorting one another, encouraging one another, rejoicing together in this *new and living way*!

Called Unto Holiness

"For God hath not called us to uncleanness, but unto holiness" (1 Thessalonians 4:7).

Our God is holy. In Isaiah's vision of the seraphim above God's throne, it was His holiness which they praised as they cried one to another, "Holy, holy, holy, is the Lord of hosts" (Isaiah 6:3). In John's revelation on Patmos, his vision was similar as he wrote of the four creatures who "rest not day and night, saying, Holy, holy, holy, Lord God Almighty, which was, and is, and is to come" (Revelation 4:8). His holiness is to be praised forever!

For those whom He has called to have fellowship with Him, to serve Him, to worship Him, His demand is holiness. Peter spoke of it in this manner: "As obedient children, not fashioning yourselves according to the former lusts in your ignorance: But as he which hath called you is holy, so be ye holy in all manner of conversation [manner of living]; Because it is written, Be ye holy; for I am holy" (1 Peter 1:14-16). Peter went on to describe the Church collectively as "a chosen generation, a royal priesthood, an **holy nation**, a peculiar [rare] people; that ye should shew forth the praises of him who hath called you out of darkness into his marvellous light" (2:9).

To *show forth his praises* is to show forth those things of which He is *praiseworthy*, or to show forth His *excellencies*. We then have been called out of sin's darkness to manifest the excellence of holiness, God's holiness.

In man's initial Creation, he was holy, created in the image of God. What a wonderful relationship Adam was thus provided! This image was marred, however, when Adam sinned, and his fellowship with God was severed. What devastation for all mankind occurred at that moment, Adam could hardly have fathomed. Human history provides a sad account of the carnage exacted by sin, by man's alienation from God.

The call of Abraham was a foreshadowing of God's graciously extending Himself for reconciliation with His creation. He called Abraham to come out of Chaldea, of which Babylon was the capital, to go to a land which we came to know as Canaan. The land of Canaan was a land of promise. We can easily equate his coming out of Babylon to dwell in Canaan with coming out of sin's darkness and confusion to dwell in a kingdom God has provided, a kingdom of life and light. We thus refer to that freedom which we have experienced through faith as we sing, "I'm camping in Canaan now."

Yet, that natural nation of which Abraham was the progenitor did not find the relationship with their Creator wherein they could enjoy His holiness. Sin was a dominating power in their lives, from which they could find no escape. Their sin stood constantly as a barrier between them and a holy God, who simply cannot countenance sin. It is repulsive to His holiness. A sinfulness from which they could not extricate themselves caused their situation to appear hopeless.

The God of hope, however, who sees beyond the limited vision of humans, inspired one of their prophets, named Zechariah, to write, "In that day there shall be a fountain opened to the house of David and to the inhabitants of Jerusalem for sin and for uncleanness" (Zechariah 13:1). This promised *fountain of cleansing* was for a future time. In fact, its fulfillment did not occur until some five hundred years later. This *fountain for sin and uncleanness* sprang forth from a place we call Calvary, outside the gate of Jerusalem. We read in Hebrews 13:12, "Wherefore Jesus also, that he might sanctify the people with his own blood, suffered without the gate."

There it happened—the sin problem was given a solution. It could now be dealt with. The *fountain* was opened. William Cowper, songwriter of the eighteenth century, caught the inspiration of Zechariah's prophecy, and wrote, "There is a fountain filled with blood, Drawn from Immanuel's veins, And sinners plunged beneath that flood, Lose all their guilty stains."

By one act of faith, we can plunge into this cleansing stream to be instantly sanctified. By abiding in the influence or the power of that stream, we can stay clean. The beauty of holiness will then be manifested in our lives. This certainly is not our holiness anymore than it is our power that sanctifies us. It is His power, the power of His blood and the holiness we enjoy, we enjoy by abiding in Him.

This is a wonderful relationship! "For both he that sanctifieth and they who are sanctified are all of one: for which cause he is not ashamed to call them brethren" (Hebrews 2:11). Estranged from God, separated by a barrier we could not surmount, hopelessly lost, not just within time but for eternity—then Jesus came! O hallelujah! The command, "Be ye holy; for I am holy," seemed impossible to obey, but God gave the command, and God made the way. And now Jesus is not ashamed to call us brethren, to introduce me to the Father as His *brother*.

Our works, our behavior, our good deeds do not make us holy. Church attendance does not make us holy. Tithing does not make us holy, dressing appropriately does not make us holy, showing kindness does not make us holy. Our holiness is determined altogether by our relationship with Jesus Christ. However, Peter found it necessary, and was inspired by God, to write, "But as he which hath called you is holy, so be ye holy in all manner of [living]."

Also, Paul was inspired to write, "That every one of you should know how to **possess his vessel** in sanctification and honour; Not in the lust of concupiscence, even as the Gentiles which know not God . . . For God hath not called us unto uncleanness, but unto holiness" (1 Thessalonians 4:4-7). While we are rejoicing in the great liberty of God's grace, may we be reminded that *liberty* does not mean *license*. Liberty of the Spirit does not mean license to sin. There is no correlation between the two. We have been called, not unto uncleanness but unto holiness.

We have the choice daily to yield to Satan's temptations to surrender to the lusts of the flesh or to continue in the grace of sanctification. Paul's reminder to the Roman Christians was "Know ye not, that to whom ye yield yourselves servants to obey, his servants ye are to whom ye obey; whether of sin unto death, or of obedience unto righteousness" (Romans 6:16). God's grace is able *to keep you from falling*. It will be there in every temptation, but it is your choice to submit yourselves to this amazing grace. We are familiar with the verse of Scripture, "Resist the devil, and he will flee from you," but the entire verse says, "Submit yourselves therefore to God. Resist the devil, and he will flee from you" (James 4:7). It is when we submit ourselves to the abundant grace which God provides that we can resist Satan. This enemy seeks to exploit the desires of these fleshly bodies we inhabit, but it is up to us to *possess our vessels* in sanctification and in honour.

We did not begin in this century as a Pentecostal church, but as a Holiness church. The church that was organized in the W. F. Bryant home in 1902 was not called the Pentecostal Church at Camp Creek. It was named Holiness Church at Camp Creek. An entry in the personal diary of A. J. Tomlinson for June 13, 1903, says, "I was ordained a minister of the Holiness Church at Camp Creek, North Carolina." Even when the name, the Church of God, was officially adopted in 1907, it still was not a Pentecostal church but a Holiness church. It was in 1908 that G. B. Cashwell, a minister from North Carolina, who had visited the Azusa Street revival in Los Angeles, was invited to come and preach in our General Assembly. The Holy Ghost fell on the General Moderator, A. J. Tomlinson, and he spoke in tongues as the Spirit gave the utterance.

The emphasis upon being baptized with the Holy Ghost with the initial evidence of speaking in tongues became very strong, and has continued until today, but not at the expense of de-emphasizing holiness. We agree with the Psalmist who declared, ". . . holiness becometh thine house, O Lord, for ever" (Psalms 93:5).

Some in the ranks of so-called Pentecostals today engage in lifestyles which fail to reflect Bible holiness. Their conduct surely must grieve the Lord. Before we judge them too harshly, however, it is good that we examine ourselves to see whether our conduct is such as "becometh holiness." Should we not pray for a purging, a cleansing, a purifying fire to sweep down upon us? Surely it is time for all flesh among us to be crucified, for everything that blurs our identity as the Church of God to be put from among us.

I still believe Jesus will "present it to himself a glorious church, not having spot, or wrinkle, or any such thing; but that it should be **holy** and without blemish."